The Art of Writing Nonfiction

The ART of WRITING NONFICTION

Second Edition

André Fontaine and
William A. Glavin, Jr.

SYRACUSE UNIVERSITY PRESS

The paper used in this publication meets the minimum requirements of American National Standard for Information Sciences—Permanence of Paper for Printed Library Materials, ANSI Z39.48-1984. ∞™

Library of Congress Cataloging-in-Publication Data

Fontaine, André, 1910–
    The art of writing nonfiction.

    Includes index.
    1. Journalism—Authorship.   I. Glavin, William A.   II. Title.
PN4781.F65   1987   808′.06607   86-30212
ISBN 0-8156-2403-4 (alk. paper)
ISBN 0-8156-2509-X (pbk.: alk. paper)

Manufactured in the United States of America

CONTENTS

Before he joined the faculty of the S.I. Newhouse School of Public Communications at Syracuse University, **André Fontaine** spent more than thirty years on newspapers and magazines in New York. He was City Editor of *Newsday,* Associate Editor of *Collier's,* Editor of *Bluebook,* and Senior Editor of *Redbook.* For more than a decade he was a free-lance writer, publishing over a hundred articles in major national magazines. He is now Professor Emeritus at Newhouse and is writing historical biographies.

William A. Glavin, Jr., is Associate Professor of magazine journalism at the S.I. Newhouse School of Public Communications at Syracuse University. He has worked as a newspaper reporter, a television news editor, and for four years as an associate editor at *Good Housekeeping* magazine, where he specialized in health-related topics.

PREFACE

This book documents a major change in journalistic practice in the United States. It is a change that has been largely unnoticed outside the profession and not understood by thousands inside. It had its beginnings nearly half a century ago in the work of exceptionally talented writers and editors, then grew slowly as more and more practitioners saw, understood, and began to use the new techniques.

The change has been called many things—new journalism, literary journalism, advocacy journalism—and definitions of precisely what it is and how it differs from earlier forms have been elusive. With a boldness not warranted by our knowledge, we would like to offer one:

Interpretive journalism is a process, based on rigorous reportage, that employs the creativity and skills of the fiction writer and presents the judgment of the writer, after he or she has objectively evaluated the facts, of where the truth lies.

Interpretive stories can range in length from a 1,000-word newspaper story to a 3,500-word magazine article or even to a full-length book. In producing such stories, the journalist may use the fiction writer's techniques of plotting, suspense, dramatic conflict, and character development, but may not go beyond the facts unearthed during the research process. Though the story must present a conclusion, a point of view, that conclusion must be reached, as in the scientific method, only after all available evidence has been weighed and after as much bias and prejudice as is humanly possible has been ruled out. Thus the idea of journalistic objectivity is vital to the process. Though the methods of presentation may differ, the process is identical in all forms of interpretive journalism. Of the creativity involved, the late Truman Capote, in a *Playboy* interview, said, "Journalism is actually the last great unexplored literary frontier. . . . It's the only really serious and creative field of literary experimentation we have today."

This book explores and describes the process of interpretive journalism, and, to the best of our ability, tells how it is done. Starting with the inception and shaping of the idea for the story, the book takes the reader through the research process, the evaluation of the evidence, the organization and presentation of material, and a discussion of leads, endings, and the body of the story. Then it discusses different kinds of writing—dramatic, descriptive, explanatory, emotional, and profiles.

Originally published in 1974, *The Art of Writing Nonfiction* in this second edition adds a co-author, William A. Glavin, Jr., and new examples of outstanding journalism. The reader will find throughout the text frequent use of the first person singular "I"; these refer to the book's original author, André Fontaine. Pronouns were a further concern to us because we wanted the language in *The Art of Writing Nonfiction* to be free of sex bias. The book's first edition followed the long-accepted convention that says "he" or "him" may be used to refer to a person of unknown sex ("If you want to convince your reader, you have to give him the fact"). Today we are all more aware of the subtle ways language can fail to reflect the experiences and contributions of women, and we sought ways of reflecting that awareness in our writing.

We hope the book will be of practical value to journalism students, to practicing journalists who seek to expand the horizons of their craft, and to all aspiring writers who want to attempt this new and demanding art form.

We wish to thank those whose thought and advice were of inestimable help in creating this second edition of *The Art of Writing Nonfiction:* Diana J. Reinstein of Syracuse University's Bird Library, who offered valuable information about databases; Dean Edward C. Stephens of the S. I. Newhouse School of Public Communications, who freely offered assistance to both of us; Mary Kate Imbolli, whose help was invaluable, and who, among other things, spent hours teaching Glavin how to use a computer (which wasn't easy); and Isabel Pearce, who typed the manuscript and whose suggestions improved the work. We also wish to thank all of the writers whose work appears in the book. They are the practitioners of interpretive journalism, and the book could not have existed without their efforts. Finally, we wish to thank our students, past and present, who provided both the inspiration and the reason for the book.

ACKNOWLEDGMENTS

Grateful acknowledgment is made to the following for permission to use copyrighted material:

Ken Auletta, "Ralph Nader, Public Eye," *Esquire,* December 1983. Reprinted by permission of the author.

Joseph P. Blank, "A Boy's Trial by Fire," *Reader's Digest,* November 1963. Reprinted with permission.

Truman Capote, quoted in "The Story Behind a Nonfiction Novel,: by George Plimpton, *New York Times Book Review,* January 16, 1966. Copyright © 1966/67 by the New York Times Company. Reprinted by permission.

Randy Fitzgerald, "Time to Crack Down on Food Stamp Fraud," *Reader's Digest,* February 1983. Reprinted by permission.

Barbara Gelb, "Mike Nichols, The Special Risks and Rewards of the Director's Art," *New York Times Magazine.* Reprinted by permission of the author.

Dan Greenburg, "The Ninth Precinct Blues," *The New York Times Magazine,* January 21, 1979. Copyright © by Dan Greenburg. Reprinted by permission of the author.

Bob Greene, "Fifteen," in "American Beat," copyright © 1983 by John Deadline Enterprises, Inc. Reprinted by permission of the Sterling Lord Agency, Inc.

Rob Hoerburger, "Phil Collins Beats the Odds," *Rolling Stone,* May 23, 1985. Reprinted by permission of the author.

Bill Kovach, "Little Man Has His Day in Night Court," *The New York Times,* September 23, 1968. Reprinted by permission of the author.

Michael Lemonick, "Voyager's Triumph," *Time* Magazine. Copyright © 1986 by Time Inc. All rights reserved. Reprinted by permission of *Time.*

Andrew H. Malcolm, "Fateful Choice in Fatal Illness: How Long to Live," *The New York Times,* February 14, 1986. Copyright © 1986 by The New York Times Company. Reprinted by permission.

The Art of Writing Nonfiction

1

A New Art Form

Almost since the days of Dr. Johnson's Grub Street, the literati have considered journalists as hacks. For the majority this is probably fair enough—even though Charles Dickens, Stephen Crane, Mark Twain, George Orwell, Ernest Hemingway, and dozens of other distinguished writers were also practicing journalists. But what most contemporary literary writers and critics have not fully realized is that during the last thirty years a new dimension in journalism has slowly emerged. Today some of the most vital and creative writing in the English language is being done by journalists. Perhaps this is insufficiently recognized because many critics, in and out of universities, don't understand the form.

For two centuries the novel has been one of our major art forms, but in recent years leading novelists like Truman Capote and Norman Mailer have turned to journalism, and other writers like John Hersey, Joan Didion, Nora Ephron, and Jimmy Breslin have worked in both forms. Meanwhile, nonfiction books have displaced novels as the most widely read and influential books on many publisher's lists.

During the sixties this new dimension in journalism became a kind of literary fad, identified by different names by its advocates and practitioners. Tom Wolfe, one of the most original of its practitioners, and Clay Felker, editor of *New York* magazine, called it "the new journalism." Harold Hayes, editor of *Esquire*, called it "literary journalism." Hobart Lewis, editor of *Reader's Digest*, called it simply "a new art form."

All except Lewis thought that this new form started in the early sixties, and all agreed that it was being practiced by a small group of New Yorkers that included Wolfe himself, Breslin, Gay Talese, and a few others. But while these men are unquestionably exceptional journalists, the list leaves out more names than it includes. Further, the history of the form was wrong.

Tom Wolfe has written that the new nonfiction was pioneered by *Esquire*, under editors Hayes and Felker in the early 1960s. He says the

1

characteristics of the new art form all developed about that time. But they actually had started to emerge at least ten and probably twenty years before. Wolfe calls one such characteristic "saturation reporting"; in it the reporter spends days or weeks with the subject of a story in order to observe first-hand the actions which reveal the person's character, the words which reveal motivation. But this kind of reportage was being done by several *Collier's* writers in the mid-forties, and I* can recall discussing with Harold Baron, of *Today's Woman,* the use of fiction plotting techniques for a nonfiction story as early as 1950.

Wolfe says all this came about in magazines, and most of it did, but the techniques also have been used in newspaper depth stories, in television documentaries, and in nonfiction books.

This type of writing is grounded almost equally in journalism and in what the English professors call creative writing—although all writing, of course, is creative. From journalism it takes the reporter's aggressive search for fact, a concern for accuracy, and a sensitive, trained observer's eye, as well as skepticism and adeptness at checking and cross-checking the things the reporter is told by his or her sources. From the "creative" or fiction writer the new journalism borrows imagination, skill at plotting and portraying character, the techniques of building a dramatic story and evoking the reader's emotions, and, most important, the imposition of the writer's judgment on the story.

The actual creative process was aptly described by the late Professor Cathy Covert of Syracuse University, herself a distinguished journalist. Creativity, she said, "is taking a bit of knowledge from one discipline, an insight from another, an experience you have lived, assimilating them in your mind, going through a process of complete chaos, and ultimately coming up with something quite new." And the chaos, she added, is absolutely essential.

This is an accurate description of what happens in the best journalism. Its practitioners—call them reporters, article writers, or nonfiction artists—go behind the facts to get the truth. They spend weeks—perhaps months—learning all they can about their subjects. They become experts by reading and interviewing experts. And they relate what they learn to the problems and worries and interests and yearnings of their readers. Then they write their stories in a way their readers can apprehend, in a way that becomes part of each reader's life experience.

Most people don't act simply on the basis of the things they perceive intellectually. They react to things they know, coupled with what they

---

*As noted in the Preface, the first person singular pronoun refers to André Fontaine.

sense intuitively, instinctually, as a result of an emotional conviction. The creative journalist looks for ways to involve these elements of a reader's personality, knowing that emotions are often more reliable than intellect.

For example, straight, factual accounts of traffic accidents are common in most newspapers:

Susan York, 7, daughter of Mr. and Mrs. Samuel York of 327 Livingston St., was struck and killed yesterday afternoon when she ran in the path of a car driven by Charles Williamson, 42, of 408 South George St.

We have all read such stories. Perhaps we have felt a pang of sadness before going on to look at other parts of the newspapers. But if we had actually seen the accident, we would have been affected far more deeply. We would have seen the little body lying the street, still and shockingly *wrong,* because a body doesn't belong in the middle of a street. Like all bodies, it looks flat, empty, doll-like. We would witness the horror of the mother, running out in the housedress and dirty sneakers she has been wearing to mop the kitchen floor, with none of her armor of makeup and with her hair in rollers. We would see her face stripped bare of the masks we all wear against the world as she kneels and picks up the child, see the way disbelief, then shock, then flooding grief wash over her face so nakedly it is oddly embarrassing, and we would want to turn away from this too-threatening emotion. And we would note the dulled expression on the face of the man whose car hit the child as he gropes to comprehend this thing he has done.

Anyone who has viewed such a scene never forgets it. Such a person is affected emotionally, and the creative journalist, in describing such a scene would attempt to make you, the reader, experience the emotions felt by a witness. The journalist does so by recreating the scene in print, making readers live the tragedy, making it a part of their view of life, and very probably causing them to think about their own driving habits.

So while the typical newspaper story conveys information that you perceive intellectually, creative journalism evokes your emotions, as the best fiction has been doing for centuries.

The difference between fiction and this type of journalism is that while fiction writers can create the characters and dramatic situations they need to get the underlying idea or theme of a story home to their readers, reporters may not. They are bound always by fact; they may make up nothing. This puts a tremendous burden on their ability to research a story and understand its depths, on their thoughtfulness in deciding what is important to report, and on their skill in organizing the story so that the essential truth they want to convey is not distorted.

To get an idea of how the two techniques differ, suppose a reporter and a fiction writer wanted to express this truth about modern living: in large, tightly structured organizations individuals are sometimes trapped between the practicalities of surviving in the organization and their own conception of what is ethical, or perhaps even lawful. The fiction writer would create a character, let's say a man in his middle thirties, married, with three children, a home in the suburbs, and all the familiar pressures to meet the ever-mounting expenses that maintain the family's position in the community, as well as his own status in the large corporation he works for. He also happens to be a man with an inordinate need for acceptance by other men because when he was six his father died, and he was brought up by a dominant and overprotective mother. After her husband died, the mother found some security in her fundamentalist religion, and as the years passed she became more and more rigid and simplistic in her ideas of right and wrong—a rigidity she passed on to her son.

When the reader discovers the man, he has just been given a promotion he has long worked for. But shortly he discovers that one part of his new job is to handle the arrangements his company continually makes with other firms in the same industry to rig the prices they charge for their products, both to government agencies and to the general public. The man knows such arrangements are a violation of antitrust laws, and his rigid conscience tells him he cannot allow himself to be a part of them. On the other hand, he knows that if he refuses to go along with the practice, his career in the corporation will be ended. He also knows enough about the lateral communication between corporations in the same industry to know he will not get a job with any of them.

There's his dilemma; what does he do? The fiction writer will work out the answer in terms of the man's character. Which of the conflicting traits will guide his decision—his need for acceptance or his rigid conscience? If the first, he will be diminished as a man; if the latter, he will be ruined economically.

A reporter, wanting to express the same dilemma, would search until he found a real situation that illuminated it. If he could find none, then he would conclude that his idea that such situations were common in today's life was false. Or if he did find one, he would dig and research and interview until he had all the factual material that would allow him to present the dilemma in terms of the man's internal struggle, just as the fiction writer does.

I ran across just such a situation while I was working on a different story. At an army base in Fort Lee, Virginia, there was a small airfield that could accommodate only light airplanes, and these only during daylight and in good weather. The commander of the base decided he wanted a larger field and asked the Department of Defense for money to build it. He was turned down, but he went ahead and built it anyway.

All base commanders have "operations and maintenance" funds of up to $25,000 a year, which they can spend without specific approval of Congress. At Fort Lee the commander decided to use these funds, but the improved airfield cost nearly $500,000. The difference was made up by falsifying invoices and purchase orders, so that airfield funds were officially listed as being spent for other purposes. After the field was built the whole scheme was uncovered by investigators from the General Accounting Office. It was reported to Congress, and special hearings were held on the affair. At these hearings the dilemma of some of the base officers was spelled out.

One colonel in the engineering office had to take care of the paper-work, developing fictitious projects to get the money and material needed for the airfield. He knew it was illegal and at one point he said to his superior officer, "I am not going to the pen for this." His superior responded ominously that he'd sign the papers.

The colonel told Congress, "I had to choose between violating the law or suffering as a result of the army's system." Those who know the "system" told me an uncooperative officer would likely be assigned to the worst posts, would get no more promotions, and would probably be discharged within a few years.

So here was the same dilemma. I never wrote the story, but if I should, I would tell it in terms of the colonel's personal struggle, I'd learn about his character and career, about the kind of thing that happens to officers who violate "the system." I'd report the things he actually did—how he struggled against the dilemma and finally reached the decision to go along, and what happened to him as a result. Nothing would be made up, but it would be necessary in the interviewing to get inside the officer himself and present the conflict from his point of view. Then the story would be organized to build up the drama of the dilemma, climax when he made his decision, and conclude with an account of what actually happened as a consequence of his choice.

To understand this kind of journalism, it is helpful to know how it came about, for it is a logical evolution in the development of the craft. In the nineteenth century journalistic writing was "personal," and much of it was magnificent. In *Pictures from Italy* in 1846. Charles Dickens reported the hanging of a highwayman in Rome with all the color and impact of his later novels. In 1865 George Alfred Townsend reported in the *New York World* on the capture of John Wilkes Booth with an artistry that put his readers on the spot and made them a part of the confusion and drama and tragedy. Writers such as these, many of whom later became outstanding novelists, used the dramatic techniques of fiction writers, evoking the emotions of their readers and certainly using their own judgment in evaluating the events they reported. The trouble was that many of them went too far and allowed their biases to override the facts. Often the ideal of objectivity never entered their calculations.

This kind of journalism was supplanted, about the turn of the century, by the "objective" reporting that dominated newspaper writing for the next fifty years. Objectivity resulted partly from changing economic conditions and partly from journalistic idealism. The first occurred largely through the growth of the Associated Press, because AP reports were distributed to newspapers representing all kinds of political opinion. Had the reports too obviously reflected any one point of view, they would have been unacceptable to many of the AP's potential customers. Objective reporting as a mark of professionalism spread largely through the leadership of *The New York Times* and a handful of other great newspapers that sought "objectivity" in pursuit of the ideal of impartiality.

This idea of "just the facts, Ma'am" added a great new ethic to reportage—fairness—and implanted it so firmly in the reporter's bag of disciplines that all journalism was elevated. But like all ideals, perfect objectivity was impossible to attain. In something as simple as an automobile accident, for example, what are the facts? Names, addresses, injuries, and what each car was doing. But if you didn't see the accident, how do you know what each was doing? You may ask the police. How do they know? They didn't see it either; they got the story from the drivers and from witnesses. So the reporter talks to witnesses and gets three conflicting stories. What are "the facts"?

Brock Brower, in *On Creative Writing* by Paul Engle, castigated this kind of journalism.

> Journalism is routinely voiceless—but far worse, journalism is routinely mindless. Its vaunted objectivity . . . is only an escape from the need to reason. When finally faced with a controversial point which demands some interpretation, the journalist is famous for the "Lib-Lab"—i.e., on the one hand *this*, and on the other, *that*, but neither hand is his. The

easy generalization . . . and the endless qualifier . . . are the two stylistic counterweights with which the journalist maintains his own commitment, and hence his own existence, at constant zero.

This type of writing became the norm, and newspapers followed it almost to destruction. Giving just the facts was fine in a simple society of uninformed people, content to be fooled and manipulated by their political and economic leaders.

But by the 1940s everything was suddenly more complicated. If a reporter were to give just the facts leading to the rise of Hitler, say, a newspaper had to find 500 pages to put them in, which it didn't have. And the endless, recitation of dry facts would not only lose readers in the first ten pages, but putting those facts in perspective would require an intimate knowledge of Germany that few readers had. Still, reporters tried to do this and newspapers stopped being pertinent and became mere news bulletin boards—a function television was soon to perform much better.

Meanwhile magazine writers had gone off on a new tack. Spurred by *Time* magazine and Henry Luce, who said frankly that objectivity was a myth and it was time to get the facts off the page and into the reader's mind and gut, magazine writers began to supply the expert knowledge and the perspective the reader needed. Nor did the best of them give up the ideal of objectivity; they simply moved it to another place in the writing process. They made judgments and expressed a point of view, but they concealed both behind the facts they selected to report. Thus they began to learn and use the skills of indirection (which we'll discuss later), and a new dimension was added to journalism.

Under the impact of this new pertinence the now familiar revolution in magazine content took place. Whereas before 1940 the mass magazines had contained about two-thirds fiction and one-third articles, they now reversed the ratio. And their circulations began to climb as readers increasingly found a medium that gave them information they needed in a way that made sense.

In the late forties a few of the top magazine writers began consciously adopting fiction techniques in writing their factual articles—which made everything more difficult, complicated, and effective. This process increased at a geometrical rate in the fifties, and the magazines ran into trouble. Spurred by their advertising departments and the competition of multimillion television audiences, magazine editors began wanting more and more fiction technique in their articles and less and less solid information. Or, put another way, in order to sell magazines, editors wanted more entertainment and less substance.

That was when readers were treated to endless recitals of the loves and difficulties of Liz Taylor and Richard Burton, to the Cinderella story of Grace Kelly and her celluloid romance with the man on top of the wedding cake, and similar vital information. Led by *McCall's*, in the 1960s many magazines also went in for packaging instead of substance, with page after page of huge, four-color pictures and little text. Magazines became more and more bland, further and further removed from the problems and triumphs and values of real people.

So, with some outstanding exceptions, magazines, too, failed their journalistic responsibility to tell people about their complicated world in a way that made sense. But a few years before, the best newspapers had caught the idea and started to do the job themselves. This was when the *Wall Street Journal,* for instance, began to carry the first "depth" stories on page one and showed the rest of the country's papers how it was done.

As the depth stories developed, they did precisely what the magazine articles had done. So did the best television documentaries, notably those produced by Edward R. Murrow and Fred Friendly for CBS. Indeed, television began to borrow magazine writers who understood the technique to do the job. Former magazine men like Arthur Morse, William Peters, Leslie Midgeley, and Gordon Manning moved to television. And several of them have said they made the documentaries the same way they had written magazine articles, except that they had available and learned to use the extra dimension of the camera and the sound track.

But of course television had its own built-in imperatives—so well documented by Friendly in his book *Due to Circumstances Beyond Our Control*—that soon caused the amount of this kind of superb journalism to decline. Then in the seventies more newspapers were getting the message, and the ten or twelve best papers in the country increasingly hired the writers, gave them the time and expenses they needed to do the job, and printed the interpretive stories that the times and their constitutional license demanded.

Today, large numbers of newspapers run sections with titles like "Style" or "Living," which contain some impressive interpretive pieces. While some of these sections also contain a great deal of pap, others contain fine stories, the result of good reporting done by reporters who are given the time and encouragement to do meaningful pieces. The increase has continued, but the need for this kind of journalism is so great that if all the mass media devoted twice the time and space that they currently do to it, the supply would still be too low.

One reason is the knowledge explosion. It has been said that the total of human knowledge since 1940 is equal to all human knowledge up to 1940.

Professor Bertram M. Gross, a noted social scientist, notes that in psychology, for instance, the amount of knowledge doubles every ten years. In this situation, the old cops-and-robbers type of reportage is as pertinent as a bicycle is to a fish. As knowledge expands it becomes more precise, more specialized, and more qualified. It gets further from the fund of knowledge of the average reader and thus needs to be related, interpreted, explained. This is the interpretive reporter's job. To do it properly he or she must master the broader implications of specialized knowledge and put them at the service of the average reader. The reporter must become a kind of communications bridge between the experts and the public.

Another dimension of the job facing journalism is the noninvolvement of people, what the social scientists call alienation. People are out of touch with their world and with other people, especially in the cities where some seven out of ten Americans live. Evidence erupts periodically all over the country. In a New Bedford, Massachusetts, bar a group of men raped a young woman on a pool table while the other patrons stood by, doing nothing. In Ohio, a woman driving to work one February morning skidded on a bridge and her car splashed into the river. The woman climbed out on the rear deck and, as the car slowly sank, screamed that she could not swim. Some thirty-five persons stood a mere fifteen feet away and watched her drown.

There are many causes of this alienation. A major one, we believe, is that increasingly over the past two or three generations, people have learned that they cannot control their own lives. With the growth of mass-production techniques, workers were no longer individual artisans who could make a chair, a suit, from start to finish, and who at the end had the satisfaction of holding a concrete expression of their work. They had become faceless parts of a great human machine. Once they sought to reassert their power as individuals by banding together into trade unions, and for a while they were effective. But the unions too grew into large, impersonal bureaucracies, at the same time the largest corporations began to operate on a multinational scale. Today unions are on the decline, and the economy is moved by forces too large and complex for most people to understand much less control.

Psychologists know that when people cannot control their own destiny, they often sink into apathy, sometimes too deeply ever to surface again. But they feel an internal, unexpressed rage, and perhaps when they see someone else being victimized, they express sadistic satisfaction by doing nothing. This process is reinforced, we believe, by the mass media. In movies, advertising, paperback and magazine fiction, and in the ceaseless drumfire of television commercials and "entertainment," people are presented from childhood with a picture of a never-never land in which all women are beautiful and happy, all men handsome, virile, and prosperous. They live in a suburban split-level with two gorgeous cars named after wild beasts and with smiling children who always learn, after minor peccadilloes, that the traditional values are best. Inevitably, after years of this, people find themselves trying to live in two worlds. They—not all and not all to the same degree—think the never-never land is the way life really is. But the realities of their own daily lives are uglier, less felicitous, pocked with loss, boredom, injustice, and problems that seem to have no solution. And when people measure this reality against the media's glamorous fictions, they feel both cheated and self-contemptuous, blaming themselves for not enjoying the kinds of lives the media portray. More apathy, more internal rage then may result.

This is one of the sicknesses of our times, and as the mass media have had a role in causing it, they have a responsibility to help cure it. It constitutes one of the challenges facing serious journalists today. To accept it and meet it successfully requires all the skills in communicating effectively that their profession has mobilized since Gutenberg.

Henry T. Yost, Sr., a biology professor at Amherst College, addressed an entering freshman class, which had been assigned to read *Don Quixote*, among other books, over the summer. His talk concluded:

> Someday we must see that freedom for the individual is not in acquiring better furniture, is not in being a success, is not in being pampered, is not even in being left alone. Our freedom lies in doing battle with giants wherever we may find them. We cannot be the New Men—a part of the establishment. We must be knights-errant and, like the Don, be willing to attempt the impossible—for that is the only true freedom. . . .
>
> For in reality, as in myth, man is always on a giant-hunt. If he does not find real ones, he will hunt mythical ones; and the role of the intellectual, be he scientist or humanist, is to replace the mythical giants with real ones, to direct the efforts of man to the searching out of those giants of our society that must be slain, and, in the process, to provide the encouragement to do battle with giants and to provide hope that the battle can be won.

No better statement of the job of the serious journalist has been made.

2

Where Do You Get Story Ideas?

*I*nterpretive writing requires changes throughout the reporting-writing process. The idea with which a story starts is a little different, the research is both broader and different in character from older reportage, the evaluation of the research is so changed it is almost a new process, and the writing itself is more highly crafted, difficult, creative.

The whole process starts, of course, with the story idea. Textbooks on magazine article writing say that ideas are everywhere, which is true but not very helpful. The problem is to know a good one when you see it. The solution starts not with the writer, but the reader.

The difference between amateur and professional writers is that amateurs write for themselves and professionals write for their readers. The reporter starting out on a newspaper quickly learns from her editor that readers are primarily interested in crime, sex, scandal, disaster, sports, society, and death, and the editors judgment of what makes up a good story is based on these values. If she goes to work for a magazine, she discovers that readers come in smaller groups and different sizes. At *Redbook*, for instance, I learned that our readers were primarily women between the ages of eighteen and thirty-five, married, with a home in the suburbs, two children, five and eight years old, and an interest in the P.T.A. If I had an idea for a story that involved teenagers, *Redbook* editors wouldn't listen to me; it was not for their readers.

If a writer today plans to sell an article to *Cosmopolitan*, she must know that *Cosmopolitan* readers are somewhat unlike the glamorous models who grace each issue's cover. The readers are primarily women between the ages of 18 and 34. They live in or near large cities, are employed, and earn about $17,500 a year. So *Cosmopolitan* is not the place for a story on how to choose the proper silver for a party at your Southampton beach cottage.

This kind of specialization, of course, was brought about not by editors, but by publishers who wanted to carve out a section of the reading audience and convince advertisers their magazine reached it more authoritatively than anyone else's. But whatever the cause, today's writers must think about their readers in more precise and subtle terms.

Thus the first, and simplest, step in writing is to know who your reader is. Is it a woman or a man? Aged fifteen, thirty-five, or fifty-five? College, high school, or grade school graduate? Skier, homeowner, scientist? Within these groupings you usually shoot for the idea that will affect the largest number the most intimately. (As Sumner Blossom, then editor of *American Magazine,* once said "I'd rather have a story on noses than on red hair: more people have noses than red hair.")

The key, as he indicated, is reader self-interest. People are primarily interested in themselves—their problems, the things they do every day, their hobbies, their relationships with others.

A good way to get the hang of this is to read and analyze some successful magazines. For example, anyone reading *Bicycling* magazine would know immediately that its editors want how-to pieces on nearly all aspects of bicycling, and pieces on fitness, bicycle trips, and tours. A reader of *Yankee* would realize that the magazine focuses on New England, and that the editors like articles on the region's history, places, and people. And a quick look at *Working Woman* tells us that the magazine wants material of interest to young, well-educated, busy career women.

A reader's self-interest may be as obvious as gender or as subtle as a psychological need. The writer must identify it and provide some satisfaction for it. When she does she will have a usable idea.

Such ideas provide a service to the reader—some simple, direct, practical, some complicated and subtle. For example, one day an observant writer may see a pet store with an unusual window display. It is the re-creation in miniature of a woodland pool, complete with rocks, overhanging branches of plants, a miniature waterfall, and a pool bright with darting tropical fish. The writer goes in, talks to the owner, and comes out with an article, perhaps for *Tropical Fish Hobbyist.*

This is fine. It has the elements of the craft: identifying the self-interest of a particular group of readers and finding new information that will serve their interest, getting it and presenting it in the proper medium and in a way that will be of value to them. It is creative in that the writer must conceive the idea, analyze the need for the information, and present it clearly and cogently. Great masses of useful information are supplied readers in this way via thousands of special-interest magazines ranging all the way from *Cats Magazine* to *Yachting.* Many features in newspapers (how to refinish your attic) and educational television programs ("This Old House") use the same basic techniques to supply similar needs.

But this kind of writing is also pretty elementary in the dynamic modern world of computers, heart transplants, and hunger that affects millions. Society is changing so fast today that none of us is living in the world we think we are, and the problems of people's relationships with each other and the systems they have created are so complex only the experts understand them, if anybody does. But people need the experts' knowledge, and it is the creative journalist's job to supply it. To do so effectively the journalist must develop skills that are considerably more sophisticated and subtle than those used by the writer dealing with the pet shop display.

This job starts in one of two ways. The writer either learns of some new information an expert has that can help solve a problem which large numbers of people face, or the writer first identifies the problem, then seeks out the information from experts to help solve it. Sometimes the two steps meld together so it's hard to tell which came first.

An example of the first is a piece I did some years ago for *Redbook*. It started with a small item in a New York newspaper, which reported a new technique some elementary school teachers were using in class. It was called sociometric testing and, like many sociological phenomena, the fancy name covered a simple process. They asked the kids in the class whom they liked best, like least, liked to work with, play with, and so on. And why.

I remembered an article I'd done two or three years before in which a sociologist at Ohio University had done a study which showed—vastly oversimplified—that the college students who had the most dates in college got the best marks. This seemed a contradiction, but when you learned why, it made sense: popular students felt accepted, secure, unthreatened; the resulting self-confidence released their energies for their studies. Question: if this was true for college students, wasn't it also true for grade school youngsters?

I went to see Dr. Helen Hall Jennings, a psychologist who had been mentioned in the newspaper story as an expert on sociometric testing, and she told me the answer was yes. But as I talked with her about the process, the subject began to broaden. When you looked at the answers of hundreds of children as to whom they liked best and least and why, you began to see emerging a whole system of values. This system was different from the one teachers and parents had for each other and, as I thought about it, I remembered that when I was a kid I felt and acted differently when I was with other kids than I did with adults. But now that I was an adult with kids of my own, I looked at them and their actions in terms of my adult value system. I never thought about theirs or that it might be different. I suspected most other parents did the same.

Now the idea began to take a different shape. Sociometric testing was a system by which educators could improve the learning ability of their pupils. But I wasn't writing for educators, I was writing for the general public. How could this insight be made valuable to general readers?

Obviously my target audience was parents and more specifically mothers, since typically they were more directly and consistently concerned with their children's development than fathers. Everybody knows that most parents want their kids to do well in school. But there was another element in the idea, too: if sociometric testing revealed the child's value system, it necessarily revealed, or could reveal, those qualities in youngsters which made others like them—made them, in other words, popular. I knew that Americans put a high value on popularity, so here was another reader self-interest that might be used.

Further research showed that there was a sound psychological reason for Americans' respect for popularity—that we all get a good deal of our feelings about ourselves from the way others react to us. If by their actions other people demonstrate that they find us valuable, respect and like us, we have a feeling of self-assurance, of confidence, a positive outlook on the world. If other people reject us, we tend to think they know what they're about and that we're not much good. So we become negative, sick with self-contempt, and we tend to withdraw.

Again the story idea changed shape and broadened. Now it would appeal not only to educators and parents, but would be of considerable help to them as they wrestled with the problems of raising emotionally healthy, competent youngsters. And it could be put to them in terms they were accustomed to dealing with, not in educators' gobbledygook. The title almost wrote itself: "What Makes Kids Popular?"

The market was also obvious—*Redbook*, because the article was a woman's piece, and because it dealt with younger children. The editors liked the idea and I went out and did the story. Here (with my comments interspersed) is the way it started and the way the original idea of sociometric testing was transformed into a story with a much broader reader self-interest:

What Makes Kids Popular?

Without meaning to, you can cripple or kill your child's chance of ever being popular. You won't do it intentionally, of course. If you do it, it's because, like almost all parents, you don't know what it is that makes one child respected and admired by his playmates and another baited and shunned.

If you'll remember back to your own school days, you'll doubtless recall that you felt and behaved entirely differently in front of parents and teachers than you did when you were alone with the other kids. You, like all children, lived in two worlds—the official one that adults saw and the "hidden" one you shared with your school and playmates. But now that you're a parent, the chances are you can't remember exactly what that hidden world was like.

Until recently, adults have never been able to enter a child's secret world. But within the past few years social scientists have developed a way to penetrate it. By means of a new kind of test they've explored that world and charted it. Their findings have surprised many who thought they were child experts.

If you want your child to be popular, you should try to understand this world, for it is often more powerful in determining what kind of person he'll be than you—or his teachers or any other adults—are.

The "you" lead was used in an attempt to get direct, immediate contact with the reader. The reader self-interest in raising popular kids is hit in the first paragraph, then expanded upon in a way designed to make the reader say, "Yes, that's the way it was." But after four paragraphs of abstract discussion I was afraid I was going to lose the reader, so I put in an anecdote that showed kids in action and also had some appeal for the reader. Of course it also indirectly made the point that kids knew how to operate effectively in their own world, which was often different from the world of the teacher or their parents.

Recently, for example, a boy in one school was fooling around and raising the roof instead of doing his work. The teacher was unable to do anything with him, even when she warned that if he didn't buckle down he might not be promoted. One day, in order to impress on him what it would be like to be left back, she said he would have to spend three or four days in the grade just below.

She told him this shortly before the noon hour. When lunch was over, she was presented with a petition signed by every member of the class except the "bad" boy. It said: "Joseph is our class member. It's our fault as much as his if he doesn't work. Please let him stay with us. We will see that he works."

Somewhat flabbergasted and a little proud, the teacher agreed. Joseph's work improved immediately and stayed at the higher level.

Now to explain the two reasons why it's important for kids to be popular, backed up by quotes from experts.

It is terribly important for a child to be popular in his own world—first, because his popularity will determine his attitude toward himself throughout his life, and second, because if he's popular he will learn more. Says Dr. Jean D. Grambs, professor of educational sociology at Stanford University, "The way one feels about oneself throughout life is affected by group atmospheres—the individual has a sense of personal security, poise, success, or the individual is suspicious, defensive, feels inferior, and dislikes others."

Thus if you can teach your child how to be popular in his hidden world you'll go a long way toward ensuring his success in his future marriage, his relations with others on his job, and his position among his friends and neighbors.

Furthermore, if a child is accepted, respected and admired by his mates, he learns more easily. Says Gordon Allport, distinguished Harvard psychologist, "The student's readiness to learn facts, it is now pretty well agreed, depends on the state of his attitudes. Information seldom sticks unless mixed with 'attitudinal glue.' And his attitudes are determined largely by what other kids think of him."

Now, after ten paragraphs, sociometric testing, which triggered the whole idea, is finally mentioned and explained. But the explanation is held to a minimum and includes no educator's jargon. To keep the reader going, there's a short, specific anecdote included. Immediately after the explanation of the device, we go back to the main reader self-interest: what makes kids popular.

A deceptively simple device has yielded these discoveries. It is called a sociometric test, and it measures children's popularity. The teacher asks each child whom he would most like to sit next to, or work on a committee with or play with.

Once she gets this information, she can draw up a chart showing which children are the most frequently chosen, and which are seldom or never chosen.

This is where the surprises start. In a New York City school, for example, there was a boy named Ronald who had an IQ of only seventy-five and whom the teacher thought "emotionally unstable, immature and below his grade level." But Ronald was chosen six times by other students, who apparently saw in him things that the teacher didn't. She put him with the six who had chosen him, and after two months she reported, "He reads nicely now and holds his own in class discussion." (Surprisingly often, the quiet, well-mannered and bright child is not wanted by his schoolmates.)

This teacher carried out the next step in sociometric testing—she rearranged the class so that the youngsters were with the ones they liked best. And, more important, she took steps to bring the unwanted children into the group.

To do this, a teacher must know what it is the other kids don't like about their less popular classmates, and this is where the testing gets tricky. Because finding out the real reasons—not the ones the kids tell you first—requires skill in what the psychologists call "depth interviewing." This may take hours, and usually the information is gotten indirectly, in reply to questions that seem inconsequential or downright silly.

It has taken years of such testing, plus the interviewing of thousands of children all over the country, for these scientists to compile any general list of the qualities that make children popular. Here are the highlights:

From here on the article lists the major attributes that make youngsters liked and respected by other kids. For emphasis the separate points are numbered and the first sentence set in boldface. In each case the point is stated, explained, then illustrated with an anecdote. There are four such points. Then there's one that lists the things that are in adult value systems, but not in the child's. Finally, the piece winds up with a "what can be done" section which suggests things parents can do to make their kids popular. This is a simple, practical structure; the artistry, if any, comes in thinking the basic idea through from a pedagogue's gimmick to something that would help parents, and in selecting and writing the anecdotes.

In the evolution of this idea, bits of information were taken from several sources and melded together to make something new. Here the process started with a new body of information from an expert; it could have started with the writer identifying a problem, a concern that is common to many readers, then seeking out the experts to find the answers, if any. But always the essential ingredient in shaping the idea is reader self-interest.

How does the writer identify self-interest? How does she learn about new information that the experts have? She arranges and maintains the broadest, most diverse intake of ideas, information, impressions, emotions that she can. She circulates and listens to people. She observes, not with the sightseer's bland gaze, but with the reporter's sharp eye that always asks why, and how does this fit. She reads enormously and as many different kinds of publications as possible. She watches television and movies, goes to plays and museums and concerts.

A writer learns to listen to everybody's shop talk as a possible source of ideas. She happens to go to a party at which are four aeronautical engineers who shortly huddle in one end of the room and talk shop. The writer probably knows nothing about aeronautical engineering, but she joins the group, listens, and gets involved, because if something concerns them, it may concern thousands of others in different jobs. It may not, too, but at least she's probably picked up some tidbits of information she didn't have before. Sometimes she tries to trigger the idea-formation process by asking a fuel oil dealer, say, what are the problems, headaches, gripes in his business. She may get a tip for an article for a home-and-garden magazine on ways to save money on oil heating or oil furnace repairs. It isn't earthshaking, but it's valuable to thousands of homeowners. Or the conversation may bring a tip-off on a racket-ridden union or city department that is victimizing homeowners and needs exposing.

A writer never knows where the next idea is coming from, so she makes the conglomeration of things she reads and experiences as rich as possible. Most writers I know read three or four newspapers a day, a couple of weekly newsmagazines, a dozen or so general magazines, plus scholarly or professional publications in the fields they are especially interested in. Medical writers read medical journals, political writers read the Congressional Record, and business writers read annual reports. Because universities are centers of research in many fields, many writers have had their names put on mailing lists of university news bureaus. All of these esoteric sources provide new bits of information which, when combined with the writer's own knowledge of people's self-interests, may trigger an idea for a new article, newspaper series, or a book.

For the creative journalist, the process of listening to people, of reading widely, of absorbing information, impressions, ideas, and emotions cannot be a passive pursuit. He or she also thinks about all these things trying to relate one to another, and juxtaposing bits of information to see if they add up to something new. It is in this process that good journalist spots trends and truths about the current scene that may have eluded others. The story idea mentioned in chapter 1, about the dilemma of a man caught in an organization trap, came while I was reading congressional testimony about the Fort Lee airfield scandal. As I thought about the situation later, it seemed likely that the colonel involved was only one of many caught in similar situations in other large organizations; checking around proved the hunch to be true.

Some years ago, the newspapers and magazines were full of stories about the horrible living conditions of migrant farm laborers. Question: Wasn't there some place in America where conditions weren't horrible, where the residents had accepted the migrants into their community's life? Some checking around revealed there was, and a report of what the town did and how it worked made an article.

Persistent thinking about what they are taking in provides writers with another great reservoir of ideas. Every writer I know agrees that some of the best story ideas can come while doing research for a quite different piece. Almost never when I have been out of town doing research on one story have I come back without an idea for one or two more. It usually happens while you're interviewing someone and the conversation wanders off the subject. Then a point she makes, an insight she shares, a story she tells opens a door to a whole new field of thought, and in the new vista you suddenly see the shape and color of a new story.

Finally, there are practical considerations in handling ideas that beginners often ignore. One of these is whether the story can actually be gotten. Many first-class ideas are too big, too diffuse to be practical. For example, medical fees had been rising faster than almost any other costs as this was written. A writer might think of doing a piece on exactly how much an appendectomy, an office visit, or a series of X-rays costs in fifty major cities across the country.

It's a good idea. It would be valuable both to document the rise in medical charges and to give millions a yardstick by which to measure their own doctor's fees. But how do you get the story? Is there time and money enough to visit each of the fifty cities and spend a week or two digging out the information? Keep in mind that it won't come easily. Most doctors won't tell you what they charge, and neither will the medical societies or medical schools. Insurance companies have schedules of fees for particular ailments, but everyone knows doctors frequently charge more than the scheduled price. Would you go door-to-door asking people? What people? How would you know that those you interviewed were a true cross-section of the city?

Labor unions might agree to poll their memberships, but less than twenty percent of American workers belong to unions, so how accurate would your sample be? Would an industry agree to such a poll? Probably not, but even if it did, wouldn't you have the same sample distortion? About the only way such an idea could be turned into a valid story would be for a magazine to hire a good polling organization to run a nationwide poll at great expense. Occasionally magazines do this, but usually the story idea originates with the editors rather than an individual writer.

A recent trend is for a publication to enlist a professional polling organization, usually in a university, to make broad, scientific studies of attitudes and happenings in its area of interest. The television networks and large newspapers like the *New York Times* and the *Washington Post* routinely use such polls to determine how Americans feel about particular issues or political candidates.

Another practical question that novice writers sometimes fail to consider is whether a story is publishable. Not whether it is well researched and written, but is the idea one that the mass media will use? The answer deals not with the audience or formula of a particular magazine or network, but with general attitudes that all media share.

The media try to be positive. A story about what's good is more acceptable than one about what's bad. Stories of a person's struggle to overcome obstacles usually must have a happy ending. Stories that explore a problem almost always must include a section at the end explaining what can be done to solve it. There are minor exceptions to this rule. Articles that expose a bad situation in the most dramatic possible terms are occasionally used for their shock value. But the market for this type of story is limited, and even then a "what can be done" section is usually included.

The reason is simple. The media are part of what we call the free enterprise system; most do not publish attacks on it. You can attack crime, labor unions, extreme leftists and rightists, politicians, and teachers, but seldom corporations or businessmen (except when some scoundrel embezzles $867,422.32 from some company, in which case you attack him, not the company). Book publishers are more likely to publish this kind of story—Ralph Nader's numerous books are examples.

Mass media editors want to keep their readers reading, their viewers watching. They know that factual, statistical presentations that appeal only to an audience's intellect are ignored in droves. So it's up to the writer to present his or her ideas and information in ways that appeal to reader's emotions and enable them to identify with the issue under discussion. One of the best ways of doing this is to personalize the situation. You write not about the problem but about a person experiencing the problem. For example, we all know that many of the people who say that the primary value of athletics is to teach teamwork and sportsmanship do not really believe that and are interested primarily in winning.

But to do an article on the subject, a reporter would have to find a way to personalize the issue. A few years ago, a student named Bob Lloyd did that. Lloyd, who came from Texas, heard about a high school football coach in the Texas town of Dripping Springs (really!) who was in danger of being fired because his team was losing. That was not unusual, but other facts were.

The coach had once been the town's hero, because he had coached the team to three division titles. He had also been praised because he had established a policy that every boy on the team would play in every game, no matter how important. Obviously his players loved him and when he was winning, the townspeople did too. But after the team was moved into a different division, containing considerably larger schools, the team started losing, and many of the townspeople turned on him. Lloyd's story beautifully captured all of these elements and showed that for some, at least, winning was the only thing. Lloyd sold the story to the *New York Times*.

With few exceptions, the mass media do not want essays in which writers expound their own ideas of the way things are or ought to be. They want reportage. Many times when I was first writing for magazines, editors tossed back a manuscript with, "This is just an essay, just you talking. Who the hell are you? The readers want to know what happened." It was hard on the ego, but it made the point.

All these media attitudes may offend your conception of journalistic truth and responsibility, as well as your ego. But a writer's obligation is to get published, and this is the way it is. If you want to write for a few select friends or people who are already convinced, that's fine. But if you want to reach millions with your message, you accept the strictures and figure a way to say what you want within their limits. In most cases it can be done. The flexibility and ingenuity required to shape your idea is also a part of the creative process.

3

How Do You Sell Ideas?

O nce a writer has come up with an idea and decided on the magazine he or she thinks will use the article, the next job is to convince the magazine's editors to buy it. To do this, a magazine writer uses something called a query letter or outline (the two terms are interchangeable).

Like one or two other things in this business, the term "outline" is confusing. It has two meanings. One is the outline you produce for your own use when you are trying to figure out how to put the article together. It's informal, written for you, and takes whatever form you choose. But the outline an editor wants to see is different. It is a selling document, designed to sell the editor on your idea. It must convince the editor of four facts: (1) that the idea is valid; (2) that the story can be gotten; (3) that it will be right for his or her audience; and (4) that you can produce it— that is, that you know how to do the necessary research, and that the quality of your writing meets the magazine's standards.

Many textbooks on magazine writing say that the outline should be as short as possible, perhaps a single paragraph, certainly no more than a page. This may be all right for an editor with whom you have worked closely and who knows how you write and research. But if you want to do major articles for large magazines, or if you are unknown to the editor, a one-paragraph letter just won't do the job.

I have written outlines that were as long as six pages. That's long—two or three pages is better—but I always feel that the assignment is going to stand or fall on the basis of what's on the paper, and this is the only chance I'm going to have to convince the editor. And not just one editor; in the bigger markets, no single editor makes the decision on an idea. He or she passes it along to three or four others, and your outline must convince them too. An outline, then, is almost a telescoped article, and because it is, there are certain things you have to do before you can produce a good one.

First, you have to do enough preliminary research to make sure the idea is valid. You have to locate sources for material you will get and make sure they have the material, know what they're talking about, and are willing to talk to you. You have to figure out likely markets, which means, among other things, that you check *Reader's Guide to Periodical Literature* to see what else has been written on the subject and who has published it. It's not the smartest thing in the world to offer an article to *Good Housekeeping* on new discoveries in dieting if they published one two months ago. You must figure out the reader self-interests of the likely markets and the ways your article will appeal to them. You must gather two or three anecdotes that illustrate the theme or some of the points the article will make. Finally you must write the outline so that it will convince *by demonstration*.

It's no good to tell an editor, "There are a lot of good anecdotes." Get a couple and write them. That way you prove there are good ones and that you know how to handle them. It's no good to say, "This will be of great interest to your readers." You must isolate the particular self-interest and make it implicit to the outline so the editor will recognize it. It's no good to say, "There are many good authorities who will vouch for this idea." You must identify a couple and quote them in support of the idea. It does no good to say, "This is a great dramatic human narrative." You must indicate it by telling some of the story, or at least listing the elements of the drama, so the editor knows that you know what they are.

Obviously this kind of outline can't be written in fifteen minutes on a Friday afternoon. It takes work and thought. Further, while you're doing it, you know it may be wasted because the idea may never sell. That's the gamble you take, the investment you make in order to get a future reward. If you're not willing to do it, forget about the major markets and the lovely daydreams about showers of gold.

A good outline, then, should contain these elements:

1. A title, if you can think of a clever one or one that expresses succinctly the theme of the piece.
2. A clear, concise statement of the idea plus ways it appeals to reader self-interest.
3. Evidence to support the idea, including a couple of anecdotes.
4. Suggested sources for the material you will use.
5. Suggestions for the "what can be done" section if it's a problem story.
6. If you have to travel at the magazine's expense to get the material, some idea of where you'll go and about how much it will cost.

Here's an example of an outline that sold an idea to *Reader's Digest*. (The title isn't very catchy, but it does express the underlying idea; it was not used when the piece was published.)

Traffic Courts Are Unfair

Motorists all over the country are being whipsawed in traffic courts that are not courts at all, but collection agencies. They retain the power of courts to punish, yet ignore the safeguards for an individual's rights that the rest of our legal system has.

Thus, a startling statement for a lead and a succinct presentation of the basic idea. Next comes evidence to support the statement, written in a way that will also promote reader identification and appeal to his self-interest.

The pattern is familiar: you answer a summons for a minor violation. You wait for hours in a jammed, uncomfortable courtroom. The arresting officer is always right; your version is wrong. If you want to plead not guilty you're given another date for a hearing, you miss another day from work, and often the cop doesn't show up so you have another postponement, and another. Often you can't afford to miss more time from work so you give up and plead guilty.

Often when you say you want to plead not guilty the judge says, "Why not plead guilty. It will only cost you $5." What he doesn't say is that it is also a conviction on your record which, in states with a point system, may be the first step in the suspension of your license—and with it your only way to get to work, or get the kids to school, or shop for food. He also doesn't say the conviction may boost your insurance premiums: if you have three speeding violations in eighteen months, for example, your rate goes up 60 percent.

All this has been general; now come a couple of specific anecdotes, written very tightly.

If you plead guilty you may well be treated like a bank robber. Recently a young man answered a summons, but he hadn't brought enough money to pay his fine. Although he said his wife was outside in the car with additional cash, he was booked, fingerprinted, stripped, searched, and held in jail for eight hours before he could reach his wife and have her bring the additional money. A New York businessman was fined $15 at 11:50 A.M.; he'd forgotten his wallet. He telephoned his office and instructed an assistant to bring down the necessary amount; nevertheless he was handcuffed and thrown into the tank. The assistant arrived at 12:20 with the money, but he was not allowed to pay it until 4:00 P.M., and the businessman was not released until 4:45.

Now, another two points the article will make, both written to heighten reader identification.

Though the chief objective of these courts seems to be to collect money rather than to dispense justice, even the simplest modern traffic violation may not be an open-and-shut thing. For instance: you're driving at the speed limit in a 35-mile-an-hour zone. When you're seventy-five feet from the corner, the light turns red. You can stop in time, but there's a car tailgating you; if you stop quickly, it may hit you. You see there are no cars on the cross street, and you decide it's safer to run the light. You have had to make several fairly complicated decisions in a split second; certainly there's room for the argument that you were right—except in the collection-agency courts.

Further, there are many unrealistic speed limits in existence, as well as many bad traffic signals and confusing signs. A person can violate a law with the best will in the world, while trying hard to be lawful. Yet none of this is taken into consideration in thousands of traffic courts. Sometimes cops have a quota of tickets to give out and lay for victims until they fill it.

Now another anecdote to prove this last point.

Recently a woman stopped at an intersection unfamiliar to her and prepared to make a left turn. She had her blinker on and waited almost two minutes for traffic to clear before making the turn. She did not see a No Left Turn sign across the intersection, but she did see a parked police car with an officer watching her. He made no move to warn her the proposed turn was illegal but after she made it, he gave her a ticket.

Here comes the "what can be done section," plus identification of a major source for the story.

But reform is possible. The American Bar Association has detailed a member, James Economos, to head up its Committee on Traffic Courts. Economos, whose headquarters is in Chicago, has traveled all over the country investigating abuses and has a store of facts about them. He has also helped communities fight to reform their traffic courts. One case I know of where he was successful was in Chenango County, New York. Here a citizens committee and the Chamber of Commerce banded together in a successful campaign of reform. But AAA officials assure me Economos has many other similar cases we could report on to tell people how to correct the abuses.

Finally, a suggestion of the travel—and expenses—necessary to get the story.

The way to do the story would be to go to Chicago and see Economos, and then if it proved necessary to visit some individual cities where abuses were taking place, do so.

After consulting with other editors, the man I worked with at the *Digest* told me to go ahead on the story. But he wanted me to get Economos to agree to sign the piece with an "as told to ———" by-line. I prefer not do that kind of story, because it restricts what you can write to what the other signer is willing to say publicly, and it means you have to do a good bit of negotiating on precisely how the final piece will be worded. But Economos proved to be willing to make many tough and truthful charges about this situation, and his name and position added authority to the piece, so that's the way we did it.

Of course, not all outlines have to be that long, and some are organized differently. Here's an outline done by one of Glavin's former students, Peter Wilkinson. The outline was sent to Christine Miles, the managing editor of *Manhattan, Inc.*, whom Wilkinson had met but had never worked with. The outline was the only basis Miles had of judging Wilkinson's ability.

Dear Chris:

Way back last year when you were still at *Forbes*, we talked about reporter/researcher jobs. I'm at Fairchild [a publisher] now and I want to propose an article that might fit in at *Manhattan, Inc.*

Al Wilburne was in the trimmings business. He sold buttons, bits of lace, piping, and ruffles to the big dress makers in New York's garment center. Through the years—Al opened his doors right after the Depression—his companies grew and prospered. But, in 1977, when in his 60s, Al saw an opportunity to increase his profits many times over. He started sending phony bills to his best customer, having them approved by a man inside, laundering the money, and using the loot to build a big house and buy furs and jewels for his wife.

In time, Al and others stole more then $4 million, pulling off the largest bogus billing scam in garment center history. Al had a partner in crime—his son Marc, who was a co-owner of several of the Wilburne companies. A shy, passive young man, Marc was a product of his father's influence and the two were nearly indistinguishable. Marc looked to Al for guidance in all aspects of business and his personal life.

Al had taken Marc into the family firm at 23—after one dismal year of dental school—and Marc performed well. But, before long, he too was consumed by the fraud. Ultimately, it would be Marc's unquenchable greed, his escalation of the scheme, that would attract the attention of federal agents. Together they were indicted, and together Al and Marc fled, first to Canada and then to Israel. And together they would come back to jail—Marc for five years, his dad for seven.

The Wilburnes had run a colorful series of crimes—hooking up with Israeli mafia figures, threatening grand jury witnesses, and framing other men. Both lived in million-dollar homes on Long Island and drove expensive cars. But later, when jail was only weeks away, the only job Marc could find was one driving an ice cream truck. And eventually, IRS agents, seeking restitution, would appraise everything the Wilburnes owned, right down to Marc's daughter's teddy bear.

Then, one night last month, Marc walked outside his "cell" at a minimum security prison in Connecticut (his father was asleep inside), tied together of couple of belts, and hanged himself from a tree. He was 35. The next day a federal judge in New York granted Al's pending request for a reduction in sentence. Al was free to go, the judge said, and Al buried Marc that afternoon.

As the court reporter for Fairchild News Service in New York, I've covered the Wilburnes since their return from Israel. I've written about their pleadings, sentencings, and Marc's death. As I see it, the article requires a detailed review of the extensive court file in the case, plus interviews with those who knew Al and his son—people in the garment center and, if possible, family members. I've gone to the prosecutor for help on this and can hope for a number of willing subjects.

Look forward to meeting with you to discuss the project further.

Note that the Wilkinson outline covers all of the basics. It tells Miles what the story is about, shows that it deals with *Manhattan, Inc.*'s area of interest (business in New York City), proves that Wilkinson knows how to conduct the necessary research, and gives an idea of the style in which he will write the story. (Mentioning the teddy bear indicated that Wilkinson had a reporter's eye for the telling detail.) No outline need do more than that. Miles says she grew interested in the story because of the outline. After reading it, she spoke with Wilkinson, gave him the assignment, and, a few months later, printed the article in *Manhattan, Inc*.

4

Research

*F*or the daily deadline reporter, research was much too fancy a word for the process of getting a story. He called it legwork and it consisted of going where something was happening, looking acutely, listening accurately, questioning participants to fill out the details, and checking what he'd seen and heard with other participants or documentary sources to make sure he hadn't been misled. In their book *The Reporter's Trade*, Washington columnists Joseph and Stewart Alsop called this "the rule of the feet" and added, "If you get out, and see what is going on for yourself, and talk to a great many people who are responsibly involved in what is going on, you can hardly help doing a good job of reporting."

True enough. The operative phrase is, "and talk to a great many people who are responsibly involved." What people? Where?

A writer answering these questions calls upon his creativity in the research part of the job. If he is going to use material from different sources, different disciplines to create something new, this is the place where he decides what sources and disciplines. If the disciplines are diverse, varied, pertinent, and the sources valid, articulate, informed, and imaginative, the resulting article will be also. If not, it won't.

That's easy to say, but how do you go about it? It helps, we think, if you go back to thinking about your readers, realizing that you are their stand-in, their eyes, ears, and nose, and mouth to ask the questions they would ask. You think what their self-interest would be in the situation you're reporting, what things would pique their emotions, why they would want to read about it. It helps, too, to envision the forthcoming story as a whole, to try to foresee all its different facts and make sure you explore them all.

How do you get started? Let's say you have an idea for an article, and you've checked *Reader's Guide to Periodical Literature* to see if any magazine has done a similar one recently (none has). But you don't know how to find out if the idea is valid—i.e., supported by fact—and you have no name or organization to start your research with.

Some of the most basic and helpful tools are located in the library. They are called databases, and they enable a writer to search through millions of documents to find material relevant to a particular subject.

There are three types of databases: bibliographic, full-text, and numeric. The first type gives you a bibliography of material that relates to your subject. The second (and much more expensive) type gives you the texts of any articles you are interested in. And the third offers numbers, rather than articles—for example, a numeric database might offer specific material from the last census.

Hundreds of databases are available, and even after you consult the directories that list them, you may need the help of an expert to decide which you should search. Ask the librarian. Most librarians we have dealt with have been eager to help.

Let's assume that you are doing a story on the problems of farmers who have lost their farms and moved to the city. If you want to know about the history of the farmer in America, you might search a database called *America: History and Life* or another called *Arts and Humanities Search.* Both will search the historical literature and offer you a list of citations to articles on the subject. You can then look up the articles in the appropriate journals.

If you wish to learn about the stress which the former farmers are experiencing, you might conduct a search of the *Psychological Abstract* database. If you wish to discover what the president of the United States has said and done about the farmers, you might search *Washington Presstext,* which contains all official information from the White House and the State Department, including presidential speeches, press conferences, vetoes, and executive orders. (It even includes State Department toasts, but they would probably be of little use in this context.)

The cost of such searches varies greatly, from $2 to hundreds of dollars, but most bibliographic searches cost between $5 and $50.

Among the cheapest of the databases are those produced by the US government. The *Government Printing Office's Monthly Catalog* lists citations to government-agency reports as well as to reports of Congressional hearings. The *NTIS* database offers more than a million citations to reports on government-sponsored research. *ERIC* makes available citations to educational research. and *Medline* contains citations to articles printed in thousands of medical journals worldwide. Remember as you conduct your research to think about the people your article is aimed at. Whose self-interest will be involved in it? Whose self-interest will be advanced? Whose injured? Once you've answered these questions you will have a direction, and most likely a source, to approach. For instance, once you have obtained the citations and read the articles, you might want to call some of the authors to get further information on the subject and to seek additional sources. One of the advantages of our overorganized world is that in America there is a society, a council, a club, for almost everything. You can find them listed in the *Encyclopedia of Associations,* which should be available in your library. You're almost certain to find one that fits your area. Call up and talk to the public relations person.

Almost every idea you get will have a starting place—a name, an organization—and this one will lead you to others. All you have to do is ask the first few people you interview, "Who else would know about this?" Their answers will start you on an interviewing chain that will lead from source to source until your research is complete. A good way to show how this works is to describe such a chain.

The trigger for the idea was a *New York Times* story which reported that the Junior Chamber of Commerce of Hopkins, Minnesota, had given one of its members, Richard Tenneson, the job of preparing a scrapbook of the group's activities. This routine job was a milestone for Tenneson, the *Times* reported, because he was one of twenty-one US "turncoats" who had chosen to remain in Communist China after the Korean War ended. He got a job because the JC members believed Tenneson, who had since regretted his decision and returned to the US, "was on his way back to healthy citizenship."

The item was interesting because ever since the war, there had been a great deal of talk in the press about "brainwashing"—making it a kind of mysterious rite akin to voodoo—and much national breast-beating about the number of US soldiers who had broken down and collaborated with the enemy or given up and died in captivity. This showed, said the breast-beaters—usually among the authoritarian right wing—that the younger generation was weak-minded and lacking in moral fiber.

This seemed to me to be nonsense. I'd read about brainwashing in books by Arthur Koestler and Joost Van Meerloo, and there was nothing mysterious about it. It was simply a clever, persistent attack on a person's psyche. It was an extension of the police method of questioning a suspect that I'd seen as a reporter. Further, I'd become convinced that no one could withstand the process if it were properly planned and continued long enough; anyone could be made to tell what he knew. The French underground, one of the toughest resistance movements in World War II, had known this so well that when one of their members was captured, that person was required to remain silent for only twenty-four hours, to give other members of the unit time to disappear. They knew no one could hold out very long under Gestapo methods. Finally, it seemed illogical that young men who had behaved so courageously in World War II, just six or seven years before, could become so weak so soon. Generations don't change that fast.

But I was working for *Redbook* at the time, and what had all this to do with our readers? How was their self-interest involved? First, Tenneson was twenty-five, married, and had a small daughter, which meant that our young adult audience could identify with him. (While most *Redbook* readers were women, we were then trying to attract young men, too). Second, many of our readers were Korean veterans, and the attack was on them; indeed, since the attack was on a generation, it impugned *all* our young readers. A defense, we reasoned, would be a service that we could and should render them. A way to do it would be to write Tenneson's story, showing what had broken him down and how and why he had ultimately rejected the Communist way. The story should explain the general methods of "brainwashing" so that readers would understand the process and by demonstrating that anyone could be broken, it would help remove the stigma from a generation.

All this made sense in editorial terms, but many questions remained. Had Tenneson's experience as a captive been representative of what others had gone through? Was he intelligent enough to understand what had happened to him and articulate enough to explain it, or had he been simply a straw blown about by different winds? How reliable was he? The Communist ideology, I knew, justified any deceit in furtherance of its goals; could you believe anything he said? Finally, was he the kind of man the magazine wanted to support—because the overall effect of an article about him would be an espousal of his story. Certainly the research on this one was going to require much cross-checking, plus a deeper knowledge of what had happened to US soldiers captured in the war.

Obviously the first thing to do was to talk to Tenneson and see what kind of man he was. I had to go to Honolulu on another story, and I stopped in Minneapolis to see him. (Hopkins, where he lived, is only a few miles from Minneapolis.) I jotted down a list of things I wanted to find out:

"Childhood? When married? Wife's reaction to past? Why didn't appreciate kind of life this country can give you? What kind of picture of US did early life give? What experience in the army? Any trouble getting jobs after came back? Any social pressure? What happened in captivity?"

When I got to Minneapolis I called Tenneson and told him we were thinking of doing a story on his experience as a way of explaining to everyone what it had been like in the prison camps. I asked to see him; he jumped at the chance and offered to come to my hotel.

Tenneson was a slight, highly nervous young man with dark short hair and large blue eyes with a semiglazed look that sometimes seems to come from thoughtfulness and suffering. But he laughed a lot as he talked. And he talked eagerly, continuously, the way some people do as a way to release inner tension. He seemed intelligent and highly volatile, either because of emotional instability or immaturity. As he told his story, I detected a good deal of self-justification (which meant I'd have to do a lot of checking), and many hints that, deep down, he felt he wasn't worth much (one of the first things he said, with an embarrassed laugh, was "My father was a bootlegger").

He left after two hours, and on the plane to Honolulu I tried to decide whether his story would do the job we wanted done. His childhood had been unstable; his mother and father had been divorced when he was a year old, and for seven years he'd lived with grandparents who, he said, were over-indulgent. At eight he went to live with his mother and her new husband, who tried to give him some discipline and teach him good work habits. But the discipline had been harsh at times, and the boy resented it. He ran away from home several times, and, though he was intelligent, did badly in school. When he was fifteen he'd gone to live with an aunt. In the middle of the school year he'd run away and wound up in jail for car theft in Nebraska, but said he was later exonerated (was he?).

He'd joined the army at seventeen, without finishing high school, and had botched up his career there. He'd been sent to Korea only a few months after induction and had never really become a part of any outfit. He'd been in combat twice, and both times his regiment had retreated. Only two months after he'd landed in Korea, when he was still seventeen, he'd been captured.

He had not been physically mistreated by the Chinese, and he didn't understand the psychological conditioning they were subjecting him to. Either through clever planning or by coincidence, the treatment the Chinese gave him had appealed to some of his deepest emotional needs.

The story seemed to have a happy ending: he had rejected communism (had he really?) and seemed to be making a strong effort to rehabilitate himself as a citizen (was he? what forces were working pro and con?).

I decided the story was a good gamble and my editors agreed. I went back to Minneapolis some weeks later with a list of people to be seen and facts to be checked. I also had a long list of questions for Tenneson. I've found that such a list, prepared in advance, serves two purposes; it ensures that you don't overlook some areas of inquiry that you might forget during the heat of the interview, and it gives you a ready question to throw in at those times when, concentrating on taking notes or comprehending what the man has just said, you don't think ahead to the next question.

The first person I interviewed was Don Pobuda, head of the Junior Chamber of Commerce (I got his name from the original *New York Times* story). From him I learned about Tenneson's activities in the JC, and how and why he was accepted as a member in the first place. As I always do, especially in the early interviews for a new story, I asked Pobuda for the names of other people who were involved with Tenneson as employers or friends or co-workers. He gave me the names of two of Tenneson's employers, as well as a couple of friends. I interviewed them to find out what kind of employee he'd been, what his friends thought of him.

Since Tenneson had told me about his arrest in Nebraska, I thought I ought to check and see if he had any other police record. I called a Minneapolis detective I'd worked with on a previous story, told him what I was doing, and asked if he'd check with both the local and state police to see if there was a record. A few days later he called back to say there was not.

Next I had a long interview with Tenneson in which I took him back over his whole life, with great detail as to names, dates, army career. I got him only as far as his capture and arranged another interview later.

During the interviewing with some of my other sources I'd heard about an incident in a bar a few months before in which a soldier had grabbed Tenneson, called him "a Communist son-of-a-bitch," and worked him over a little before Tenneson's friends had pulled the man off. As far as I could tell, it had been the only incident of its kind since Tenneson had come back. So I talked to two men and a woman who had been there, to get the story straight.

These contacts gave me the names of other people who knew both Tenneson and his wife, and I later talked with several of them. Obviously I had to talk to Tenneson's mother who, I learned, was living on a farm some miles from Minneapolis. I called and made a date to visit her. Then I interviewed Tenneson again for several hours, not only getting more details of his experience, but questioning him specifically about "brainwashing" techniques I'd noted down from books on the subject.

The next day, I drove through the cold, barren, snowy country to see his mother. Again in detail, I took her through Tenneson's childhood, his arrest in Nebraska (and got the name of the lawyer who had defended him), her own trip to Japan to try to talk her son out of joining the Chinese Communists, and the long period after his return when he stayed with her and her husband. She also gave me the name of a doctor, Philip Bloemsma, in Washington, DC, who had himself been a prisoner of the Japanese during World War II and had subsequently made a study of the psychological effects of prison life on soldiers.

Back at the hotel that night I called the lawyer in Nebraska and got his story of Tenneson's arrest, time in jail, and subsequent release. He said Tenneson had been an innocent victim. I asked him if he'd send me copies of the court papers on the disposition of the case, because the only testimony I'd gotten had been interested—Tenneson's, his mother's, and the lawyer's. Later the lawyer sent the papers, and the stories checked out. Also that night I made another list of questions to be covered with Tenneson, his wife and friends, questions that had been raised in previous interviews.

The next day I talked with a young woman who was a close friend of both Tenneson and his wife and got an outsider's view of their personalities and their marriage. I also talked with another man who had been present at the fracas in the bar. And then Tenneson again—this time mostly on his experience in China after the war, his decision to return home, and what happened thereafter. I also got a dates-and-places chronology of when he came to Hopkins, where he lived and worked, how he met his wife, got married, and so on. (I've learned that in a story like this the inteviewee tends to skip around in time, so that it's hard to put together a chronology later when you're assembling the story. But if you try to pin them down to specific dates and places at the time you're interviewing, it tends to stop the flow of talk. So I try to do the whole chronology later at one time.)

Next I had a long talk with Tenneson's wife, Jan. Obviously a man's wife is not an objective witness. But I've learned you can offset the bias somewhat by putting the proposition to her that you're trying to understand this man, to learn what goes on beneath the surface, and since she knows him better than anyone alive, she can help. Usually she'll try to level with you as best she can. You start by asking questions about specific incidents: What did your parents say when you told them you were going to marry Rick? What was his reaction to meeting your parents? And so on.

Then I had a final interview with Tenneson, in which I cleaned up loose ends and again checked things I'd learned from others.

Before I left Minneapolis I called the late S.L.A. Marshall, in Detroit, and asked if I could see him the next day, a Sunday. Marshall was a newspaperman, a reserve general, and one of the best military historians writing. I hadn't met him, but I'd read a couple of his books, knew he was deeply interested in what makes men fight—or not—and that he had been in Korea interviewing combat soldiers.

I had asked for an hour; we spent seven together, and it was one of those rare and wonderful times when two minds mesh—exciting, stimulating, and for me, at least, rich in new insights. He also gave me the names of some officers in Washington who had conducted with Korean War soldiers one of the most extensive investigations the army had ever run on why men fight or give up. Finally, he gave me the name and address of the general commanding Tenneson's division in Korea, which was to prove invaluable.

Marshall also advanced a reason why the army had supported the attack on a generation of soldiers as weaklings; the army knew perfectly well the techniques of "brainwashing" that would be used on captured soldiers ("Hell, we'd used most of them ourselves on Japanese prisoners in World War II") but had failed to train its own soldiers in what to expect if captured or give them any defenses against the psychological pressures they were sure to meet.

Then I flew to Washington and went to the Book and Magazine Branch of the Department of Defense in the Pentagon. I told them about the story I was doing and asked to see the official records of the regiment Tenneson had belonged to, in order to check his story of what had happened during the two battles he'd been in. After a couple of days word came back that I could not have them; they were still classified (despite the fact the war had been over for five years, and presumably the enemy knew what had happened). So I tried another tack: I made up a list of specific questions covering the major points of Tenneson's story and asked if they would check the records and give me the answers. (I received the answers some weeks later, after the story was written.)

I wrote the commanding general whose name Marshall had given me. This time I wrote exactly what Tenneson had told me about the battles (briefly), explained why I wanted to check the story, and asked his help. He replied immediately, told me what he knew himself, and said he was writing to the commanding officer of Tenneson's regiment for fuller details. Shortly I received a detailed reply from this officer as well. Both men were most appreciative that I'd written. Thus was it possible to get around Pentagon red tape.

One thing the Book and Magazine Branch did do that was most helpful was give me the name of a navy lieutenant who had been a prisoner of the

Chinese and who had successfully resisted their efforts at "brainwashing." I found him not at all smug about his accomplishment. He was full of knowledge about how the Chinese had worked (which checked with what Tenneson and others had told me) and compassion for those men who had not been able to withstand the pressure.

Next I talked to two officers—one a psychiatrist—who had conducted the long investigation of the prisoners mentioned earlier. They added new insights into the psychological pressures the Chinese had used and into the different backgrounds, both in the army and before, of both the men who had broken under the pressure and those who had not. They also denied, as Marshall had, that there had been significantly more collaboration with the enemy in Korea than in other wars.

Finally I went to see Dr. Philip Bloemsma, who had been in a prison camp for three and a half years in Burma during World War II. He told me that prisoners of war commonly experienced a definite psychological sickness, which he called "the fence complex." This sickness, he said, had been studied by Dutch and British doctors during World War II, and its syndrome was explained to him when he headed a hospital in Bangkok after the war. The symptoms of the sickness exactly fitted some of the feelings and attitudes Tenneson said he'd had. They also jibed with things the army men had told me.

(A year later I described the sickness to an expert on civilian prisons in the US. He had never heard of it, but said it matched his own observations of what happens to long-term civilian prisoners. And thus another story idea was born.)

That completed the research for the story. What does this rather lengthy process demonstrate?

That writers shouldn't panic when they start on a story and don't know where the parts to it are coming from. Almost always there's one source at the beginning (Tenneson, Pobuda), and if you ask questions, this one leads to others until you have a long and complete chain.

That you usually start in a library, getting background information so you know what your sources are talking about.

That you check things a source has said against documentary records whenever there's a chance that his or her self-interest might lead you astray. And do it anyway if such records exist.

That while you're researching you keep alert for other names, other sources that will add new facets to the story—and follow them up.

That you don't take an official no for an answer. Find another path to the information.

That you prepare a list of questions that your reader would want answered before you start, and draw up other, more specific lists before you go into each interview.

That you go there, see your sources in their native habitat, if possible see where the action took place. (Once I drove 160 miles to visit a diner where a murder took place so I could describe it in the story.)

That research takes a great deal of time if the story is to have any depth. Once I spent a full day in research to get one line in a story; often a two-hour interview will yield only one colorful, felicitous phrase, but it is still worth it.

That you keep interviewing until your sources begin to repeat each other. This accomplishes two purposes, and possibly a third. If two or three experts, with differing points of view, agree on a fact or a principle, you can be pretty sure it is accepted in their discipline. Second, the agreement tends to offset personal bias by any individual source. The third? It has been my experience that when your sources are no longer telling you anything new, your research is about finished.

One of the pitfalls of this kind of writing is that you can over-research. The chief reason, I think, is that it's easier to interview people than it is, finally, to sit down alone before that terrible blank sheet of paper and start writing. But the loss of time from over-researching is only the lightest penalty that writers pay. The serious one is that they can get so much material that they lose sight of the story line, wallow in confusion for days trying to recapture it, and sometimes never do. When that happens the story fails.

But beginning writers are more inclined to do too little, rather than too much research. So the final rule is, interview, observe, and keep at it.

5

Interviewing

*T*here's an ancient gag in the newspaper business that goes: "So this guy wanted to be a reporter, but he couldn't because nobody would tell him anything."

Like most one-liners that survive long enough to become ancient, this one has truth in it. One of the most persistent failings of unskilled reporters is that they don't see enough people about a particular story, don't ask the right questions and thus don't get the right answers. The art of interviewing breaks down into two parts: how do you get to see people, and how do you get them to tell you the things that will make a story pertinent, lively, readable?

In solving the first problem it is important to understand what you have going for you. It is not difficult to get to see most people for an interview, because essentially what you're doing is asking for their opinion or their expertise. And asking people their opinion is flattering. Most of us spend our lives being told things—by our colleagues, our bosses, our husbands, or our wives—and have to fight to give posterity our own special wisdoms. So when somebody comes along and asks us to tell them what we know or what we think, especially if it's going to be published so the whole world will benefit from our advice, we are delighted to agree. Thus, in many cases, the only thing a reporter has to do to see a person is call up and ask.

But, particularly in depth stories and magazine articles, many of the people you want to interview have days and nights already full of requirements imposed by their jobs, their families, their own interests or ambitions. You have to break into their schedules—which is troublesome for them—and to do it you have to convince them it will be to their self-interest to take the trouble. There are various types of leverage you can summon to help.

The late Dan Mich, one of the great editors of his time, made a basic point a few years ago when he was talking to his writers:

Before starting out on . . . interviews, I would read every available word on the personality or situation involved. I would make notes on what I read. When I reached the point of asking questions, I would know what questions to ask. Instead of boring my source of information with dull routine, I would be able to make the interview challenging and interesting for him.

The last few words are the operative ones, both in getting to see your source and after you are in her office. You accomplish this, as Mich said, by preliminary reading, but also by thinking about the coming interview from her point of view. Not yours, *hers*. What's in it for her to give you time from her busy schedule? Will it help get her a promotion? Will it enhance her reputation? Will it help her defeat a rival? Will it increase the profits of her business? Will it help her solve a problem? Will it help get her votes, or a larger audience for her next show, or more readers for her book?

Once you've figured out what her self-interest is, make your pitch on that basis when you call to ask for an interview. Say, "I'm doing an article for *Reader's Digest* on the increase in crime, and, based on your statement in the *Times* a couple months ago, you disagree with the attorney general and many others about the causes for the increase. I'd like to talk to you further about this; can I come and see you?"

This does several things for you. It tells her you are not some unknown hopeful, but a writer good enough to have an assignment from a well-known publication. It tells her you have done your homework and know enough about the subject to know her position and the attorney general's and thus won't waste her time with a lot of uninformed questions. It gives her an opportunity to attack or answer or defeat her professional rivals—in an influential medium. And it suggests that you will do all this for her with the least possible inconvenience to her—by coming to her office at a time she sets. She'd be a fool to refuse.

But suppose you don't have an assignment from the *Digest* and thus don't have the prestige of the magazine's name to increase your leverage. This happens often, not only with beginning writers, but also with established journalists who are doing the preliminary research necessary to validate—or knock down—an idea before they present it to an editor for approval. You can't count on your name being known to the person, even if you've published a hundred magazine articles, because people rarely pay attention to writers' by lines. But you can use other kinds of leverage, and one is flattery.

It is difficult to overestimate the average person's capacity for flattery. For years I have used the most blatant kind: "I'm working on an article on air pollution, and I understand there isn't anyone in the country better informed on it than you. Can I come to see you?" Usually I do have decency enough to say the last part in a half-kidding way, but it is surprising how many people aren't bothered at all by the exaggeration. Usually they say, delightedly, "Oh, I don't know about that—but sure, I'll see you." Or if you can't bring yourself to be this obvious, you can say with complete sincerity: "I'm trying to get a true picture of air pollution in this country. I've talked to people on all sides of the question, and certainly I can't do a complete job without talking to you." This has the advantages of being both true and consistent with the best journalistic ethics.

Or you can use a variation of the old reporter's hook: "I've got Joe's side of the story, what's yours?" In this one you play one person's self-interest off against another's. If you want to talk to the Republican county chairman about politics in court appointments, you tell him you have talked to the Democrats (if you have) and now want to talk to him. Or you tell a union leader you've already seen the management people and want to get her side. Once I wanted to see an expert on juvenile delinquency who had just gotten a top appointment in Washington and was extraordinarily busy. From background reading I knew he disagreed violently with parts of a study done by Sheldon and Eleanor Glueck of Harvard, which was what I was writing about. I simply told him I was doing a piece on the Glueck study, knew he didn't agree with parts of it, and wanted to talk to him about it. It worked. And it also added depth and balance to the final article.

I learned one of the most unexpected and effective hooks some years ago. I'd read in the paper that a sociologist at Ohio University at Bowling Green, Samuel Harmon Lowrie, had done the survey of dating habits mentioned in Chapter 2, which showed that the kids who had the most dates got the best marks. Obviously I needed to spend a good deal of time with Professor Lowrie to learn about his study. I called and asked for an appointment; he was not interested.

I suggested that publication of my article would broadcast his findings; he didn't want this, at least at the moment, because he wanted to have his study published in a professional journal first. Besides, he said, he was highly dubious about the popular press, and thought it too sensational. Although he was too polite to say so, I got the idea he thought I would cheapen his study. I tried to tell him I was not a sensationalist (how do you convince a stranger you're an honest man?) but wasn't getting very far. Over the phone I could feel his resolve not to see me hardening, and I grew desperate. Finally I said, "Look, you've got an answer here that will help thousands of kids. Most parents think dating hurts their youngsters in school. You've demonstrated the opposite; if we can convince parents of this, we'll not only be removing a source of family friction, but we'll be improving the kind of education thousands of kids will get."

It did the trick. The appeal to his altruism, the suggestion that he could help others, was strong enough to overcome his perfectly legitimate reservations. Since that experience, I've learned that this appeal to a person's altruism is one of the strongest arguments you can use. It has won me access even to convicted criminals in jail, who were going to stay in jail no matter what I wrote, and even though the basis of the appeal was insulting: "If you talk to me maybe it will prevent some other guy from becoming a bum like you." (Of course it was never phrased that way, but the implication was there.)

Another very simple, and often overlooked, device is to put your body in the man's office. You ask to see him. He's busy. Okay, you say, I'll wait. So you sit. What's he going to do with you, throw you out? That would be pretty drastic, especially since all you want to do is ask his opinion about something. You may wait two or three hours, but almost inevitably you'll get to see him.

For one thing your presence puts pressure on the receptionist. She starts out by resenting you for not leaving the way you were supposed to when she turned you away. But the longer you sit there being polite and pleasant and silently importunate, the more sympathetic she gets. After all, you just want to see the man and what is he, some kind of god that he hasn't a couple of minutes to talk to a perfectly nice writer? So she starts working for you, phoning in at intervals and saying, "That writer is still waiting for you." Pause. "I know you did, but he won't leave." And pretty soon you get in.

A similar kind of pressure can be put on the man's secretary, who is paid to keep you from seeing him. You do it with phone calls. First call, she says he's not in, which may or may not be true. So you tell her who you are and what you want to see him about. (Secretaries are usually more impressed by writers than their bosses are.) Ask what time he'll be in; if she says eleven o'clock, call back at about 11:15. Now she's on the defensive: she can't tell you he's not there without some explanation, because it makes her look as though she doesn't know her job. Furthermore, if he is there, she resents having to lie for him when you have done exactly what she told you to. Don't push her; be amiable, flexible, and politely ask when he's likely to be in. You want to build the feeling that you understand her problem and that you and she are working together toward a common goal—to talk to the man. Keep repeating the process and sooner or later, you'll get to talk to him.

Maybe on the first call she says she doesn't know when he'll be back, but she'll have him call you. Don't do it. Say, "Well, I'll be moving around town, so I'd better call him." Then call in about two hours. Keep on calling at intervals for the next day or two; you are putting on the same kind of pressure as when you sit in the office. Most times you'll get to talk to the man before too long.

You have to be imaginative in adapting your techniques for getting to see a source to the particular situation. Writers have come up with dozens of different devices, and here are a couple that I've run across that apply leverage in particular situations.

Once I was in Hollywood to do a story for *Redbook* on Red Skelton. I'd spent two or three days at CBS talking with his producer and director, his writers, some of the people who worked on the show with him, to a couple of vice-presidents, and to the public relations people. Now I was ready to talk to Skelton, but his public relations man wouldn't make an appointment for me. I tried for a day or two, meanwhile talking to friends and other associates and continuing to call the PR man. He gave me nothing but excuses. There was no way to bypass him and go directly to Skelton, because his estate is fenced and its gates locked and he won't talk on the telephone to strangers.

I didn't know what to do. One afternoon I was griping to an editor at CBS, who finally said, "I don't know if it will work, but why don't you try this? Get people to send telegrams to the PR man. We'll send him one saying you've finished your work with us, and we know he wants to cooperate by getting you to Skelton as soon as possible. I'll get our vice president to send him one. Get Skelton's business manager to send one. Get your editor in New York to send one, and anybody else you can think of."

I did. Most of them arrived the next morning. At eleven o'clock the PR man called me to say I had a date with Skelton for that afternoon.

Mort Weisinger once told the members of the Society of Magazine Writers about a hook he used to reach VIPs by phone that worked "nine out of ten times.'"—at least for out-of-towners. From a public phone booth, he said, he would place a long-distance, person-to-person call to the celebrity at his office. "When I reach him, the operator invariably says, 'I have your party. Please deposit $3.25.' Then I go into my ritual of inserting 13 quarters. If I had phoned him from my home phone, he might curtly tell me he's busy and to send him a letter. But when he knows I've shelled out hard cash, a fact which has registered on him via the tolling of the coins, he is sympathetic, helpful, and most cooperative."

Telephones are fine for making appointments; they are no good for the actual interview, unless you have no time or simply want to check a point you forgot in an earlier face-to-face interview. (Everybody forgets sometimes.) They're no good because they don't let you see what your source looks like or watch the expressions and mannerisms which help reveal his or her character; because they're always hurried and you need time for depth interviews; because they don't let you see the person's home or office; and because they're a barrier to the interplay of your two personalities. And this is important, as we'll see in a minute, in getting you the kind of detail and color that creative writing requires.

Most important of all, they're bad because they're inaccurate. While working for a master's degree at Stanford University, Fred C. Berry, Jr., made a study of accuracy in three San Francisco area newspapers. He did it by sending copies of 270 news stories to the people mentioned in them for comment, and he found that 46 percent of them were completely accurate. But, he found, "the most frequently used sources of information were not the most accurate sources. Personal interviews produced about one and a half times as many accurate stories as telephone interviews." (*Journalism Quarterly*, Autumn 1967, p. 482)

One of the wisest things ever said about accuracy is a remark made by a British official to a reporter: "You think," he said, "that we lie. We don't, really we don't. But if you count on that, you make an even bigger mistake: you think we tell you the truth."

Once you get in to your sources, how do you get them to talk? Many people are happy to talk forever about things they want to talk about, but creative journalism requires that they talk about the things you want, that they reveal themselves in many ways—perhaps their deepest inner conflicts, their opinions on touchy situations that they prefer to conceal, their emotions, sometimes even things they have done that will get them in trouble with the law or colleagues or friends. Often you have to carry their thinking on a problem further than they ever have before, by presenting it from an angle they've never considered.

Once, for example, I had to get a young woman to tell me, step by step, about a mental breakdown she'd had, about her feelings and experiences during nine months in a mental hospital, about her adjustments and deceptions in fighting her way back into normal life. Another time I had to induce the mother of a man who had murdered three people in a week to tell me about his childhood troubles with the law and even the things she and her husband had done that had damaged his personality.

It helps in this kind of depth interviewing if you understand the dimensions of the problem you are facing. In their book *The Dynamics of Interviewing*, Robert L. Kahn and Charles F. Cannell, of the Survey Research Center at the University of Michigan, list the barriers we all build against communicating with each other:

Under the continuous impact of sales pitches in newspaper and magazine, radio and TV advertising, we build a tidy skepticism of the things people tell us. We learn to disbelieve as a form of self-protection. This carries over into all our daily conversations but makes us especially careful when we're talking to a journalist whose obvious motive—to get us on record, in print—may be entirely consistent with our own best interests.

We build defenses against another's ill opinion of us. We don't want to appear in a bad light, especially to a reporter. This is a hurdle public opinion pollsters have had to learn to get over. For example, an early survey, trying to find out what features in newspapers people liked best, startled everyone by showing that most readers turned to the editorials first. This, of course, was nonsense. It took a while for the pollsters to realize that people were saying this because it was intellectually classy.

We don't listen to what the other person is saying. We pick up the key words or phrases, then assume we know what the rest of the sentence is going to be. At that point we tune them out and start thinking about what our answer will be.

Our memories are selective. Many of us have psychological reasons for not being able to remember something or remember it accurately. Often the conclusions we draw from a set of facts lead us to change the facts themselves. This is not intentional, but it is nearly universal—which is why good reporters always must check things they're told against documents or other evidence.

Kahn and Cannell write, "The way each of us sees the world or anything in it depends in part upon external objective reality, and for the rest on our individual needs, goals, motives and past experiences." Someone who is paid $50,000 a year as a publicist for an automobile company is unlikely to give you an unbiased version of the safety of American cars.

Most of us aren't very articulate. Kahn and Cannell say the average person knows fewer than 10 percent of the half million words in the English language. So even when someone is trying hard to explain something to you, he or she may not have the words to do so. Further, most of us have particular habits of speech resulting from our backgrounds, our jobs, our hobbies. This is especially pronounced, in our compartmentalized world, among various kinds of experts; a sociologist talks an entirely different kind of language from a jazz musician. A reporter, interviewing either, must first learn the lingo.

To overcome these barriers to communication, "the interviewer," write Kahn and Cannell, "must create and maintain an atmosphere in which the respondent feels he is fully understood and it is safe to communicate fully without fear of being judged or criticized. . . . An interviewer focuses on *content*, and the respondent is encouraged to explore fully and frankly his own position."

Psychologists list three qualities that produce good interview results:

1.   Warmth and responsiveness. This shows you're interested in and accept the person. The interview should resemble a conversation, not a grilling.

2.   Permissiveness in letting respondents express their feelings. Give them the idea they can say anything at all without penalty; maintain that attitude whether you agree with them or not. You almost never argue with a source; if you must disagree with something they say, quote an authority—a book, an article, an expert you've interviewed earlier—and ask for a comment on that. This lets you off the hook; *you* aren't attacking them; you're simply asking them to explain an inconsistency. (Sometimes it is valuable to argue but only if you want to make the person mad enough to say something he shouldn't. In thirty years of interviewing, I've done this perhaps half a dozen times.)

3.   The atmosphere you want to set up is: "We're a couple of responsible people exploring this issue together."

Beyond the general atmosphere of the interview, there are a number of specific techniques that have worked out for me. For example, when you first walk into a person's office, there usually is some small talk to ease your strangeness with each other. You can make this work for you by taking a quick look around the office and spotting something your source is interested in. It may be a golf trophy on a file cabinet; say, "You must be a pretty good golfer." It may be pictures of children on her desk; as, "Are those your youngsters?" Giving a person a chance to talk about something she's interested in warms her up and also gives you insights into her personality and some facts about her nonbusiness life.

When the small talk is finished, outline the basic idea you're working on so the interviewee knows specifically what areas you want to talk about. Very often the idea involves a problem or public issue; outlining it invokes the impulse, widely shared by Americans, to try to solve problems. It also gives the person a creative role consistent with point number three, above: she can bring her own knowledge to bear in a way that may help solve the problem.

Then you proceed to explore the problem together, with you being the interested, intelligent, but uninformed student who wants to learn from this expert. Don't hesitate to ask her to explain further if you don't fully understand part of what she tells you. And use your prepared list of questions to lead her into other dimensions of the problem. Don't argue, discuss, and bring your own background knowledge to bear: "I saw a report from the Council on Family Relations the other day that shows—— ——. How does that bear on what you just said?"

Having the facts is excellent leverage for prying out information the person is reluctant to reveal. Once I was doing a story on sweatshops in New York City. It was built around the experiences of a young man named Francisco Mangual, who had courage enough to fight against both the labor union and the company management that were exploiting him and his co-workers. He led a walkout one day in defiance of both and was promptly fired. He took his case to the State Labor Board and, after a hearing, the employer was ordered to rehire him. I had, of course, read the record of the hearing before I interviewed the employer.

He was unfriendly. He didn't want an article written about sweatshops generally and especially not about his own. I made it clear to him, politely, that the article was going to be written anyway and asked him why he had fired Mangual. "Oh," he said, "he was no good. He was a lousy worker, always goofing off, and several times the girls in the shop complained to me that he'd been bothering them. Which," he added virtuously, "was a damn shame, considering that nice little wife of his." (The Labor Board had considered and rejected these same charges.)

"Then why did the State Labor Board order you to rehire him?"

"Oh, you know about that, eh?" Pause. "Well, you know how these labor boards are, a bunch of bureaucrats who don't know anything about business. Besides, they're all run by the unions."

Obviously the employer had no specific rebuttal to Mangual's story and, since the Labor Board had confirmed it, I could assume it was true. But of course it had been necessary to give the employer a chance to knock it down.

It also pays off if you take the time to frame very carefully, in advance, the tough questions you are going to have to ask in an interview. This not only helps you pin down precisely what you want to find out, but also enables you to build in psychological hooks which will help guarantee an answer—and many people, particularly politicians, are adept at evading tough questions.

One key to these psychological hooks is self-interest. Think carefully what your respondent can get out of the interview, and make sure your question suggests it. For example, I was doing a story on John F. Kennedy while he was still in the Senate. It was obvious he was preparing to run for the presidency, and when he did his Catholicism was going to be an issue. I wanted to get him on record on the subject. The night before the interview I spent more than an hour wording the question. It went:

"Senator, before I could vote for you, I'd have to have the answer to one question. If the dictates of your church conflicted with the demands of your public office, which would you follow?"

The "before I could vote for you" bit was the self-interest hook; all politicians want votes. I debated this, because the senator ran from Massachusetts and I lived in New York; it opened the door to a quibble on his part. But I figured he was intent enough on the presidency, where I would be eligible to vote, to overlook it. The word "dictates" took a lot of thought. It was a nasty word for a Catholic, suggesting his church was a dictatorship. Yet I knew many non-Catholics felt this way about the church, and I finally decided that the nastiness would work for me; it would irritate him and thus might provoke him to answer seriously instead of evading.

It worked. The first thing he said was, "In the first place my church doesn't dictate to me." Then he went on and answered the question, saying much the same things he said a few years later when he was actually campaigning for the presidency. But my article was the first that put him on record on the subject.

During the whole interview listen actively. Reporters can't afford to listen like normal people; they must work at it. You recognize that most people aren't very articulate, that their words are a screen that often shadows or distorts information which is very clear in their own minds. You have to penetrate this screen and see the idea as clearly as your source does. It takes work.

You must concentrate hard on each word the person says, probing for the precise meaning behind it. You watch his face, his gestures, the movements of his body, the expressions in his eyes. You follow his thoughts and complete them for him. You pin him down, but not aggressively: "I don't understand. You said ———." "But how does that work in this situation?"

And let the man know you're listening to him; it flatters him and makes him try harder. Quote himself back at him: "You said a minute ago that —— ——. Does that mean ——?" Keep your eyes on him so he knows you're paying attention. Encourage him to continue talking by making neutral comments that show you're with him. Things like, "Boy, I'll bet that hurt." "What happened next?" "How did that work out?" Should you let your man wander off the subject? Not if you're pressed for time or if you need only specific, factual information from him. But if you have time and need depth, I've found that often when a person gets comfortable with the subject and starts to wander, he gives you not only unexpected information but also new insights into his personality and viewpoint. And it is precisely these nuggets that make your story broader and deeper than the usual newspaper or television interview.

Of course you do have to keep some kind of control over the interview, otherwise you won't get what you came for. This is especially important if you're interviewing a glib PR man who wants to fill you up with commercials about his company, or a political wheelhorse who learned long ago how to evade a question by snowing you under with a blizzard of unresponsive words. You know the type.

REPORTER: Senator, we all know how bad the drought has been in your state, with farmers having to buy water to keep their cattle from dying, with crops dried up in the fields, and families facing the loss of all their savings and perhaps even of their farms. Since this is so, Senator, why did you vote against disaster crop loans for your state?

SENATOR: Miss Marsh, I want you to know that nobody knows better than I the plight of farmers in my state. Why, I grew up on a farm, and I've put in my days pitching had and milking the cows. I venture to say, without being immodest, that I know as much about the problems of farmers as anyone on Capitol Hill. And I respect them. The farmers are the backbone of this country. We have the situation of this great industrial country with its 230 million people all depending for their very lives on the work and skill and faithfulness of only about a million dedicated farmers. No, ma'am, there's nobody who knows better than I how important our tillers of God's soil are to all of us.

REPORTER: Then why, Senator, did you vote against the bill?

SENATOR: Vote against it? Where did you get that idea?

REPORTER: Each week the *New York Times* publishes the voting record of Congress on important bills. That's where I got it.

SENATOR: Now, Miss Marsh, I'm not going to be put in the position of criticizing the *Times*. To my mind it is one of the great—I'd even go so far as to say the greatest—though I'm not criticizing the papers we have in my state, mind: some of the finest journalism in America is being practiced in the papers of my state. No ma'am, I will stand up for the rights of a free press and especially the record of the papers of my state against all comers. I'm not afraid, ma'am, to take a stand!

REPORTER: But Senator—

SENATOR: Now, Miss Marsh, I've got to run along; I've got a very important committee meeting that started ten minutes ago, and I can't shirk my duty to my constituents. I've enjoyed talking to you, and I want you to know that anytime you've got any questions you just come right along to me. My door is always open.

What's a reporter to do? This is one time when I'd stop being polite. The senator was obviously caught and was trying to weasel out; further, he was showing contempt for the reporter's intelligence. Along about the middle of his second peroration, I think I'd have broken in with a polite remark like, "Senator, cut the crap!" Respect is due high office, but not when its holder demeans it. Another option is to print a transcript of the interview, as I did above, to show readers how unresponsive your subject was.

But usually you can control the interview in less drastic ways. You can be sure the interviewee is watching you. If she wanders too far from the subject, you can often call her back simply by leaning back in your chair and looking out the window in obvious boredom. You can exert many degrees of influence by the way you take notes. Normally the subject will watch what you write down and what you don't. This serves as a guide to her; she wants to say things that will make you take notes and once she sees what you write down and what you ignore, she'll try to feed you more of the significant material. You can use this: when she wanders, simply stop taking notes. She'll get the message. If she doesn't, I've sometimes gone so far as to close my notebook and toss it disdainfully on the desk. That rocks her.

The way you take notes can have other important effects on the interview. Every experienced reporter knows you can't take down everything the interviewee says; it takes too long and stops the flow of talk. It keeps you so occupied you haven't time for the other two important jobs you should be doing—watching and evaluating the person and thinking up the next question. You make notes on the operative words and phrases, on names and dates and addresses and figures. You remember the rest, and you have to train your memory to do it.

It's not as difficult as it seems. For one thing, a good part of the interview is commonly spent in inconsequential talk. For another, if you're concentrating on the interview as you should be, the person's words are deeply imprinted in your brain, and you recall them automatically later on. And it will not be much later; as soon as a noteless interview is finished, I have gone somewhere nearby—a library, a restaurant, my hotel room—and written down the entire interview in detail. Sometimes this takes almost as long as the interview itself, but it's worth it. You may not be writing the story for a couple of weeks and you won't remember the details that long, especially since you'll be doing other interviews in the interim.

Finally, there is another truth that I learned from Chester Barnard, then head of the Rockefeller Foundation and one of the most brilliant men I've ever met. Barnard had come up through the Bell Telephone Company and at one point had been one of the youngest presidents of a phone company—Pennsylvania's—in company history. On this job he had to visit offices and installations all over the state, then write reports on what he'd learned. He told me later that at first he was scared he'd forget something important and would take extensive notes on every visit, every interview. But after a while, he said, he discovered that the facts and figures that ultimately ended up in his report were those he remembered without consulting his notes. From then on he took only the sparsest of notes.

After he told me this, I reexamined my own experience and discovered the same thing. The points, the quotes, the anecdotes that wound up in the finished article had come full-blown into my mind when I was writing. Almost invariably when I checked them against my notes, I found I had remembered them accurately. (In spite of this, of course, I was never quite sure enough of myself to take no notes at all.)

Why should you ever attempt a noteless interview? Because sometimes your notebook scares the interviewee so badly that he or she never relaxes and talks freely. This usually happens with people who have never dealt with a reporter before, but sometimes notebooks create discomfort even in those who are used to journalists. When I was doing the story on Red Skelton mentioned earlier, I assumed that a man who had been in show business as long as he had—since the age of ten—and had been interviewed as many times as a star has, would be perfectly at ease in the situation. So when the first interview started I hauled out my notebook and went to work.

After about fifteen minutes it began to dawn on me that things weren't going well, and I took a good look at Skelton. He was sitting in his chair with his feet together and his arms pressed to his sides, as still as a department store mannequin. I couldn't believe it, but it was obvious the man was scared. So I ostentatiously closed my notebook, put it in my briefcase, and pushed it aside. And we just talked. Slowly he began to relax, and after about ten minutes he was at ease and talking freely. For the next five hours we had a marvelous time, and I learned a good deal about the man and his world. That was one of the times when I made the notes back at the hotel before I went to sleep.

What about tape recorders? The jury is still out on this one. They have definite advantages: you get the full interview, with all of the man's individual ways of saying things and many more details than you could possibly take down in notes. You also get complete accuracy: if there is ever any question that you have misquoted him, you have a record to prove your case. You are freed from the job of taking notes and can concentrate wholly on drawing the man out.

They also have disadvantages: every time we have used them we have found they inhibited the interviewees. They were always conscious of the recorders. Maybe this is not true of all interviewees, especially those who are interviewed often. There's a certain amount of bother; you have to stop the interview to change tapes. One of the biggest difficulties is that when you are ready to refer back to the interview for a quote or an anecdote, you have to play the whole tape, which takes as long as the original interview. When you make notes, you edit and take down only the important stuff; it is much easier and quicker to find the exact quote you want later on.

Also, there are built-in mechanical difficulties: We've found recorders to be useless when you're interviewing someone over lunch; the machine picks up so much background noise the words are often lost. And a recorder can fail in the middle of an interview without your knowing it. When you get home you discover you have nothing. One television reporter we know solves this by using the recorder *and* taking notes. This seems a little elaborate.

But there is no doubt at all about one aspect of recorders: if you use one you must let your source know about it. It is highly unethical and in some states illegal to tape an interview secretly.

One interviewing problem that every writer we know has difficulty with is getting good anecdotes. An anecdote is a little story that makes a point—like the one about interviewing Jack Kennedy. They are absolutely essential in mass media nonfiction because they explain or illustrate a point in specific, concrete terms instead of in abstract generalities—and most readers aren't accustomed to handling abstractions. They are also convincing to readers because they evoke emotions, making them say, "Yes, that could happen to me." Because they are what makes the piece readable, one of the most frequent instructions of editors is, "Get some more anecdotes into it." They are also hard to get.

When being interviewed most persons tend to get pretentious. After all, their own words are here being recorded in deathless prose for all future generations to delight over. They talk in broad generalities and profound philosophies, most of which have been said earlier and better by someone else. It's our job to bring them down to earth, to make them talk like people instead of books, to lead them to reveal their uniqueness of thought and experience.

The major problem is that the person you're interviewing is not thinking in terms of specific stories, case histories, experiences, and so when you ask him for a story, he or she can't bring it to mind. The other night a television reporter was interviewing a man who was retiring after forty-two years as sheriff. The reporter said, "There must have been many humorous things that happened during your long experience." The sheriff answered, "Oh, there were. Many" Pause. Smile. "But I can't think of any right now." The reporter's job is to trigger the man's mind so he will remember.

One of the best ways to do this is to tell an anecdote yourself. This not only gets his mind working in the right direction and defines for him the kind of thing you want but also provokes his old competitive urges to top your story. The stock reporter's question designed to produce anecdotes is, "What was the funniest thing that ever happened to you as a life-guard?" But this usually doesn't work very well because it requires the man not only to cast his mind back over a long series of experiences, which he can't remember very well, but also asks him to consider many and select one as the all-time great. That's asking too much all at once.

It's much more effective to narrow the area for him. For example, when I was doing the sweatshop story mentioned earlier, it seemed to me the people who worked in them lived in a constant miasma of fear. Everything in the society preyed upon them—employers, unions, the police, land-lords, criminals. I was talking to my man's wife, an extraordinarily beautiful young woman. I mentioned the police lock on the front door of their apartment and asked why they had it. Because of the danger, she said. What danger? Men. Banditos. Dope "addicks." Had they ever bothered her? Oh, yes. When? Lots of times. She thought a moment. "But it's not as bad here as in the project where we used to live." What happened there? Then she told me the anecdote. Once when she had got on the elevator to go up to her apartment, a man was already inside, and on the way up he tried to rape her. She had fought him off, and when they reached her floor she ran to her apartment, yanked open her window, and screamed to her husband, Francisco, who was sitting on a bench outside, what had happened. Francisco ran in when the elevator came down, he caught the man and beat him.

There was a story; now it was just a question of taking her back over it and getting the detail that would make it come alive for the reader. Had the man raped her? No. What did he look like? How was he dressed? When did he attack her—as soon as the doors closed? What had he done—had he wrestled her to the floor? What had she done to fight back? And so on. What you must do is keep questioning about even the most minute details—what color were the walls, what furniture was in the room—until you get a clear mental picture of the scene and the action. Only then can you recreate it so the reader will see it too.

S. L. A. Marshall, the late military historian, told me about an interviewing technique he had used with success when he was writing *Pork Chop Hill*, a detailed report of a single patrol action in the Korean War. He had gotten all the men together immediately after the patrol and taken them over the action minute by minute. Where were you at that moment? What did you do? Did you see Smith? In this way, he said, the men checked on each others' memories of the events, and he got an unusually complete and accurate account of everything that happened to each of them.

I tried it later and found it worked very well. But it took hours to do because the individuals sometimes argued about whether Tim had done exactly that at that moment, and you had to let them resolve it before you could go on. And there may be another weakness: for the method to work, I think the members of the group have to trust each other. I tried it again with a group of people who did not, and the session wound up in a cat fight, with individuals attacking each other, working out their hostilities and gripes instead of telling the story.

Often it helps to get anecdotes if you apply the subject under discussion to the interviewee's own life. Have you had this problem? How did you handle it? Have any of your friends faced it? What did they do?

Also, of course, official records are full of case histories—police, court decisions, social agencies, congressional hearings. From them you get the main lines of the story, then you flesh it out by talking to the individuals involved. Officials can help you locate anecdotes if you simply ask for case histories to illustrate specific points in the story. And they speed the process, because their own experience has included many such stories; once you get them thinking in these terms, they remember the outstanding ones.

Public relations people can do the same thing for you. But, of course, you have to remember that their job is to build a favorable image for their organization, and you must check whatever they tell you with others who are involved. PR people can help you in another way, too: If you tell them the idea you are working on, they can pinpoint the people in their organizations who would be most helpful and arrange appointments for you. Of course they will select the people who will give the positive picture; if you rely on them alone, your story will be unbalanced. Only the very best PR people, knowing a reporter's need for balance, will give you both favorable and unfavorable facts about their organizations.

The requirement for balance in a story is, of course, one of the cardinal rules of ethical journalism. It is also good practice. If your story is too one-sided you sacrifice credibility. Readers are not dopes; they know that every question has two sides, that ointments come equipped with flies, that no human being is all sweetness and light. If you give them only one side, they think you're trying to gull them and they stop believing in you. The moment that happens you're out of the communications business.

Further, by interviewing the other side, you often get material you could get no other way. Whenever I've been doing a piece that was going to hurt someone, I've had to walk around the block five times before I could get up courage enough to go in and see that person. There's an awful temptation to skip it, figuring you've got all you need anyway, and why put yourself through what is bound to be an unpleasant scene. But you can't afford to give in—and not only because if you give the person a chance to tell his or her side you'll be in an infinitely stronger position if the person sues you for libel.

Once Lester Velie, one of the country's best reporters, was doing a story on Artie Samesh, a lobbyist in California. The title, "The Secret Boss of California," gives the idea; Samesh had built up so much power in the state legislature that he could have it pass almost any law that would favor one of his clients. Velie had spent weeks digging up evidence to prove this, and the time came to see Samesh himself. Velie walked up to his house in what four-syllable writers call trepidation.

Samesh met him with a big smile: "Come in, come in. Sit down. Have a drink."

After the niceties were over, Velie brought up a case of influence-buying and asked Samesh about it. Samesh verified every item Velie had dug up and went on to add some details Velie did not have. It went on like that in case after case, so that by the time it was over Velie had facts and figures that no one else could have given him. Indeed, Samesh was so cooperative that he even allowed a photographer to pose a ventriloquist's dummy, with "The State of California" written across its chest, on Samesh's knee and shoot the picture.

Velie's story cost Samesh his influence with the legislature and probably helped send him to jail. Why was he so cooperative in his own destruction? The only reason Velie could figure out, he said later, was that while Samesh had this tremendous power, he felt neglected because nobody knew it. He wanted a little public appreciation of all his hard work.

6

Evaluating the Research

*E*valuation is the heart of the interpretive writing process. It is also the most difficult part for the writer, for it is here that we must finally make a judgment, here we must identify truth. It is not only a rigorous intellectual exercise, it is the core of the creative part of this kind of writing. For this is the period of chaos, mentioned earlier in Cathy Covert's definition of creativity.

At this point, when you have finished your research, you must summon to your mind the huge mass of facts, figures, statistics, expert opinions, conflicting viewpoints, anecdotes, tangential information, the motives and emotions of the individuals in your story—summon all these to mind and make a judgment about where the truth lies. This judgment will be the "something new" that is the end product of creativity. And you must do this, not as an omniscient and impartial god, but as a fallible human being, complete with faulty logic, prejudices, opinions, intellectual hobbies, emotional bents. All these must be surmounted, as best you can, for you're going on record with your judgment, and your work, in turn, will be judged by it.

Consider the dilemma of the writer. He or she—let's say he—starts out with an idea for a story, an approach to a set of facts. He has validated the idea in his preliminary research. Yet he knows that a cardinal sin of journalism is to collect only those facts and opinions which support his original idea. So he does a thorough research job, amassing all facts, both pro and con. Inevitably he discovers that his original idea has changed under the impact of the research. Now what does he do? Does he hew to the line and forget the inconvenient facts? He knows this is dishonest journalism, so he can't. But how much is the original idea changed? Where? This is what he must decide, and this is where his personal integrity enters the picture.

As always, integrity has a heavy price. Sometimes the price may be the loss of the story and the necessity of explaining to your editor that you were wrong: the idea you worked so hard to sell him is not supported by the facts. This is a particularly unhappy spot for a writer, because not only does his ego take a fall, but there is always the suspicion that if he had worked a little harder, seen more people, been more successful in eliciting the required information from them, the story would have come through. The temptation is almost irresistible to fudge the facts and save the story.

Once, for example, I went to India on assignment for *Reader's Digest*. One of the stories I was working on was about a missionary-agronomist from Massachusetts who, in twenty years of work in one of the country's worst famine areas, had introduced modern farming methods and enormously increased crop yields—a major success in a country that was chronically unable to feed its population. I had gotten the basic facts of the story from the church official in charge of Indian mission activities, and one of the main points was that the agronomist had introduced new methods of rice growing that had doubled or tripled harvests. Since rice was a staple in the diet of millions of Indians, this was vastly important.

But when I got to the mission station, I discovered the agronomist had not introduced the new rice-growing methods: the church official had been wrong. The agronomist had taught the Indian farmers many other modern methods—irrigation, terracing of fields, crop rotation, better plowing methods, use of pesticides—which had increased yields, but not rice culture. It was not a rice-growing area.

Normally I would immediately have called the editors and told them what I'd learned, but I was 8,000 miles away, there were no telephones, and letters would have taken too long. So I went ahead and gathered all the information on the other things the agronomist had accomplished. The story failed. The editors bought it because they were responsible people, but they never published it.

I think the reason it failed was that there was nothing in it quite so dramatic as the rice-yield increase, nothing as significant in terms of the country's overall food-production problem. I recognized it when I was in India, and when we discussed my findings after I got back and before I wrote the story, this was the point the editors instantly fastened on.

Editors are not stupid; if a story has a factual weakness they can spot it immediately. Thus to the ethical argument against fudging facts is added a very practical one: it doesn't work.

What does the writer do in this situation? Two things: he tries to find a replacement story while he's in the field—either a completely new story or a new approach to the present one that is factually sound. If he can't do either, he immediately phones the editor, explains that the story has failed, and comes home. If he has found a replacement, he explains this to the editor, tells why it was necessary and hopes the editor agrees to let him go ahead on it. The whole process is traumatic, and it indicates the stark, objective questioning the writer must apply to his own work, even while he is subjectively involved in it.

It seems to us there is a parallel between this process and the scientific method. One of the best descriptions of the scientific method, especially as applied to the social sciences, is in Stuart Chase's book, *The Proper Study of Mankind.* He lists ten elements of the method:

1. A problem to be solved . . . maybe cosmic rays, maybe juvenile delinquency.

2. Gathering the available facts about it, searching the literature.

3. A theory to explain the problem, a pattern sketched.

4. Rigorous verification of the theory by other scientists. Emotion and bias ruled out.

5. A stubborn atmosphere of doubt. The cheerful ability to say, "I was wrong."

6. Prediction in terms of probabilities, not absolutes.

7. Thinking more in terms of process than of linear cause and effects.

8. Thinking in terms of *structure.* How things are related to one another; the order in which they come—the structure of a skyscraper, a corporation, a community, a conference, an argument, an agenda.

9. No closed solutions; room always for new data which may give a closer fit.

10. No secrets, no monopolies, no pay-offs.

This is a pretty good definition of the process of interpretive journalism. It demonstrates that in journalism, as in scientific research, the place for objectivity is in the mind of the writer. In the old "just the facts, Ma'am" kind of journalism, reporters discharged their obligation to objectivity by presenting all sides of a question, without drawing any obvious conclusions. But, as we have seen, this approach is inadequate in today's complex world. On the other hand, if you throw out the ideal of objectivity, reporters become mere propagandists. So the ideal is retained, but inside the mind and conscience of the reporter, and it comes into play when he or she is evaluating the facts the research has turned up.

Erwin Canham, the great editor of *The Christian Science Monitor,* pinpointed it: "Background, motives, surrounding circumstances, related events, and issues all need to be understood and appraised as well as the immediate event. . . . But interpretation requires integrity and knowledge and understanding and balance and detachment."

To achieve complete objectivity when you are evaluating your research is obviously impossible. We are human beings, with prejudices, preconceptions, and opinions, and, as journalists, we usually feel strongly about public questions. Yet while the ideal is impossible of achievement, we are all obliged to come as close to it as we possibly can. Checking your research to make sure your facts *are* facts is the most obvious way. But an attitude of consuming skepticism also helps. So does noninvolvement.

Federal Judge Learned Hand made it a rule never to join any organization—political, economic, civic, even social, like a country club—because he never knew when some member of the organization might come before him to be judged. He said it was hard enough to be objective in passing judgment under the best circumstances, and being a member of the same organization might lead him to be either too lenient or too severe on the individual before him. The rule may well apply to journalists, too.

We think it helps, too, to remember that you have prejudices and consciously to try to offset them when you're making judgments. Are you a political liberal? Then when doing a political story, make sure you spend at least mas much time getting the conservative side as the one you naturally lean to. Do you believe the blacks have been exploited by the whites? Then do as much research discovering and understanding the white point of view as the black before you commit yourself to the main line of your story.

This is not only ethical journalism, it is self-protection. You will be judged by editors, other writers, and the public by what you write—not by whether you are a good parent or have soulful eyes. You will be forgiven some mistakes and some sins of omission. You will not be forgiven sins of commission.

The thing that makes this evaluation process so difficult is that you have to *think*. You are forced to analyze your facts and decide what they mean, what pattern they shape. That takes thinking. You have to compare conflicting bits of evidence and decide which is overriding. That takes thinking. You have to weigh the pros and cons of a situation and decide which is dominant. And that takes thinking. Finally, you have to decide what truth the dominant facts add up to. What's my story here? What am I saying in this piece?

I have spent a full week on this process, and all the while I appeared to be doing nothing. During it I might have scribbled a few sentences or paragraphs on copy paper—most of which were thrown away.

For me this was the hardest, most frustrating, most infuriating, most demanding part of the whole job—much harder than actually putting the words on paper. What I was trying to do was to write one sentence, one sentence that would give the main point, the message that all the research added up to. It had to be a sentence that encompassed all the findings and that contradicted no solid fact. It had to be short and not diluted by qualifications. It might end up as the title; surely the title would encompass its idea. But only after that sentence was written did I have the main theme of the piece, and only with the main theme before me could I go ahead and organize the bits and pieces that would make the final article. Without the sentence the article would have no unifying theme, no focus, and hence no single, compelling message. It would sprawl. Instead of hitting the reader with the force of a jet from a fire hose, it would have the impact of a lawn sprinkler.

Some other devices can aid the process. When they have finished their research, many writers I know spend a day or two retyping all their notes. They make little or no attempt to organize or expand them; they simply retype. This, they say, does two things—it makes them put everything they've learned through their minds again, and it gives them material *on paper*, which they can then cut up, rearrange, expand, or throw away. It is laborious, but they say it helps.

Because I'm congenitally lazy, I don't do this, but I do go through all my notes at one time and mark in red the nuggets that seem too good to leave out of the finished piece. One advantage this shares with the other process is that by reviewing at one time bits of information you may have collected three weeks or two months ago, you can see patterns and relationships you might otherwise miss.

Here's another trick: without referring to my notes, sometimes I simply sit down and recall those things in my research which stick in my mind and jot down, in no particular order, a few key words that identify each. (The things you recall immediately probably have some universal appeal that made them stick in your mind; if they impressed you, they'll impress your reader.) Then after I had organized and outlined the piece, I checked the outline against the list to see if it omitted anything important; if it did, the outline was probably faulty.

The business of distilling out the essential message from the mass of your research serves a double purpose. It not only gets you to the truth about the facts, but it also helps to shape the story, for only after you have written the single sentence can you decide what among your research supports the message and what doesn't. And only then can you decide the most effective way to get the message into the reader's mind and emotions. Probably the best way to illustrate this process is to describe a case.

When I was at *Redbook* the newspapers carried a story about Charles Kelly, who had won the Congressional Medal of Honor for his heroism in World War II. Ten years later, Kelly had just come out of the hospital, where he had nearly died from a burst appendix and ensuing peritonitis. The story revealed he had been down on his luck for years; he was living in a municipal housing project in Louisville, Kentucky, and had had a long run of joblessness. And there had been sickness too, not only for himself, but for his six young children. He had come to New York to be on one of the television giveaway shows that were edifying the soap opera set in those years, and the editors suggested I go see him. We had no definite idea for a story, but he was in our readers' age group, and we thought we might do a piece somewhat along the lines of how a hero readjusts to normal life.

The show was being produced at one of the midtown theaters, and Kelly was on when I arrived, so I stood in the wings and watched. The more I saw, the madder I got. They were humiliating him. Kelly was a proud, independent man who had fought his way out of the back alleys of Pittsburgh, and he had to tell the story of his own failures. In return, they showered money and gifts on him. But the jolly master of ceremonies, in "intellectual" black-framed glasses, let his contempt for Kelly's failure show. I suppose it made a good show, something like a public hanging, but it infuriated me to see a man who had won the nation's highest honor for valor exploited for the purpose of selling more deodorants, or whatever.

Kelly was a small, wiry, thin-faced guy with a nose like the blade of a hunting knife, and he'd lost so much weight in the hospital that his out-of-style suit hung on him in folds. When he came off the stage I was shocked to see he had tears in his eyes. I talked to him for only a couple of minutes—partly because he was obviously on the thin edge of control, and also because I didn't want to commit the magazine to doing a story until we were surer. But all the way back to the office I was telling off—in my head of course—the wise-guy master of ceremonies, the producer, the director, the network, the sponsors, and the whole television industry. It was pretty devastating.

I suppose it was anger as much as anything that made me decide to do the story—on the idea that this is what happens to a hero when the war's over—and the editors agreed to go along.

I dug up Kelly's service record and got the commendations for his Medal of Honor and other medals. They were impressive; obviously here was a man who, in a crisis, could act fast and effectively and with great courage.

I picked up the story, as usual, in bits and pieces—in Louisville and St. Louis, where Kelly was working on the new job he'd gotten after the publicity about his plight. Here are my notes on the story. While they may seem voluminous, they are about average for an article. My own comments, written at the time, are in brackets.

Following the notes is the article I wrote from them. Comparing the two illustrates part of the writing process. You can see how disjointed the information is as you get it, and how it still must be assembled to make a readable piece. You can see how much of what you get never ends up in the article. Most important, by going through the "chaos" process with one writer, you can see how identifying the underlying theme of the story can give direction, movement, and unity.

FIRST INTERVIEW, AT TV SHOW: Chas. Kelly, 36, 137 lbs., first wife died of cancer '51—I watched her die for three years. Was chauffeur for Attorney General of Pennsylvania . . . married second wife '52, she from Louisville . . . couldn't make living Pittsburgh—$125 month for apartment, $40 month gas, $7 electricity . . . Clothes burned up in construction shack Frankfort . . . Baby to hospital with pneumonia; wife to hospital for sixth kid . . . her doc had emergency operation; his replacement delivered her . . . she in Tues., out Fri. . . . I ruptured appendix Sat-Sun, given three days to live, lost 28 lbs. Got Louisville job $1.25 hour, pick & shovel—furniture in storage, bill $350, couldn't raise; had save 3-4 weeks. [He should never have sent furniture; can't plan.] When baby in hospital—no insurance—cost $97—knocked on ass again.

Moved form Pittsburgh because couldn't make ends meet.

Watched first wife die cancer three years, giving increasing doses morphine.

Couldn't collect unemployment insurance since operation because not fired, not laid off. No workmen's compensation because not hurt on job. [If this isn't true it doesn't make any difference because he *thought* it true.]

[This is the story of the little man—limited, unsure of himself, with all the fears and limitations—but the man who perseveres, who is indomitable at last. He has courage and warmth and he survives.]

Used to say marriage was 50-50; well, today it's 75-25—75 for wife and 25 for man. I get up at night when kids cry; my wife needs her sleep. She has a bum ear, sleeps on the good one. But that's good. When I was sick I tried to get up but couldn't make it . . . shook her. She told me, "Why you not wake me? Kids my job." But they mine too.

[Chews tobacco and is self-conscious about it.]

KENTUCKY UNEMPLOYMENT INSURANCE DIVISION: Kelly unemployed "through no fault of own." Can't draw while unable to work and can't get workmen's compensation unless hurt on job.

BETTY (KELLY'S WIFE): Met Ft. Knox in '45 . . . Married Jefferson-ville, Ind., in '52, November . . . first wife died '51 . . . Children: Virginia, 10; Charles, Jr., 9; Michael, 5 [Mrs. K's by early marriage—divorced]; Lee, 3; Wm. Bennett, 1; Jerrie Lynn.

[Kelly's] father died '41, mother, '55 . . . worked in gas station for year after leaving Army in '45 . . . Worked four years as "investigator" for Pa. Attorney General, the late Chas. J. Margiotti, then four years as painter . . . to Louisville March '55.

June '55 Army sent him Bronze Star and second Silver Star; has about 10 medals . . . Here May '55 [housing project] he worked till Nov. '55, drew $14 unemployment from Pennsylvania; not here long enough for Kentucky.

[Betty's] uncle, the foreman, told Chuck would work that winter, but partnership [in company he worked for]splitting up; expected work again in Dec. No call. Decided wait until Jan. 1. No call. He told Kelly he didn't know when would reopen business. Kelly got odd jobs—not much paint-ing; the previous year he was off 2–4 months because of bad weather. In June he went to work as a painter . . . from Jan. to June mother, friends, neighbors kept us in food; Harry Holt [an insurance agent and friend] kept Kelly in spending money . . . William [called Bennie] got bronchial pneumonia in June '55, shortly after Kelly's mother died . . . When Kelly had appendix flare-up in August he wouldn't complain—he never does. Saturday night he crawled from living room couch into bedroom and asked me for the pain tablets; they in cabinet over kitchen sink; he crawled in but couldn't stand up to reach them . . . next morning he so white, said he couldn't move . . . Holt had said he had appendix the night before . . . I called Henry [Holt] and asked him to call the Veteran's Administration Hospital because a Medal of Honor winner can get in anytime. Henry came over and argued with Kelly an hour and 15 minutes before he'd agree to go. Left here Sunday morning at 9:30 . . . I alone; mother was in the country . . . Harry back at 5:30 with Kelly's clothes, they had operated . . . 8:30 I called hospital, talked to nurse, she said he fine . . . I saw him on Monday, 4:30 to 9:30 . . . He under dope for three days . . .

Sunday night I was in the kitchen from 12:30 to 3:30 praying, crying, smoking . . . I went to the hospital every day for 3–4 hours; he was unconscious . . . he came out of it Thursday, got no food until Friday . . . He in hospital 12–15 days. He in hospital 10:30 A.M., they didn't operate until 4:30 P.M.—thought he didn't have busted appendix; when operated found peritonitis had started. He put ice packs on belly Saturday night.

When he came home why they give him keys to the city? That won't feed us; give him a job. It has been 12 years since he came home from the war, now after 12 years they want you to come home to go to work . . . At breakfast you sit down and give the kids cereal; they want more; no more to give . . . My uncle took Virginia for the summer; mother took Chuckie; this was a big help.

The story of Kelly's sickness was on the wires—AP, UPI, the *Courier-Journal*, the New York papers . . . I flabbergasted; nothing like this had ever happened to me before . . . Kelly was scared to death to go on

TV . . . He was going to have to tell a story he didn't want to tell. It took a lot of courage to do it.

People are wonderful; it makes tears come to your eyes . . . the kids are upset; photographers here all the time . . . wake the baby up . . . we both lost 10 lbs. over it.

In Pittsburgh I had to pawn a diamond engagement ring for $34, and couldn't redeem it. Got another when Kelly working in Frankfort; had to pawn it just before the baby was born and couldn't redeem that, either. I never want another.

"When a baby is born you can well understand who makes it; there's only One Person who could."

When Kelly working Frankfort he come home Saturday and couldn't wait to wake the kids up from their naps, take outside and romp with them for a couple of hours . . . He shows affection by cleaning the house, taking care of the kids while I go to the show a couple of nights a week. I'll go play cards with a couple of girl friends; he puts the kids to bed. He's older, he had his running around, so he lets me have mine. That's the way he shows love.

What do I want? A home with enough ground so that I know I can put the children out safely, that some other kid won't walk up and beat the kids up or take their toys . . . What does Kelly want? To be left alone.

After all the publicity we got a letter from an old lady in an old ladies' home; she enclosed a dime . . . One woman brought that couch, that chair, those two lamps; another gave us a youth bed, two hats and some clothes for Virginia . . . St. Vincent de Paul brought groceries and notified the welfare department; welfare paid the rent and gave us $20 a week until late September.

Name: Betty Dugzinski, born Michigan. From Mt. Vernon, Ky., 120 mi. from here. Came Louisville '49. Florida State University Fall '49. Got married '50, back Louisville '50. First husband's name; don't use. Got job photo studio in '50; worked two years, married Chuck '52.

Had met Kelly when about 14 when he on bond drive, asked autograph. He said cute kid, gave me nickel, told call when grew up. Here again on Veteran's for Eisenhower campaign in '52; friend was entertaining one night, asked me over. I said, you owe me another nickel; phone calls cost a dime now. "What?!" He didn't remember; we talked all evening, he kept calling me later.

Mother: Mrs. Robert Cummings, works Louisville. Father, Michael D., Detroit. Grandfather in Lily, Ky., Ed Newland. He sends food canned stuff from garden. Uncle, B. H. Hall, Corbin, Ky., stayed with him when K. in Frankfort. Met K. Oct. '52, married six weeks later. She stayed here. In March, convention in N.Y.C., she there, then marriage announced.

Sends two oldest children to Hazelwood Baptist Church. His first wife was Catholic, had kids in Catholic boarding school. She wants small farm. Has twin sister, 15, Margaret and Mary. Mary helps care for children. Diamond engagement ring $275, pawned in Pittsburgh when broke for $37. Got second one cost $150, pawned for $11. Kelly offered a total of seven jobs [after publicity about his illness] from $40 to $75 a week. Gov. Chandler made him a Kentucky colonel, offered him a highway job; he refused. Offered lifetime membership in Moose. Betty, 24.

Saturday night in kitchen [day K. went in for operation] 12:30 to 3:30, saw him before me. Was like he said, "Betty, take my hand." I started cry and I never prayed so hard in my life. Sat there smoking and crying and praying until 3:30.

[Quote her saying he scared to death to go on TV and he having no education, wanting her with him, but show wouldn't pay her expenses. He had to tell a story he didn't want to tell. Tears in eyes when came off.]

KELLY (in St. Louis where he working): First wife May Frances Boish, married '45 in Phoenix City, Ala., stationed at Fort Benning. About '48 had two children. She had backaches, took to doc—family—he sent us to a specialist, Dr. Shubb, Pittsburgh. He examined, Medical Arts Bldg., called me aside, said wife has cancer, like to have her in hospital, tomorrow? Fine. Walked out, in elevator wife: "What he say?" "Said you have cancer." She didn't cry, say anything.

Didn't bother her until later. Had hopes could beat it in hospital. After hospital said, "We can keep her alive a few years." It in womb. She only 25. She died '51. We living home, 713 Annandale St. She kept working until about '50, taking X-ray and radium treatments. Then 1–2 day's work, she felt pretty good; she danced, went to card parties. Later '50, couldn't walk up the stairs, had to carry. Went to see Ed Sullivan show, felt fine, but I had to carry her up the stairs.

Each day it got worse, Doc giving her shots; nurse, friend, came in to do it. I bathe her, feed her, massage her. Weighed 118 lbs., at death weighed 45. She had cravings—strawberries, ice cream. I get them for her, sometimes in middle night. I took the kids to her sister's home, Betty

Fullerton; Virginia about 3, Chuckie 2. This about two months before her death. Before, I took care of kids, gave her morphine shots; doc showed me how. Used to buy it by the bottle. Shots every four hours, then increased amount morphine, then shots closer; finally 1–½–2 grains every hour; every 45 minutes at end.

She'd ask to see the kids, then say, no, don't want them to see me like this. I catching a sandwich when I could, got very little sleep. Slept in chair by bed. We had a cocker spaniel, Cindy, got killed. She said get another—a mutt—about year before she died.

I working from 9 to 6–7 at night, sometimes later. Sometimes out of town for a couple of days, maybe a week. She died April '51, buried Westview Cemetery.

Sold house, lived hotel; children went to brother Edward, Westview. He crippled, worked in post office, has two girls younger than Chuckie. He next to youngest brother. Every time I saw the kids they wanted to come with me. Mostly on weekends, sometimes not on Sunday because working.

Fall '52 Jim Duff had appointed Attorney General Charles J. Margiotti (died '56). Duff in Senate. Had campaigned for Duff when ran for governor. Clarence Adams, Veterans for Ike, in Chicago. He invited me to GOP convention in June—parades and stuff. Started traveling through 17 states [67 speeches] for Ike. Did some traveling before 17-state tour.

Met Betty first in '44 when on bond tour. She 14. Gave nickel, said call when grow up. Called her every night for 3 weeks from whatever town I was in. Married Nov. Indiana. She back to Louisville. I in Pittsburgh, she met the kids. Had had to sell all furniture to pay bills for May's sickness and death. So no furniture, nothing except clothes and two kids. Now a wife and three kids. Had sent money to Betty, to brother Ed for the kids— about $50 a month for kids; I had to buy clothes and live myself. In Jan. '53 Betty came up, we picked up the kids—Virginia was in boarding school and the headmistress called Betty. Chuckie was with Ed. We picked up both and brought to a hotel. Betty and kids slept in bed, I in a chair. Next day I left, she took them back to Louisville. She had 4-room apartment on West Market St. Two bedrooms, living room, kitchen. The lady downstairs had been taking care of Mike [Betty's son]. Betty quit her job. I sent her money. Once I flew down to see and couldn't leave—stayed three days. I looking for furnished apartment. As fast as I'd save money, she'd want to come here or want me to come down. Fare $43 round trip.

In December they came to Pittsburgh. I borrowed a car, drove down, loaded all her belongings, all the kids, including a playpen, and drove back, 800 miles, no sleep. A guy promised to rent me his apartment—he, wife split. They made up; no apartment. We stayed at my mother's a three-room apartment. Mother slept on the couch, the kids in the bed, I on the floor. There about two weeks.

Found a 2–½ room apartment, furnished. Bedroom, kitchen, alcove with a couch, for $12 a week. Were there couple months. Found a furnished apartment for $125 a month. Two bedrooms, living room, kitchen, bath, sunporch. Had own furnace—gas—hot water heat. Water wouldn't circulate. Gas bills were $40 a month or more. Later moved down to a basement apartment—two bedrooms, living room, kitchen, bath. It was warm, had a backyard. $100 month.

I quit Margiotti in Spring '53. worked as a painter, P. A. Freyvogel, painting contractor and joined the union. I had belonged before and it cost $100 plus dues of about $12.50 every three months. Now it costs $150 plus dues. I making $2.95 an hour minus 10 cents an hour insurance. Making $114 a week, take home about $100. I worked nights, worked six hours and paid for eight. My wife scared be alone at night. I worked Saturdays, then she got pregnant and I had to cut down overtime.

There was a strike—out two months in the summer—I stayed home, had no money and borrowed. I laid off three weeks before Christmas, but all the presents had been bought so we had a good Christmas. I picked up a job painting an apartment next door. But I was out of work four months. Some guys will work overtime for straight time pay; they'd get the winter work. I was a foremen. Had been a wall-washer before the war and became a foreman. After I quit Margiotti I started at the bottom and became a foreman again. We painting five and dime stores. We had stool pigeons. We took half an hour for lunch; you take five minutes more and they told the boss. They told that I letting the men smoke—a man smokes all his life, how's he going to stop? We finished on job, I told the guys if they finished in eight hours we'd be paid for eleven. We finished in seven, I called it eight. I got chewed out for it and from then on I was on the outs. Got bad jobs. This in Fall '54. Betty kept wanting to go back to Louisville. One Friday night just before Christmas, she had a suitcase packed and train tickets. We went on Saturday, said she had a place; her mother had called. I'd had no job because the weather was too bad for nearly three weeks. We stayed with her mother, who worked. I stayed with the kids and when the twins came home I'd go look for a job.

Her uncle, J. C. Newland, was·superintendent of a construction gang. I got a job with him as laborer on the roads at $1.25 an hour; dug ditches. In two weeks I was raised to $1.45 and when the weather got better, to $1.60. Owner, G. D. Davies, Frankfort, Fuller & Davies. I painted his house—a new house. By then the road was done, Newland went to Greenville,

Ohio, on a road job. I went along as labor foreman. We were raising manholes and catch basins two inches and black topping over brick. I was raised to $2.25. Worked about a month, then operated a gravel machine filling ditches at $2.50 an hour. We were there two more weeks, then back to Kentucky to the airport at Frankfort. I in charge of heavy equipment, laying rock and so on. I was next to Newland, who in charge of job.

A month after I started work Betty and the kids came down from Pittsburgh. [He was confused; Betty and kids already in Louisville.] Had bought furniture in '54. I had the money to bring them down, but not the furniture. One outfit would move the furniture down and put it in storage—which didn't cost anything then. Betty flew down—Lee had chickenpox and she was pregnant. She stayed with her mother for about six weeks and had the baby. Right after that we got in the [housing] project but couldn't get our furniture. We'd been delayed about three months getting into the project because we had to wait until somebody moved out. Her mother said it was okay to stay with her, but it wasn't—with all of us, it was too much for her. They talk about when a girl marries her mother doesn't lose a daughter, she gains a son. Well, she sure was getting a daughter.

I had to pay a hospital bill of $105 for Benny. I paid the doctor off for Benny, and Jerrie at about the first of October '56. We owed $300 for the furniture; I borrowed it from my boss and paid two months rent—$82. Furniture bill was $360; Betty borrowed $60. There was much missing— clothes, tools. But we finally got into the project and everything was pretty good.

I was now working in Frankfort, in a cabin with six men in three rooms—two bedrooms and a kitchen. I worked steady at $2.50 an hour, knocked off for rain, averaged $85–90 a week. So things were pretty good. Benny got bronchial pneumonia in the fall of '55. Had to go into the hospital for about a week. In one hospital, didn't like it; the baby would cry and nobody would care for him—at $11 a day. Baby was 4–5 months old. Took to another hospital where they had specialists—Benny's windpipe would close. After that the roof fell in.

I had all my clothes in Frankfort. On weekends when I came home I brought nothing but the clothes I wore. Monday morning I brought some jeans and a work shirt, walked in to get my work shoes and the cabin was gone—burned. Everything was gone, my medals, clothes, razor, shoes. Only thing I found was a pair of pliers. I had $5 to last me the week. The cabin owner had no insurance and neither had I. He said we'd have a place to stay, so four of us slept in a trailer. I lived in it for a month. No heat. Washing in a gas station, took baths at the airport.

About two weeks before Christmas the job folded—bad weather. The boss said the company was dissolving; as soon as it was settled up we'd be called back. I waited about two months for the weather to break. The boss didn't have enough work. I went back to $1.25 an hour putting in driveways and such. I went around to the factories trying to get a job—Dupont, Ford, Naval Ordnance—nothing. Drawing $14 a week unemployment from Pennsylvania. In the spring I got two houses to paint and we had enough to live on—with everybody helping out.

I got a job working for Leroy Heighbaugh—$1.45 an hour for a nine-hour day, 7–4:30, and five hours on Saturday. 50 hours a week. We were maintenance men. He owned houses, apartment houses, and we'd paint. Worked there 5 weeks. Betty went into the hospital to have Jerrie, in on Tuesday, out on Friday. I had to borrow $97.20 to get her out. She felt lousy; her doctor was in the hospital when she called Monday; she called a replacement, and he was in the hospital. She called all day Monday for a doc and finally got one. She went in Tuesday, baby born Wednesday and her doc not there when baby started.

Friday night she took sleeping pills. I felt lousy Saturday and didn't go to work. The pain kept getting worse; I was at Harry Holt's house and we thought it was my appendix. I went back home. Harry and I walked up the street for a Coke; I was full of pain. I bought an ice pack; the pain was worse. I filled the ice pack and put it on my belly while guests were there. Harry said go to the doctor. No; too many bills. He said we better leave. I went in and lay down; I had the ice pack, a towel wrapped around the ice trays from the refrigerator and a water bottle frozen solid on my belly. After everybody went to bed, it got worse so I crawled into the bedroom to get the phenobarbital—I couldn't walk and Betty wouldn't wake up, she'd had a pill too. After she did she said it was in the cupboard over the sink in the kitchen. I crawled back, but couldn't pull myself up to reach it. I lay on the floor. After about half an hour the pain left. I went into the living room and sat in a chair with the ice packs. She came out at 8, asked, do you want breakfast? No. She called Harry. He came. I couldn't get up—weak. Finally got dressed; Harry took me to the VA hospital; they examined me—blood counts and so on. Said no appendix. After other reports came in they decided to operate. I didn't know anything until Tuesday. I had peritonitis; I think it broke about 2 A.M. Sunday. They operated about 4:30 P.M. In hospital 12 days until about Aug. 15.

How he met Betty [this by Betty]. Friend called, said having K. and others over for supper. I hunted up my nickel and went over. He out walking dog. Came in, I up and said, owe another nickel. What? Do I know you? You gave me a nickel to call you when I grew up, but now it costs a dime. Later he called me from St. Louis, Washington, Detroit, Massachusetts.

Kelly won Congressional Medal of Honor, Silver Star, Bronze Star, Italian Cross of Valor, British medal for bravery—can't remember name.

First story (of their trouble) broke when Jerrie born. *Saga* had story, N. Y. *Post* called, *Louisville Courier-Journal*. All told he got about 100 job offers—Texas, Utah, Calif., Fla., Pa., Mo., N. Y., Ky. "Strike It Rich" paid $500; got $100 from hotel chain. Pittsburgh City Commissioner John Walker announced a Kelly Fund be started in Mellon Bank; about $2800 in it—from all over.

Started St. Louis job Oct. 12. Betty to hospital for operation about Oct. 1—complications resulting from babies—cyst. When the *St Louis Dispatch* had the story Jerry Cataldi came to see me and offered the job. Was going to form a corporation and make K. part of it; Betty checked the corporation. Now making about twice as much as before; also will move family up here.

Facing the enemy was easier than the terrible six months. In battle you have a job, you know it, can do it. The other way, hands tied; you have a thing to do, can't do it. Go ask a man for a job; he says no; turn around and walk out. You walk 3–4 miles and they say the same thing. I'd have 50 cents in my pocket, no cigarettes or chewing tobacco. I'd go see men 3–4 times, then have go home and face wife. She: do any good? Naw. Next day, same thing.

You sit and try to think what can I do. You can't talk. You get so many no's. She sees this, says let's talk out. There's nothing you can grasp. You are asking for a job, you don't know if you can do it. Never had a high school education. Don't know much. But will try; every job I had I ended up on top of it. Seems every time I have to start at the bottom. Would walk out of house with a bus ticket and 15 cents for chewing tobacco. Sometimes I didn't have enough to get a room, so I'd sleep in a truck instead of borrow off the men. I just don't like to borrow.

The most important thing in my life is kids and wife. I took my bumps from when I was a kid. I want them not to make the same mistakes I did. Chuckie wants to go to West Point; I help as I can. I'm not brilliant, but I do what I can. Sons of Medal of Honor winners can get a special appointment to the Point, but must meet the same qualifications as anyone else.

I want to get my wife and family into a home of our own. At "Strike It Rich" I was scared because of no education. They said tell what you want: 1. job; 2. operation for Betty; 3. a sewing machine.

I try to help others. I've raised money for Red Cross, Salvation Army, war bonds; they use my name for fund drives and so on. I did practically nothing else for two years except go around and help raise money. It cost me money; I got $6 a day and transportation. $3 for a hotel and $1 for meals. So it cost me; I never had a hotel for less than $6 and sometimes up to $14. Nothing for cleaning, l had to buy own clothes, take care of tips. I used up all my Army pay and had to dig down for other money.

My notes ended there. Of course they are fragmentary, mere triggers to make your memory supply the full sound and flavor of what they said. For example, Kelly's account of the night he had the appendicitis attack was a long story with many more details; the notes merely give the progression of the action. the rest was so colorful and moving that it was deeply imprinted on my mind; after years, I can still see and hear him as he described it.

And now back home, the evaluation process started. What did all these bits and pieces add up to—what did they say, what single message could be drawn from them that would be important to our readers? What self-interest of theirs would be piqued so they would say, "Yeah, that could happen to me"? What emotions would the story evoke, so readers would not find it a dry recital of another's experiences with no real pertinence to their own lives? How should the story be constructed—what should come first, what next? What should be used, what left out? What would the story *say*?

I thought about Kelly, that cocky, vulnerable little man with the wad of chewing tobacco tucked in his cheek. I remembered the way his voice deepened with self-importance when he talked about the parades he'd been in, his visits to the White House, the obvious relish with which he described the cheering crowds that surrounded his car during the war bond tours. I recalled the big cigar he had that day at lunch in St. Louis, and how he talked importantly about forming a corporation, when he obviously didn't have an inkling of what a corporation was or entailed. I thought he was being used for his publicity value, and when that died away he would be eased out onto the streets again—and he didn't know it. I thought, the guy is a phony; he was really taken in by all the public relations razzle-dazzle; he believed what the press agents said about him (which is fatal). And I thought, why should we add to this? The man is not worth doing a story on; he's hollow.

And then I remembered the tears in his eyes at the TV show; they, by God, were no press agent's gimmick. And I remembered that he had known he was going to be humiliated at the show and had gone anyway. Why? Because he needed the money, because his family needed the money. I remembered Betty saying that when he was working in Frankfort and came home weekends, he was so anxious to see the kids he'd wake them up and take them outside to romp. I remembered that during the bad times, he must have known that all he had to do to start the golden shower of money and jobs was to go to the newspapers with his story. And he'd had too much pride and independence to do it. I remembered his face, blank with concealing his emotions, as he said, "When you give the kids a bowl of cereal for breakfast and they ask for more and there isn't any more, you don't feel like much of a man."

I thought, he may have been taken in by the razzle-dazzle, but there are damn few men who wouldn't be, and he has shown that he's a tough man, he keeps on fighting. Is that what the story says—that a man ought to keep fighting? Big deal, who *hasn't* said that before?

Is Kelly the kind of man we want to do a story on? Look at all the mistakes he made, like paying $275 for an engagement ring for Betty when he should have known that kind of money was way out of his class— and then having to pawn it a few months later for $34. Yeah, but look at it another way: maybe he *did* know it was out of his class and bought it anyway because that was way of showing his love for Betty. Or take that marvelous little story about Betty and the nickel and the way they met. He was being lionized—the big hero accepting the homage of the natives. So why did he take time out from being lionized to walk his hostess's dog? Doesn't this show a kind of simple helpfulness so strong in him that it overrode his vanity?

Or take the time when the doctor told him May had cancer and advised him not to tell her about it. Kelly told her immediately, before they even got out of the building. Wasn't this callousness? Maybe. But also maybe it was a kind of faith in her—faith that she was strong enough to take whatever she had to take. Certainly the business of sitting by her bed for three weeks, giving her morphine injections every hour, grabbing a sandwich when he could, catching naps in the chair, going out for strawberries at 1:00 A.M.—all that didn't indicate callousness. Probably the man was speaking the literal truth when he said his kids and wife were the most important things in his life. Maybe this is a love story, a man's love for his family. *That* certainly would be pertinent to our readers' lives.

And so the process goes on—weighing, evaluating, analyzing. I spent two or three days at it. Once I went out into the backyard and walked back and forth for three or four hours thinking, "This has obviously got to be a narrative; how in hell am I going to get narrative into it? What's the problem to be solved? What are the conflicts and suspense in it?" And suddenly it began to come clear that this was a story of courage, of two kinds of courage—the kind that enables a man to win the nation's highest honor for valor and the kind that sustains a man through the grinding attrition of day-to-day living, running a marriage, raising kids, meeting the bills, coping with sickness and emergencies, keeping the whole shebang going against the slings and arrows of outrageous fortune. Remember how Kelly himself had said that just living was harder? That business about when you are in battle you have a job to do, you know it, and know you can do it; but the other way your hands are tied—you have a thing to do and can't do it. That was it.

I went into the house and scribbled on a sheet of paper: "We're showing that it takes more courage to live an everyday life, raise a family, and take on all the things life can throw at you than it does to win a Medal of Honor." And I wrote the title: "A Hero Is Many Men." (Later the editors changed it and rightly so. The title was ambiguous I knew what it meant, but the reader wouldn't.) The story was, it turned out, a simple straightforward piece.

At that point, I could start to organize the story, to select and assemble those bits and pieces that would get the message across to the reader, that would make the narrative flow, evoke the readers' emotions so they would see themselves in Kelly's struggles. I'm not very happy with the result—I think in many places I failed to make it as strong and compelling as I should have, and I didn't make Kelly as rounded a character as he really was—but here it is:

A Man's Fight for His Family

"Commando" Kelly had earned the Medal of Honor, but when misfortune struck his home, he needed even more courage— just to live from day to day.

The door to the office opened, and the doctor appeared with May at his side. He told her to take a seat for a few moments, then looked at Chuck Kelly and said, "Will you come in, please?" Kelly knew instantly that it was bad, but he didn't say anything as he walked in and sat down in the chair next to the desk.

The doctor's face was solemn. "I'm afraid I have very bad news for you, Mr. Kelly. Your wife has cancer; I believe she has only a few years to live."

Kelly blinked, but his voice was level, almost uninterested. "Wouldn't an operation stop it? What about X-ray treatment?"

The doctor shook his head. "You can try them, of course. An exploratory operation would show how bad it is, but I think we already know that. I doubt that X-rays would help. I haven't told your wife—I think it would be better not to."

Kelly didn't say anything more. On the way down in the elevator May asked what the doctor had said. Kelly, who believes that people can take what they have to take, answered, "He says you have cancer." May didn't say anything, didn't cry or do anything at all. They walked out of the Medical Arts Building and went home to their two children and their house on Annandale Street in Pittsburgh.

Probably you have heard of Charles Kelly. A few years before that day at the doctor's he had become one of the 15 living Americans to receive the Congressional Medal of Honor, the nation's highest decoration for courage.

Kelly was 22 at the time, a slim, tough kid who'd grown up in a back alley in Pittsburgh and learned a cocky independence from his blacksmith father, from earning his own way as soon as he finished grade school, from being able to handle himself in street fights.

He went in on the beaches at Salerno, Italy, in September 1943, and in two days of furious fighting around Altavilla, he led volunteer patrols against entrenched German machine gun positions and wiped them out and took another patrol through two miles of enemy-held territory under constant sniper, mortar and artillery fire. When his company was surrounded in a house, Kelly ranged from window to window pouring a torrent of fire into the enemy. In a few hours he burned out nearly half a dozen Browning automatic rifles and then used, in succession, a Thompson submachine gun, Garand and Springfield rifles, carbines, a 37 mm. anti-tank gun and a bazooka. Once he repelled a German assault by picking up 60 mm. mortar shells, pulling the safety pins and hurling them like hand grenades.

Later Kelly led 44 men across the bloody Rapido River and brought eight back. Three time his outfit was in the line at Cassino—for 15, 43, and 36 days at a time, under fire so terrible that once Kelly, a sergeant, was the highest-ranking officer left alive.

Kelly's exploits won him the nickname "Commando" and constitute a record of courage that seldom—if ever—had been surpassed in U. S. history. But is the kind of brilliant courage that carries a man to the peaks in a flashing moment of war the same kind that sustains him in the slow, grinding attrition of everyday troubles that so many heads of families must endure?

In the five years after his date with the doctor, Kelly was to find out—was to have his courage tested to the utmost. For there is nothing in the world that is more important to Chuck Kelly than his wife and kids—not his job, not his war record, not even his own well-being.

At first the cancer didn't interfere with May's activities much, and Kelly stayed at home at night to look after Virginia and young Chuckie in order that May might go to the movies or play cards with her friends. But increasingly, before the movie or card game ended, the pain would hit her. After a while she gave up the nights out. About a year before she died she couldn't walk upstairs any more; Kelly carried her. And sometimes she'd get great cravings; Kelly went out and hunted the city for strawberries or ice cream.

After she became so weak she had to stay in bed most of the time, Kelly hired a nurse to come in and bathe, massage and feed her—and give her the morphine shots that were steadily increasing in size and frequency. Finally May got so thin and was in such pain, she didn't want the children to see her; they were sent to her sister's to live. But she never cried.

At this time Kelly was working as bodyguard and chauffeur for the late Charles J. Margiotti, then attorney general of Pennsylvania. He was making a fair wage, but long sickness can devour any income. When the money ran low, the doctor taught Kelly how to give the injections. May required almost constant attention now—injections every 45 minutes—and Kelly's boss let him stay at home all the time during the last weeks.

He often slept in a chair and grabbed a sandwich when he could. The rest of the time he sat with his wife, talking to her, holding her hand, watching her die. Finally death came, in April 1951.

Kelly had to sell the house and furniture to pay the bills. He moved to a hotel and his brother Ed, who worked in the post office, took the two children. Kelly's job kept him out of town a lot, but he visited the kids as often as possible. Every time he left, they wanted so badly to come with him that he felt like a criminal.

The following year, Kelly was asked to help campaign for General Eisenhower's first term as a "Veteran for Ike." While in Louisville, Kentucky, he met Betty Dugzinski.

He had met her once before, during the war when he was on tour trying to boost War Bond sales and she was a star-struck kid of 14. She'd come up for his autograph, a cute, blonde youngster, and he'd whistled to make her feel good and pulled out a nickel. "Here," he'd said, "call me when you grow up."

Now he was in Louisville with the campaign troupe, and she was running a photography studio there. A friend called her, said she was having the veterans over for dinner and would Betty come to help entertain them? Betty hadn't forgotten Kelly. She went home, dug out the nickel and was at the friend's house when he walked in the door.

"You owe me another nickel," she said.

"What!"

"You owe me another nickel. Telephone calls cost a dime now."

"What? Who are . . . Do I know you?"

Then Betty explained.

Before the evening was over, Kelly told her seriously, "I'm going to marry you." Betty didn't believe him, of course. The next night the troupe was in St. Louis; he called Betty and talked for half an hour. He called next from Detroit, then Worcester, Massachusetts, then Washington, D.C. Six weeks after they met they were married in Jeffersonville, Indiana.

But they couldn't be together right away. Kelly had to find a place to live and save money for furniture. So Betty went back to her job in Louisville, and he stayed in Pittsburgh. Kelly looked for a furnished apartment big enough for three kids—his own two and Mike, Betty's son by a previous marriage. Finally he found one that was big enough, but it cost $125 a month and had a gas furnace which cost $40 a month to run during the winter and even then didn't heat the place.

To get more money, Kelly quit working for Margiotti and went back to his old trade—house painting. He was bringing home about $100 a week, but he had to work at night to do it. Being alone frightened Betty so that after a while Kelly switched to day work, even though it meant a cut in take-home pay.

There was a strike that summer which meant no pay for two months, and Kelly was laid off three weeks before Christmas when the weather turned bad. Still, since they'd already bought the kids' presents, Christmas was all right that year. Weather kept Kelly out of work four months that winter— about average for painters—and although he managed to pick up some jobs on his own, there was barely enough money to go around.

Prices kept going up. Lee was born in the spring, and Kelly started having trouble with his boss. A misunderstanding arose and Kelly started losing good assignments. Finally he had to pawn the diamond engagement ring he'd given Betty. He got $34 for it.

One night Betty said it seemed to her they weren't making any headway; they couldn't keep going into debt. She thought they could do better in Louisville where her uncle, who was superintendent of a highway construction crew, could help Kelly get a job. She also counted on finding a much cheaper apartment in a municipal housing project.

They went to Louisville, Kelly did get the job and—eventually—they moved into the housing project. Kelly started as a pick-and-shovel man at $1.25 an hour and worked his way up to foreman in charge of the heavy machinery, just under Betty's uncle.

The job was at the airport in Frankfort, Kentucky, about 50 miles from Louisville. Kelly was living in a cabin near a gas station down the road from the airport and coming home only on weekends. He missed the kids so much that, if they were still napping when he got home Friday afternoon, he immediately charged in, woke them up and took them all out in the yard to romp for a couple of hours. They had five youngsters now; Bennie had been born that spring.

Kelly is not a man who thinks that kids are a woman's business. When one of them called out in the night for a drink of water or a little reassurance, he was the one who got up. Betty has one bad ear and Kelly teasingly says she always sleeps on the good one so he'll hear the kids first. "I used to figure that taking care of kids was a 50-50 proposition," he said, "but now I know it's a 75-25 deal. Seventy-five for the wife and 25 for the husband. Betty has them all day long; the least I can do is get up with them at night."

What he doesn't say is that he's so crazy about them he's delighted to see them any time.

Then, suddenly, there was trouble. The baby, Bennie, started to run a high fever. He became flushed and still. The doctor said it was bronchial pneumonia and ordered him into a hospital. The hospital was overcrowded and understaffed; when Bennie woke up and cried, no one came to care for him. Betty and Kelly couldn't stand it; they bundled the baby up and took him to another hospital.

It was touch and go for a while. The baby's windpipe would close up and specialists had to be called in. But Bennie pulled through. The bills knocked a hole in the Kellys' budget that wasn't repaired for more than a year. And shortly after Bennie came home, bad fortune struck again.

Kelly stepped off the bus one Monday morning on his way to work and turned to go up to the cabin. It was gone. There was only a pile of ashes and a few charred bits of wood. In it had been all his work clothes, tools and some of his personal belongings. The only thing he could salvage was a blackened pair of pliers.

Under his arm, Kelly had a new pair of jeans and a work shirt; in his pocket was $5. He went into the men's room at the gas station, changed his clothes and went to work. That night he and three other men slept in a trailer that belonged to the gas station owner. Later, the other men rented rooms, but Kelly couldn't afford one. For a month he slept in the unheated trailer, washing in the men's room of the gas station and taking baths at the airport. Replacing only those clothes he couldn't do without put the Kellys further into debt.

There was one bright note; Betty's uncle had said he was sure there'd be work all that winter. Two weeks before Christmas the weather went bad just as the airport job was finished. Before another one could be started, word came that the two men who owned the company were dissolving their partnership. However, one of them said that, as soon as they got the legal details settled, he was going to continue the business alone and he wanted Kelly to come back to work. He said it would take about three weeks. Nine months later work still hadn't been resumed.

Things quickly became desperate. Kelly couldn't get unemployment insurance in Kentucky because he hadn't worked there long enough. Because he hadn't worked recently in Pennsylvania, he could get only $14 a week from there. And the weather stayed bad, preventing work in the construction trades.

Meantime he made the rounds looking for some kind of factory job. Nobody was hiring.

"You go out of the house in the morning with a bus ticket and 15 cents for chewing tobacco in your pocket," Kelly said, "You ride downtown and walk into the first place and ask the man for a job, any job. He says they're not hiring right now, so you turn around and walk out again.

"Maybe it's three, four miles to the next place and you walk because you don't have the money for a bus. It's the same thing over again. You do that three or four times and then you have to go home and face the wife.

"You walk in and she looks up with a smile that's got hope in it and asks, 'Did you do any good?' And you have to say, 'Naw,' and go sit in a chair.

"Next day it's the same thing again."

And that's the way it was—for nearly four months.

In 1944, when Kelly came home from Italy with the Congressional Medal of Honor, he was a national hero. He talked to the President in the White House and they had a parade for him in the nation's capital. Pittsburgh gave him the keys to the city and everywhere he went the crowds of cheering people were so thick they had trouble forcing the cars through. He traveled the 48 states and everywhere it was the same. He was interviewed, photographed, honored at banquets.

Now, 10 years later, he knew that, if he told the newspapers about the trouble he was having, the golden flow would start all over again. But he couldn't bring himself to do it. Around Pittsburgh they used to say his father was "independent as a hog on ice." Chuck Kelly had the same independence, or pride, and he couldn't ask for help—yet.

When the good weather came that spring, he applied for work with all the painting contractors, but had no luck; they were hiring back their former employees first. When he was working in Frankfort, Kelly had bought Betty a diamond ring to replace the one they'd pawned and lost in Pittsburgh. Now they had to pawn the second; Betty said later she never wants another.

Betty's family helped out during these dark weeks. Her grandfather, who has a small farm in Lily, Kentucky, sent some food he'd raised and canned, and her mother and sisters helped, too. Harry Holt, an insurance agent and

Republican precinct worker who had become Kelly's closest friend, helped out most of all. He hired Kelly to paint his house, which really didn't need it, and paid well for the job.

Kelly found another house-painting job and then in June he finally went to work as a painter-maintenance man for a real estate operator. He made $1.45 an hour and worked 50 hours a week.

Five weeks after he got the job, Betty went into the hospital to have their sixth child. The bill was $97.20, which Kelly had to borrow to get her out of the hospital.

The next day Kelly had a sharp pain in his stomach and didn't go to work. As it grew worse, he decided it was not his appendix. That afternoon, when Harry Holt came over, they walked to the drug store and Kelly bought an ice bag. Harry told him to go to a doctor, but Kelly, thinking of the bills, refused.

Betty went to bed and Kelly stayed in a chair in the living room. The pain was getting intense, and pretty soon Kelly had the ice bag, a water bottle that was frozen solid and three ice trays wrapped in towel, all on his abdomen. There weren't enough. He remembered that Betty had some sleeping pills for her own post-childbirth pain. He started to go for them found he couldn't walk. He crawled into the dark bedroom and had a terrible time waking Betty, who had taken some pills herself. She mumbled that they were in one of the kitchen cabinets, but she didn't wake up enough to comprehend Chuck's agony.

He crawled into the kitchen, but couldn't hoist himself up high enough to reach the pills. He lay on the floor, drowning in the pain; then he blacked out.

Later the pain broke. He looked across and there was the familiar living room chair under the cone of light from the lamp. In his abdomen now was only a dull ache. He got up and lurched over to the chair and sat down and dozed.

At eight o'clock Betty came in, took one look at his drawn, white face and went downstairs to phone Harry Holt. Harry came over and took Kelly to the VA hospital. They checked in at 10:30 in the morning and Kelly told the doctors he thought his appendix had burst the night before. They took tests and operated at 4:30 that afternoon; by then peritonitis had set in.

Betty couldn't sleep that night. Harry had come by and told her about the operation and said Kelly was fine, but something about his manner kept her from believing him. Finally at about 12:30 she went into the kitchen for a drink of water. She was standing by the sink looking out the window at nothing when suddenly,

"I saw Chuck," she said, "and I could feel him there in the room. He was reaching out to me, and I knew something was terribly wrong.

"I started to cry and I don't think I ever prayed so hard in my life as I did right then. I stayed in the kitchen for three hours praying and crying and smoking cigarettes."

The next morning, Monday, she insisted on going out to the hospital, although it was not yet seven days since she'd had the baby. Kelly was unconscious and stayed that way until Thursday. Each day Betty was beside his bed for the full four hours that visitors were allowed.

Kelly was in the hospital 12 days and lost 28 pounds. When he came out, the nation had heard of his trouble; Harry Holt told the newspapers when he went into the hospital. Then the golden shower began as the American people poured out their generosity on a family that needed help. One woman brought a chair, a couch and two lamps; another brought a bed; another gave clothes. After Kelly appeared on TV, letters with money poured into the Mellon Bank in Pittsburgh until the total reached $2,800. The most touching letter came from a woman in an old ladies' home; she wished the Kellys well and enclosed a dime.

Kelly received more than 100 job offers from all over the country, and the Governor made him a Kentucky colonel. The tiny Kelly apartment was swamped with reporters, photographers and broadcasters. President Eisenhower sent Kelly a telegram and later invited him to take part, on TV, in one of the question-and-answer shows that were a part of his campaign for reelection.

But the golden shower was not without its dark clouds. Kelly was invited to appear on the "Strike It Rich" television show, and it was this appearance that swelled the money and job offers into a flood. But it was also an ordeal.

"He was scared to death," Betty said. "He knew he couldn't answer the questions they'd ask him, because he never forgets that he didn't even go to high school. And he had to go up there before all those people and tell a story about himself that he didn't want to tell. He's an independent man and he was ashamed.

"He hated it, yet felt he couldn't refuse to go because we needed the money so badly. He very much wanted me to go with him, but the people wouldn't pay my fare and we had no money of our own. So Chuck went alone and it took a lot of courage. I watched the show; at the end I could see he had tears in his eyes."

One day last fall Kelly was talking about courage. I asked him which took more—to face the Germans that day at Altavilla, or to live through the past few years. He answered instantly:

"The past years took much more. When you're in combat you have a job to do, you know how to do it and you know you can do it. So you just go ahead. Besides, when you're in a fight, you get so hopped up you don't even think about the danger.

"But these years have been rough. Your hands are tied. You have a thing to do, but you can't do it. You go in and ask a man for a job. It's a job you never had before and you're asking for it, but you don't know if you can do it. And you get so many 'No's.'

"Then there's your family. You give the kids cereal in the morning and they ask for more and there isn't any more. When you tell them, you don't feel like much of a man.

"But you just have to keep on and do what you can."

This article, of course, is flawed. There are minor failures, such as not noting that it was after midnight the time he went out for the strawberries for May, not realizing that most readers think of housepainting as an outdoor, daytime job and that I should have explained that Kelly was painting the interiors of apartments at night. I should have used the date of the summer strike, and I should have noted that it was wintertime when he slept in the unheated trailer. But the greatest failure was that I didn't present the side of Kelly that was seduced by the razzle-dazzle, didn't show his vanity, his self-importance. In the evaluation process I decided this wasn't as important as other things he did and was, and left it out in order to hew to the stronger line. Since then I've read better journalists than I who found ways to include this kind of material without destroying the main theme of the story and thus produced a finer, deeper, truer piece.

7

Organization

M ost of the textbooks on writing that we've read have sections on organization, and most didn't help us when we faced the actual job. Most start by saying organization is vital to good writing, which is true, then go on to talk about jotting down sections of the piece on 3×5 cards and arranging them in order, or scrawling ideas, quotes, and facts on butcher paper and tacking them up all around the room, or similar mechanistic approaches. None dealt with the basic problem: how to assemble all these bits and pieces into a compelling article?

Perhaps one reason for this is that each part of a piece is different— the material you have, the feel of the story, your objective in writing it. Good organization must reflect all these, must grow inevitably out of the story itself, and while the manipulation of pieces of paper or cards might help, it doesn't get to the heart of the problem. For while organization *is* part mechanics, it can also be where the writer's creativity shines through to make a collection of facts glow with a special warmth.

When you're writing a typical news report, organization follows a pattern, and it takes place more or less automatically in your mind. But when you face a longer piece like a depth story or a magazine article, the familiar system doesn't work. You have many more facts to contend with, some of them contradictory. You have abstract ideas, suggested by the facts, to be distilled out and stated clearly. You have to sustain reader interest over a longer period. All this means that you have to analyze and plan—consciously.

This is creativity. For writers who are very good, talent dominates the organization process, and they may come up with something so new and effective that people still remember it years later. But most of us aren't that talented—or that talented every day—and as journalists we have to keep writing. So when inspiration fails, craftsmanship can move in to fill the gap. Your piece may not be brilliant, but it will be sound.

The heart of the organization process is first to refine out the single theme or idea that the facts indicate, as we discussed in the Kelly story in Chapter 6. Once you have this, the job is to summon all the material—statistics, quotes from experts, anecdotes—that support the single message. Everything in the piece should support or relate to it; anything that does not should be left out, no matter how attractive it is in itself. But how do you arrange the material? What comes first, what next?

All our training in linear thinking and logic pushes us to arrange a story chronologically. Are you writing history? You start at the beginning of a century and work through to the end. In recounting a series of events you report what happened first, then next and next until the story is ended. One of the best examples of chronological organization is in Jim Bishop's "day" books. In the first, and perhaps best, of these, *The Day Lincoln Was Shot*, Bishop started his story twenty-four hours before Lincoln's death, then carried through hour by hour until the end. This gave the whole series of events immediacy and allowed him to build an unusual tension as characters and events moved toward the climax of the assassination in Ford's Theater.

But the book also illustrates the weakness of chronological organization. In order to let the reader understand the motivation of his characters, Bishop had to break chronology and go back in years to report the events that shaped their lives. For example, Bishop had to go back almost to John Wilkes Booth's childhood to explain Booth's frustration and bitterness. These excursions broke the tight chronology and, though Bishop handled them well, tended to relax the tension of the book.

This same problem was illustrated much more concisely in an excellent little piece in the *New York Times*. Here it is:

Little Man Has Day in Night Court

By Bill Kovach

He was a small man, the plaintiff, and standing before the bench looking up at the judge, he seemed even smaller. His hands trembled as they darted from his black rimmed glasses to his silver hair and back again.

It was not just the courtroom, wood paneled and large, that emphasized the smallness of Isaac Spira, but also his adversaries. Mr. Spira, the owner of a small cleaning establishment, was challenging the New York Telephone

Company, with its attorney and battery of experts holding folders of wonderfully detailed technical information.

Like many of those who have been using Night Court in steadily increasing numbers to try to right what they consider wrongs, Mr. Spira was unlearned in the law.

Armed with only his complaint, he jumped to the attack, pouring out a torrent of words. "They cost me business, Your Honor," he argued. "I was without phone service for three weeks because they cut off my phone at my old place—I even had to go next door to a neighbor's to make my calls and my customers told me they tried to call and couldn't get me—and when they put it in at the new place it rang in the old place, too. It was from July 26 to Aug. 14 before I had decent phone service, Your Honor."

Patiently, Judge Andrew R. Tyler let Mr. Spira make his complaint in his own words, not allowing technical details of legal procedures to interfere with his telling of the story.

Isaac Spira, who was born in Germany and spent more than five years in German concentration camps, was having his day in Night Court.

Each year thousands of New Yorkers like Mr. Spira go from the streets and the marketplaces into court with their arguments. It is in this courtroom on the ground floor of the Civil Courts building at 111 Centre Street, in lower Manhattan, that literally thousands—the total last year was 65,000—get their first experience in court.

The night sessions of Small Claims Court, a part of the Civil Court, were organized in 1957 by Judge Daniel Gutman. Realizing that a man suing for $100 (which was the limit of the court in 1957, but is now $300) could probably not afford a day off from work or business to press his claim, Judge Gutman struck upon the plan for a night court.

The success of the court has generated widespread sentiment to raise the maximum claim to $500 or even $1,000. For $2.91 to pay for a summons, anyone can bring suit for civil damages. There are no other costs.

Neither is there a need for an individual to bring a lawyer.

"This is simply a people's court," Judge Tyler said. "Many come here as a matter of principle. We let them tell their story in their own way—all we are after is the truth, and we let each side tell that as best they can and as best they see it."

Judge Tyler is one of the regular judges of the Small Claims Court, which meets on each weekday. Each judge, on a rotating basis, sits for a week in Night Court.

Similar Night Court operations are maintained across the street in the Criminal Courts for those accused on criminal charges.

Many Get There Early

Night Court convenes at 6:30 P.M. A hand-lettered sign notes that that means "6:30 sharp." But, many plaintiffs and defendants arrive early. They stand about, their voices subdued and small in the marble and glass expanse of the two-floor lobby.

If the weather is nice, some wait on benches outdoors, employees head for home, or go across to the Court View Bar for a quick drink.

As they gather, most of them segregate themselves into little groups: here a plaintiff and some friends; there a defendant casting sullen glances at his accuser.

Sometimes they are friendly. One night recently, a typical night at the court, one of the 60 new cases docketed that night was settled in a friendly discussion in the lobby. A store owner, sued by a customer for a defective air conditioner, met her as she went into court.

He had explained he "could do nothing personally" about the machine, but her suit had brought in the manufacturer. On this night a representative of the manufacturer was present and in a conference in the lobby, agreed to send the machine back to the factory for service and repairs.

Satisfied with the arrangement, the three left, no longer needing the services of the court.

How the Court Works

Promptly at 6:30 Joseph Hyland, clerk of the court, opened the doors to begin the preliminaries before Judge Tyler assumed the bench.

"What we try to do," Mr. Hyland explained to a hundred or so people, most of whom had never seen the inside of a courtroom, "is to expedite your cases. We have two choices available to you. If both sides agree, your case can be handled quickly by arbitration. If you cannot agree to arbitration, we can try the case before the judge."

The distinction, he went on, is that arbitration—conducted by an attorney with the same qualifications as a judge—is final. There is no appeal. At trial, a transcript is kept and an appeal is possible, although with a maximum claim of $300 the cost of an appeal is generally prohibitive.

Mrs. Shirley Eisner, a Manhattan housewife, considered the alternatives. Carrying her evidence—a blue and white suit coat, marred, she said, by her cleaner—she hoped to avoid a trial.

"I still do business with him. I don't want to have to go through that," she said. "Maybe we can settle this."

Mrs. Eisner and her cleaner ("Let's leave his name out of this," she said. "It couldn't be helped and we still get along") agreed to arbitration. She settled for less than the $509 she originally sought, and the two left, apparently pleased with the results.

Most of the litigants agreed to arbitration, but the few who insisted upon a trial presented for Judge Tyler a series of problems.

One woman sought a postponement: "I had all my evidence in my pocketbook," she told the judge, "and I changed pocketbooks to come down here and left them in the other one."

He put the case over to October 16.

Another, an elderly woman who appeared confused by the proceedings, presented the judge with a fistful of papers—42 in all.

"If you'll read these," she said, "you'll understand my case."

Quietly and patiently, Judge Tyler waded through the documents, some of them handwritten.

"Don't you have an attorney?" he asked the woman, the defendant in the case.

After a moment she answered: "My attorney could not come. He is a lovely old man and he is in the hospital dying of cancer."

Both Sides Are Ready

Over the protests of the other side, Judge Tyler ordered the case set over: "She cannot handle this alone," he said, "I'm not going to let this case go to trial in this manner."

By the time Judge Tyler came to the case of Isaac Spira, doing business as Jac-Le-Valet, vs. the New York Telephone Company, the docket had almost been cleared.

Both sides were ready in this one, and the issue was joined immediately. Accustomed to a more formal procedure, the company's attorney began on several occasions to rise and object to the statements of Mr. Spira. A calm wave of Judge Tyler's hand, however, kept him in his seat.

"Just let him tell his story," the judge said quietly.

And when he was through, the judge similarly overlooked Mr. Spira's dramatics in his cross-examination of defense witnesses.

In the end, the court reserved judgment. "We never give a final decision the night the case is in court," explained the clerk. "They've had their opportunity to present the case and they will call back later for a decision."

Few are disappointed, he said, no matter how the decision goes.

It's the Principle

"Most of these people are in here as a matter of principle." he explained. "It is not so much the money involved, but their right to sue anyone they believe has wronged them. But, in the heat of a courtroom argument—when they are re-enacting the wrong they feel done them—tempers can build. We don't add to that by ruling for one side or the other the same night. It seems to work very well; we have very few complaints."

A janitor was sweeping away cigarette butts in the hallway at 11:30 this night when Night Court ended. He paused for a minute, leaning on his broom, and shook his head with a smile. Mr. Spira, who moments before condemned every phase of the telephone company's operation, was walking out with the company attorney.

"Sure," he was saying, "I understand your problem. Come on, I'll take you home in my car, your place is not far from where I live."

Here Kovach uses a kind of chronological organization. He starts by showing Isaac Spira in action, pleading his case before the judge. He gives readers a single man to identify with and evokes their underdog sympathies—the little man versus the giant corporation. But after seven paragraphs, he must depart from the Spira story to sketch the larger significance of his piece—what the night court is and how it works. Then he goes back to the chronology again, under the subhead "Many Get There Early," by picking up the story as the court opens. He follows through with succeeding cases and finally winds up with the rest of the Spira story and the closing of the court.

If our training pushes us to chronological organization and the requirements of comprehension prohibit it, how does the writer solve the dilemma? I got the first glimpse of the answer from an editor with whom I worked. I had done a piece and while he liked the idea and the research, he didn't like the way it was put together. He was trying to tell me what was wrong with it. "You've got to organize it by concepts," he said.

"What do you mean? I don't understand."

"Well, look: You make certain points here—or the facts you report do. But they're not clear; they're not stated clearly and then each point driven home with facts, supporting evidence. That's the way you put a story together; you make a point—tell the reader what it is—then prove it with evidence. Then you go on to the next point and do the same thing."

To make this new approach penetrate my dim brain, he had to take the manuscript and point out specific instances of what he meant. Finally I got it and ever since when faced with the problem of organizing a piece, I have gone back to his formula for guidance. It works. It works for all kinds of stories; it is almost infinitely flexible. Even stories that seem to be put together chronologically are in fact organized conceptually. Like the Kovach piece, above.

The first six paragraphs are the lead in which Kovach catches the reader's interest and presents, by illustration, the theme or idea; here's a way little people who feel they have been wronged can get justice. Then he goes from the specific to the general to point out the significance of the court and, briefly, its history. After three paragraphs he makes his first point: "Neither is there need for an individual to bring a lawyer." He nails this down with a quote from Judge Tyler, then gives two more paragraphs of background explanation.

Under the subhead "Many Get There Early," he goes back to chronology and makes another point: some cases are settled in the lobby outside court. This one is not stated explicitly, but is implicit in the reporting and in the last paragraph:

"Satisfied with the arrangement, the three left, no longer needing the services of the court."

The next point—claimants have two choices—is made in the next three paragraphs and driven home with the anecdote about Mrs. Shirley Eisner. The next—Judge Tyler has to handle many human problems—is made in the paragraph starting, "Most of the litigants agreed . . . ," which does double duty by also carrying the chronology forward. Then he goes back to the Spira case and, in reporting it, makes the point that the judge won't let legalisms overwhelm a lawyerless claimant nor let an emotional claimant subvert the law. His final point is made by the night clerk: "Most of these people are in here as a matter of principle."

The chronology is ended with the last two paragraphs, which also restate the theme that little people can get justice by showing Spira satisfied and friendly.

The skeleton of a piece that is organized conceptually, then, can be simply stated:

    * Lead—to hook the readers in, get them emotionally involved.

    * Statement of the theme/idea what the story is about and why the reader should read it. Answer reader's question, "What's in it for me?"

    * Point number 1 to prove theme/idea, supported with evidence: facts, quotes, anecdotes.

    * Points number 2, 3, 4, etc., similarly supported.

    * Ending—summary, wrap-up anecdote, snapper, or restatement of theme/idea.

After you have used this formula a few times you'll begin to get disgusted with it; it will seem too simple, mechanical. You'll think, "Hell! I've got more artistry than that," and you'll be right. So start experimenting with it; put in your supporting evidence before you state your point and let the evidence lead up to the point; let one of your characters make the point, as Kovach did, if you have a suitable quote. Try other variations (some are noted later on). You don't have to be a slave to your outline, but be very cautious in departing from the formula; it can be clothed in many different styles and types of writing, but basically it is sound and will produce for you a solid, compelling piece.

Howard Whitman, who was to become one of the country's outstanding magazine writers, talked about this when he was just making the switch from newspaper to magazine writing. We were talking about organization, and I asked him if he outlined his stories before he wrote them. He said yes, always. Why? "Well," he said, "I don't have much confidence that I'm a genius. I think my writing is OK, but not great. But when I organize and outline a piece carefully I know that at least it will have everything in it it ought to have—the editor won't be able to fault me on that."

("Look, Ma, No Hands" Department: the paragraph above is an example of a variation. It does three things: I am about to move to a section on outlining; this introduces the idea. It validates the idea of outlining by quoting the experience of a good writer. It breaks the impersonality of the chapter by getting people into it.)

I hadn't written many magazine articles when Whitman said this; later, when I was writing full-time, I stole his idea and always outlined a piece before I wrote it. I still do. The word "outline," incidentally, has two distinct meanings in the magazine business. The first is what an editor asks you to prepare when he or she interested in one of your ideas; this is a two or three page item designed to sell the editor on the idea. It's also called a query. The second meaning is what we're talking about here—the skeleton of your piece. Nobody else ever sees it; it's a memo from you to you. The memo can take almost any form; it need not be the kind of thing you English teacher taught you in the fifth grade, though some writers do follow this form. Others simply jot down notes on the lead, the theme/idea, the points with supporting evidence, the ending.

There's a reason in addition to Whitman's that outlining is valuable. It breaks the writing process down into two parts. In the first you distill out your theme/idea and the various points you're going to make in the article. You arrange them in order and decide what facts, quotes, and anecdotes you're going to select to make each one convincing. Once this is finished you know you've touched all bases, you know what you're trying to say. Then when you start to write you don't have to think of any of these things, but are free to concentrate on putting the right words on paper in the right order. This freedom lets you get more pace, drive, flow in the writing; you can concentrate on the effects you want to create and on building clear, concise sentences and paragraphs.

Of course, once you get the story moving you may find you want to depart from the strict outline. Go ahead. But remember the outline represents your cool, logical judgment of what ought to be in the piece; in the heat of creation, when you're really rolling on a section, some item in the outline may seem inconsequential. Leave it out and keep going. But later, after the whole piece is written and the creative drive has been spent, go back to the outline and reconsider. That way you get the best of both worlds: the ecstasy of creation and the coolness of deliberation.

One of the troubles with talking about outlines is that the talk is too general, while in trying to put a story together you're dealing with very specific and often intransigent facts. So it may be helpful to use the journalist's trick of illustrating the general with the specific.

The following article, which appeared in *Reader's Digest*, does several of the things articles should do. It personalizes a major problem facing the country. It involves the readers' emotions, by showing how the farm crisis has affected a small group of people. And, it is clearly organized and written. The writers used the conceptual organization mentioned earlier in this chapter.

Hard Times in America's Heartland

by Carl T. Rowan and David M. Mazie

Some evenings, Dennis Tangeman, 34, looks out his window at the corn and soybean fields that he—and his father and grandfather before him—used to farm in northwestern Iowa. "They've taken farming from me," he says softly. "They've taken farming from my kids."

Mike Mahlendorf, 36, spends anguished evenings too. He's president of the Sibley State Bank and must decide whether area farmers will get money for operating expenses. "You sit in the office and tell people they're facing severe financial problems, and then you go home. You can't forget it," he says.

Sibley, the seat of Osceola County, Iowa, is not the bustling town it once was. Its main street isn't filled with shoppers these days. "For Sale" signs are common in store windows and on front lawns of the tree-lined residential streets. Merchants are worried. "Right now, living in rural America is not the American dream," says supermarket owner Steve Davidson.

For much of rural America, the dream has indeed been shattered by the worst economic crisis to hit the heartland since the Great Depression. It has made once-proud farmers angry and despondent, and threatened them with the loss of land that their fathers and grandfathers farmed and that they in turn had hoped to pass on to sons and daughters.

Family farms and rural towns have been bulwarks of American life for generations, a treasured part of our heritage that not only has fed this nation abundantly but has personified its social and cultural values. Now many of these communities are fighting for survival.

The crisis has reached beyond fields and barns—to those nearby small towns where hardware, clothing, implement stores are hurting, banks are squeezed, schools are consolidating, homes are up for sale; and to larger cities where farm-machinery manufacturers are laying off workers. It has created divisions and distrust—but at the same time brought people closer together to battle adversity.

The seeds of this bitter harvest were sown in the 1970s when America's agricultural exports quintupled, commodity prices hit historic highs, and farmers were urged by government, bankers and agricultural experts to expand their operations. To do this they had to borrow at skyrocketing interest rates, but with the price of land shooting upward, farmers simply used that as collateral. And lenders—whether local banks, cooperatives such as the Production Credit Association (PCA), or government agencies like the Farmers Home Administration (FmHA)—were more than willing to loan money. A farmer might ask the bank for $500 and be told no. "Better take $1000." Farm debts soared from $53 billion in 1970 to $216 billion in 1983.

Feelings of Frustration.

Those golden years finally ended in the early 1980s, when the grain embargo against the Soviet Union crippled the export market, new nations entered as sellers of agricultural products, and the strong dollar made U.S. commodities more expensive. The value of Iowa's agricultural exports plummeted from $3.76 billion in 1981 to $2.85 billion in 1983. At home, commodity prices tumbled. So did land values; an acre of Iowa farm land that sold for an average of $2147 in 1981 was going for barely half that in 1985.

Net farm income declined 50 percent between 1981 and 1983. Suddenly, many farmers found it difficult to earn enough to live on, let alone repay debts.

One of those was Dennis Tangeman, who lives with his wife, Beckie, and sons, Matt and Josh, in a mobile home on his father's farm, ten miles southeast of Sibley. For 52 years the Tangeman family had farmed the same 160 acres. Each spring, like most of his neighbors, Dennis would borrow money to buy seed, fertilizer, fuel and other supplies to plant crops and raise hogs; each autumn he would pay it back. The profits were not great, but the family got by and loved living on the land.

Then, in 1983, with crushing, 18-percent interest rates adding to his expenses, Tangeman barely broke even. He sold some of his hogs to pay off FmHA and other loans, but debts still piled up, and crop prices continued to fall. In June 1984, at the FmHA's insistence, he sold all his machinery. The sale brought only about one-fourth of the $96,000 Tangeman owed. Then a few months later the bank took possession of his breeder pigs, and shut off his credit line. Last December he filed for bankruptcy.

Feelings of frustration, bitterness, confusion fill the Tangeman home. "It's a real slap in the face to have the farm taken away," says Dennis. "Everything I did, I did with approval of the FmHA and the bank."

While a few farmers went overboard during the expansion of the 1970s, many of those who are in trouble were considered among the best farmers—young, college-trained and innovative. "They started playing under our set of rules," says Richard Haack, PCA loan officer," and the rules simply changed on them."

But that's little comfort to families like the Tangemans. Today Beckie is a secretary for a fertilizer dealer and has swallowed her pride to accept free cheese offered to families in need. Dennis, who has had two part-time jobs off the farm, is deeply bothered by having to tell merchants he has known all his life, "Hey, I can't pay you." However, he intends to repay everyone. "It will take me a while, but they're gonna get paid."

25 Cents on the Dollar

Actual bankruptcy and foreclosure are still relatively rare. Iowa State University reported last spring that only four percent of Iowa's farms were insolvent, with more debts than assets. But another 28 percent had a debt-to-asset ratio greater than 40 percent, considered serious. A Des Moines *Register and*

Tribune Iowa Poll found that one out of six farm operators reported having sold off assets during the previous two years. Only 32 percent said they were making a comfortable living or prospering.

Of all the hardships, probably the most agonizing for these farm families is the feeling of having broken faith with generations past and future—the continuity upon which family farms are built. In many cases, fathers borrowed money in the 1970s to help sons and sons-in-law get started, or they bought a piece of land next door to their own to bring children into the operation. Sometimes grandparents co-signed on the notes, and suddenly three generations were dragged down.

Besides financial problems, the agricultural recession is wreaking emotional havoc. Requests for help have risen 40 percent at the Northwest Iowa Mental Health Center in Spencer. "Children as well as adults feel a great anxiety about the future," says Pete Zevenbergen, former director of the center.

The suicide rate in some farm counties has climbed to twice the national average. In one town in west-central Iowa, three farmers killed themselves in an 18-month period. A few weeks after losing his farm near Sibley, Dayton Monier suffered a fatal heart attack. "They say he died of heart failure," observes one of Monier's neighbors. "I know it was a broken heart."

The tension also has eroded some of the friendliness of rural America. Many families have become more withdrawn. "We just don't neighbor as much as we used to," lamented one Osceola County farm wife. In some cases, neighborliness has given way to hostility and distrust—most of it directed at the lenders, "That tears at a community," says the Rev. Durwood Clauson of Trinity Lutheran Church in Sibley, who senses feelings of discomfort when a farm family share a pew with someone they owe money to.

Not every farmer is the sworn enemy of his banker. "They've got their problems too. I'd hate to be in their shoes now," says one farmer. But many feel that bankers could have handled them with greater respect and understanding.

Actually, farmers and business people are in this crisis together. Larry Swanson, an economist formerly with the University of Nebraska, calculates that for every seven farms that close, one commercial business goes under.

Oliver Leu, who's been selling farm equipment in Sibley for 31 years, got only 25 cents on the dollar at an auction sale he held to get rid of his inventory. "It was either sell low or pay interest for another two years," explained Leu.

Hotline

Sibley's two banks also have serious problems. Reports published last April show that their troubled debts (those more than 90 days past due) significantly exceeded their capital—an indicator of potential danger. As a result, bankers like Mike Mahlendorf feel "caught in the middle." On one side is pressure from the bank's owners and federal examiners, who are worried about too many shaky loans; on the other side pressure from farmers who desperately need money to keep going. But Mahlendorf and other lenders insist they are doing all they can to help farmers. "We spend hours trying to find a way to make it work," he says. "My goal is to get them through these hard times in any way we can. Survival is what we're aiming for."

There are others working to help farmers survive. In recent months several states have stepped in with actions such as a moratorium on farm repossessions, training farmers in finance and law, and loosening rules that govern eligibility for certain financial assistance.

Iowa has been among the most active. It set up the Rural Concern Hotline for farmers and communities to use if they have financial or emotional problems. Last year, project ASSIST was initiated to inform local leaders about farm problems, provide individual financial counseling to farmers, and help communities marshal their resources.

One of the most significant efforts in Iowa is a network of peer counselors organized by the Northwest Iowa Mental Health Center. Farmers generally are stoic people who don't talk easily about their problems. But support groups are attracting more and more participants. "We can't save their farms," explains clinic caseworker Joan Blundall, "But at least we help ease the pain and depression."

Difficult Decisions

Despite all its damage, the farm crisis may have positive effects. Both townspeople and farmers show a new awareness of their interdependency. A farm wife who admitted she had not been very concerned when four businesses left in three months now grants that "Main Street is important to the entire economy." Although on the brink of financial collapse himself, Sibley fuel dealer Frank Leu extended credit to one struggling farm family. They eventually pulled through and now feel much closer to Leu and others in town who stuck with them.

Sibley's business and professional leaders have organized a development corporation to find ways of bringing new industry and jobs to their town. Says grocer Steve Davidson, "If we work together, we can save the small-town way of life. Everyone is ready to do something. Trouble is, no one is sure exactly *what* to do.

That same dilemma is evident in Washington. Many policy-makers have argued against any new government subsidies on the ground that farming is a business like any other. Why, they ask, does Uncle Sam have any greater responsibility to save family farms in Iowa than, say, steel mills in Pennsylvania?

For one thing, comes the reply, the government helped to create the problem with past policies and misguided advice. Also, despite bumper crops this year, there is no assurance that agriculture's troubles are over. Moreover, it is argued, family farming is *not* like other businesses.

The Administration, Congress and the states must give high priority to resolving these arguments. Short-term help is needed to get hard-hit farms and communities through the current crisis. At the same time, difficult decisions must be made about a long-term agriculture policy that would serve both rural America and the national economy. One suggestion is to target subsidies to struggling family farms, not to large agricultural enterprises.

Most of the crops are harvested now, but many of the farmers working in the fields in Oxceola County on chill autumn days are not sure they will be driving tractors through them again next spring. Yet for all the pain and sorrow they've endured, these farmers and townspeople are determined to fight for their cherished way of life—and for their futures.

It's possible to outline this article in a way similar to that described on page 88. Such an outline would look like this:

Possible Outline

Bam-bam-bam lead (see Chapter 10) shows the dimensions of the problem.

Theme statement: "The worst crisis to hit the heartland since the Great Depression." Effects summarized in a sort of road map to the article.

Point 1. How the crisis arose. Figures on decline in exports, commodity prices, farm income, land prices. Tangeman anecdote and government quote.

Balance paragraph: Bankruptcy is rare.

Point 2. Broken faith with past. Three generations hit. Emotional costs. Suicide rate.

Point 3. Community damaged. "We don't neighbor." Clauson quote. Farmers and businessmen in it together. Swanson quote. Leu quote. Mahlendorf quote.

Point 4. States help, moratoria on repossessions, training farmers, easing financial assistance. Iowa's Rural Hotline, peer counselors, Blundall quote.

Point 5. Positive effects. Recognize interdependence, Sibley Development Corps.

Point 6. Washington's role. Some oppose help, others say farmers special and government helped create problem.

Point 7. What can be done. Needed: short-term help, long-term policy.

End: Back to Osceola County.

8

Presenting Your Findings

*I*t is a comforting conceit of writers and teachers to pretend that ideas and processes flow in neat and logical order—for instance, that in putting together a magazine article you first get the idea, then do the research, then evaluate the research, then plan the organization, and last, figure out exactly how you are going to write up your findings. Trouble is, it doesn't work that way in real life. Things happen simultaneously: you are often evaluating your research while you're doing it, you plan the *kind* of article it's going to be while doing the organizing, and so on.

What do I mean—*kind?* Well, after a good many years of writing I learned that it helped in shaping a piece if I thought, "Yeah, this is going to be *that* kind of story." Once I identified the kind, I knew pretty well what it should contain and how it should be shaped. So I made up a list of categories. Of course, it's only one man's opinion, but here it is:

Here's Something New Stories

A new piece of information, a new idea, a new process. An obvious story of this type might be about a new medical discovery or a new way that educators have discovered to help disabled children learn. Newness is important to editors, and there are many more "new" articles in magazines than there are discoveries to justify them (new ways to lose weight, to make your marriage work, to advance your career, stop smoking). So when a writer comes up with a genuine new discovery that affects the lives of millions, he or she has a world-beater. The "What Makes Kids Popular?" story, in chapter 2, is this kind of piece. In developing such an article, the points to be covered are obvious: Here's what it is. Here's why it's important. Here's how it affects you. Here's how it works.

Adventure Stories

These use the old fiction writer's plots: man against nature, man against man. (A good many of these stories are about women, of course.) The outdoor magazines are full of man-against-nature stories—the man-with-gun against a 1200 lb. grizzly bear, or man-with-fly-rod aginst the wily old brown trout. But other magazines use them too: stories about how an island family survived a cataclysmic hurricane; how a woman lived and worked alone for months in the African bush in order to study chimpanzees; how a town fought a flood.

Man-against-man stories are even more varied. Most detective stories are in this category, from true crime yarns to pieces about a special prosecutor's fight against the Mafia. Many business and political stories fit here, too—pieces about how a man battled his competitors to establish a new firm, or fought the establishment over a better way of running things. The Fort Lee airfield story, described in chapter 1, is such an article. Even love stories sometimes fit into the group: boy gets girl, or vice versa. And husband vs. wife pieces on marital relations. Self-improvement pieces also fit because man vs. man includes man vs. himself.

These stories are dramatic narratives that make full use of characterization, conflict, suspense. We'll talk more about this later, in the chapter on dramatic writing.

Problem Stories

In a sense, of course, all articles are problem stories, but this category refers to public issues or broad social problems. The piece may be about how a concerned group saved a Florida river from destruction by the army engineers or a power company, about cash-register justice in traffic courts and what to do to eliminate it, about the millions of youths who are out of school and can't get a job and how they can be helped.

Essentially the points this kind of story makes are: here's a problem that affects you; here's how it affects you; here's what it's about; here's what can be done about it. You start by defining and dramatizing the problem, go on to explore its dimensions in terms of people, then suggest possible solutions.

A subsection here is the *microcosm* story—in which you focus on a particular situation to illuminate a larger one—which you see over and over again in newspapers and magazines. It is discussed further in chapter 15.

How to Do It Stories

This is another big category that includes everything from how to build a backyard pool to how to win a guerrilla war. These pieces are used by the hundreds in business journals—how to save money on materials handling, how to train new salespeople; the women's magazines—how to stay slim, how to make your eyes sexy; the men's magazines—how to stay slim, how to dress sexy; shelter books—how to add space to your closet; sports books—how to perfect your golf swing, how to navigate in a sports car rally; and general magazines—how to recruit better cops, how to communicate in a marriage. This book is a how-to book.

Mostly they're unfancy, factual, and follow a simple step-by-step organization plan. "First you buy the lumber: twelve two-by-fours eight feet long, twenty-four three-quarter-inch common pine boards in ten-foot lengths. . . ." You must be specific and always give prices. You illustrate ways to overcome obstacles by telling how someone actually did it. You assume the readers already know why it's important to do what you're telling them to do, so you don't have to waste much time selling the idea, though you do include some of the rewards of the process, usually in anecdotal form. When you have finished describing the last step of the process, you stop.

Personality Pieces

These, obviously, are stories about people who are important to the reader for some reason. When they are the familiar puff pieces about television or movie or sports stars, they satiate the reader's curiosity and help sell magazines. But the better ones are written on two levels; ostensibly they're about a personality, while actually they illuminate a human dilemma, impart some new information, explore some aspect of the common condition. If they do this well, the personality does not have to be well known; reader identification is satisfied by the other aspects of the story.

To me these have always seemed the hardest of all stories to write. The reason is that you are trying to put on paper the true essence of the person with all his or her variety, contradictions, complex motives, neuroticisms, failures, and aspirations. Yet, as in every other kind of article, the piece must also have a single underlying idea. Satisfying the second requirement, however, sometimes tends to make your subject a two-dimensional, cardboard character. Preventing this is a major challenge to the writer's artistry.

In addition to the *kind* of article, it helps if you identify the *story* elements in the piece you're going to write. Is it a detective story, which presents your readers with a crime, then takes them, with the detective, through mystery after mystery until the criminal is caught? Is it a narrative, in which a woman has an objective and overcomes obstacle after obstacle until she achieves it? Is it a love story, in which two people slowly lose their loneliness in each other's trust? The characteristics of several of these stories will be discussed in the later chapters on kinds of writing.

Though each of these types of articles has its own approach and content, there are techniques of good writing that apply to all.

Number One: write about people. The newspaper reporter covering an event doesn't have to worry about this; there's no way to avoid it. But the interpretive journalist and the magazine writer often start out with an idea instead of an event and, being intellectuals, tend to write directly about the idea. That's OK if they're writing for *Harper's* or *The Annals of the American Academy of Political and Social Science*. But it's not for the mass media.

What you do is translate your idea into a report on people doing things by thinking how it affects them. What kinds of people? People over sixty-five? Vacationers? Homeowners? And how does it affect them? Go and ask them. When you've talked to enough of all the different kinds affected, you've got your story. Write it in terms of what happened to them. The story on Chuck Kelly in chapter 6 is an example; so is the one in chapter 4 on the soldier who was brainwashed in Korea.

Number Two: use specific details. For years fiction writers have said there are no new plots in the world; after years of work, nonfiction writers *know* there are only a limited number of basic ideas about the human condition. What makes a story fresh and new and colorful are the details. People have struggled for courage to meet adversity for centuries; what makes *this* story different is the way *this* unique individual struggles to overcome *this* particular kind of adversity. So the good creative writer spends hours and thought and effort to get details that demonstrate the person's uniqueness.

Further, it is the specific detail that convinces the reader that you know what you're talking about. You don't write, "Income tax returns were filed by millions of Americans this year." You write, "Income tax returns were filed this year by 67,327,000 Americans, one of every three men, women, and children now alive." And you don't fake the details; you do the research necessary to get them accurate.

Once I did a three-part story on the number of kids who are out of school and out of work. It was titled, "We Waste a Million Kids a Year," and I wanted to make the point that a nation's young people are its most valuable resource. Writing it just that way would have been true enough, but pallid. So I spent a day going through an exhaustive study of the distribution of talent among the various socioeconomic groups that make up our population. At the end of the day I was able to write this one line: "Among them [the million] are 50,000 of the finest minds in the country." I thought the day well spent.

Number Three: be precise in the words you use. There was a professor at Amherst who made a big thing of this in his freshman English classes. He'd get the class to define a simple word like "door." After wrestling with it for a while they'd come up with something like, "a door is what you use to enter a room." So the next time they met, the prof would climb in through the window and say, "I just came in the door."

"No, that's a window."

"Okay, then what *is* a door?"

It would go on like this until they had a definition that was completely unambiguous. Sometimes a week's homework assignment would consist of writing one sentence; then each student would have to defend every word in it from attack by the rest of the class. What the professor was teaching was precision in using words.

The late John Ciardi, speaking before the American Society of Journalists and Authors, emphasized the value of using just the right word this way. He'd been working with some original manuscripts of John Keats's poems, and he picked these lines from "The Eve of St. Agnes."

> Anon his heart revives: her vespers done,
> Of all its wreathed pearls her hair she frees;
> Unclasps her warmed jewels one by one;
> Loosens her fragrant bodice; by degrees
> Her rich attire creeps rustling to her knees. . . .

The girl, Madeline, was undressing while Porphyro peeked from the wings. The fourth line was originally written, "Loosens her bursting bodice . . .," but Keats had wanted to preserve a tone of purity in the scene. "Bursting" had been crossed out, Ciardi said, and "fragrant" inserted instead. You can see the different impression the change accomplished.

If this kind of precision is effective for Keats, it's just as important for you and me. Gay Talese once said in an interview that he rewrites sentences up to eighteen times before he is satisfied with them. His craftsmanship shows, as the Talese lead in chapter 10 proves.

There's an adjunct to this rule of precise word use that's made especially well in that little classic, *The Elements of Style*, by William Strunk, Jr., and E. B. White: "Write with nouns and verbs, not with adjectives and adverbs. The adjective hasn't been built that can pull a weak or inaccurate noun out of a tight place."

An adjective is defined as a "modifier" of a noun, and that's exactly what it does—modifies. It detracts, takes away the word's strength, reduces it. Adjectives are the lazy writer's out. Of course, they're necessary, but most of us use them as crutches. Once when I was trying to learn to write, I decided I wouldn't use a single adjective in anything I wrote for a month. It made the job about twice as hard, and everything I wrote took two or three times as long, but I think the exercise was worth it. Once you do it you find that your prejudice against adjectives carries over, and you use them sparingly ever after. Your writing improves as a result.

Number Four: take advantage of the connotations of words. Even the simplest words trigger different pictures or impressions in different people's minds. Psychologists who give word association tests see this every day. The word "color," for instance, will make many men think "red," many women think "blue" or "green." Skilled writers use these connotations to get their meaning implanted in the reader's mind.

In her book *Saying What One Means,* Freya Stark says it about as well as anyone:

Accuracy is the basis of style. Words dress our thoughts and should fit; and should fit not only in their utterances, but in their implications, their sequences, and their silences, just as in architecture the empty spaces are as important as those that are filled. The problem of all writing is the same as that presented by the composition of a telegram, one has to convey a meaning with the use of few and always inadequate words, and eke it out with what the reader, drawing upon his own reserves, will understand. The number of words that even the most profuse writer will dare to use is always insufficient for a complete impression, but the reserves he can draw upon in the reader's mind are lavish indeed. The whole generalship of writing is in the summoning and marshaling of these unseen auxiliaries.

Number Five: don't use gobbledygook. Every book on good writing says this at some point, and who needs to be left out of the parade? Besides, the gobbledygookers seem to be winning out over us purists. The reason, we suppose, is the increasing specialization of our society and the determination of every woolly-thinking "expert" to protect the barricades of his or her specialty by using language that mere humans can't understand. Writers who interview the specialists must, of course, become acquainted with the jargon, and after you've spent a week interviewing, say, social psychologists, phrases like "interpersonal valences" or "negative reinforcement" fall trippingly off the tongue, but you should never let them fall onto the page.

When Malcolm Baldridge was named Commerce Secretary, he decided to weed out some of the jargon that littered the department's letters, memorandums, and reports. Among the words he barred were *finalize, interface, parameter, prioritize, optimize, impact* (as a verb), *specificity,* and *utilize.* As writers aiming at the general public, we must also edit out such pompous, confusing, and even silly terms. We do not interpersonally communicate with one another—we talk.

We don't know why people use such words. Some of it, of course, is pure snobbery; when you first learn a lot of big words, you want to use them to show the world how educated you are. But after a while you realize that a better test of your education is whether you can communicate with people so they can understand. That's when you grow a little alarm bell in your brain that pings every time you use a word with more than three syllables. At each ping you stop short, go back, figure out exactly what you're trying to say, and find a way to say it simply and directly.

We think the two most important rules for good writing are: be simple; be clear. They are also, of course, the two hardest to apply, because it takes a great deal of hard thought to say a complex thing simply. And it takes a long devoted love affair with the English language to be able to use words with precisely the right meaning and connotation so they convey to your readers what you want them to know and feel. To get an idea across clearly and forcefully, nothing has ever been invented that beats the simple declarative sentence.

Hemingway understood this. He could load more meaning onto simple, short words than they had any right to carry, and I think he could do it because he was so very precise in using them. I think writers ought to study how he does it. For years I have reread *The Old Man and the Sea* because I think that, for technical brilliance, this is the capstone of his work.

A friend who knew him told me years ago that Winston Churchill had a rule about word use. He thought that the old Anglo-Saxon words had more power and guts than latinized words, and he tried to use them as much as he could. Consider, for instance, the raw sock of, "I have nothing to offer but blood, toil, tears and sweat."

Most books on writing say you ought to vary the length of your sentences and paragraphs, which, of course, is true. It keeps the reader awake. It's like the difference between driving on a narrow country road—where you have to contend with sharp curves, hillocks and dips, small-town speed limits, and straight open stretches—and driving on a super-highway, where you can pass anytime you like, where curves and hills are long and gentle, where you can maintain an unvarying fifty-five miles per hour, and where the monotony makes you fall asleep—or almost.

Figures of speech are one of the most useful tools a writer has to explain complex ideas or inventions, to marshal reader identification, to brighten dull explanations. In hack journalism most metaphors are clichés. Everybody wants to avoid them, but studying clichés can tell you something about how a successful metaphor is made. (After all it wouldn't have become a cliché if it hadn't been so apt.)

Take "cold as a dog's nose." A dog's nose isn't really cold at all, but it seems cold because we expect it to be warm like the rest of the animal, and when we touch it we get a shock. So a metaphor must be used on a common and memorable experience. How about "cold as the bathroom floor on your bare feet"? That's a common experience, but it's not much of a metaphor because it requires too much qualification: "cold as a bathroom floor" doesn't do it.

So you need shock, and conciseness in addition to common experience. Often you can get it by reaching halfway to Boston for your figure of speech. Raymond Chandler was master of the colorful metaphor. Once he wrote, "She had a voice you could use to split stove wood," thus using an image of physical action to describe a sound. Another time he wrote, "He was a big man, but not more than six feet five inches tall and not wider than a beer truck." The first part isn't so good, because it makes the reader do a mental computation—"Let's see, I'm 5'10" so he must have been . . ."—which drains the instant impact. But the second half is good;

a beer truck summons up exactly the effect Chandler wanted—massive, irresistible, and slightly disreputable.

In his play, *The Real Thing*, Tom Stoppard has one character, a playwright, refuse to help another playwright, Brodie, improve his work because of Brodie's insensitivity to the power of words.

[Words are] innocent, neutral, precise, standing for this, describing that, meaning the other, so *if* you look after them you can build bridges across incomprehension and chaos. But when they get their corners knocked off, they're no good any more, and Brodie knocks the corners off without knowing he's doing it. So everything he builds is jerry-built. It's rubbish. An intelligent child could push it over. I don't think writers are sacred, but words are. They deserve respect. If you get the right ones in the right order, you can nudge the world a little or make a poem which children will speak for you when you're dead.

9

The Uses of Indirection

S everal years ago I visited several air force and navy training bases to get material for an article about a new citizenship training program that the armed forces had developed. It taught me a basic lesson about creative journalism.

I was at Lackland Air Force base, in San Antonio, Texas, watching an instructor teach a class in something called the "Rule of Law." He gave no lecture; instead he gave each man a printed sheet on which was this story:

> There is a thief in the barracks. Of this there can be little doubt. For the last week the men have been missing small items such as cigarettes, candy bars, and razors. Then yesterday Jim Brown had his wallet stolen while he was in the shower. All efforts to trace down the thefts have failed. The men are angry and sullen. Every man is suspicious of every other man.
>
> Today the men return to the barracks from drill five minutes early. Jim Brown is the first man in the door. Upon entering he sees Tom Baker, who was excused from drill because of blisters, taking a pack of cigarettes from another man's footlocker.
>
> "Here's the thief, men," Jim Hollers. "I caught him in the act. Let's give it to him."
>
> Jim drops his rifle on the floor, clenches his fists and, with his right hand cocked, moves in on Tom. Several men join Jim. The others watch intently.

After they'd discussed this story for ten minutes or so in small groups, the men were asked whether they would help give Tom a licking. The men said yes in various ways. One said you should have a kangaroo court, another said you should report it to the flight chief and let him handle Tom. But most disagreed and said a good beating would teach Tom a better lesson than any flight chief could.

Then a slight, dark-haired youth in glasses stood up and said, "But this is mob violence!" in a surprised tone and sat down again.

The discussion continued, but once the idea had been presented it began to grow. At first every third or fourth speaker would say something like, "Well, you ought to let a court martial handle it." As the argument continued this idea crept in more and more, and finally a rangy, ginger-haired man in the back stood up.

"I saw mob action once," he said. "A man and a woman had been murdered—robbed, I guess. And here comes a couple kids down a dark alley—they didn't have nothing to do with it, but they were kind of tough kids and they came down this alley. So the crowd saw them and right away decided they were the murderers." He took a deep breath and let it out. "They strung 'em up right there. Two weeks later they found the murderer."

In the silence the instructor said, "I've got a film here I'd like to show you." The film was MGM's *The Ox-Bow Incident*, cut to twenty-eight minutes. It tells of a posse that hanged three innocent men for a crime the members of the posse only thought had been committed. It had the wallop of a Missouri mule; when it ended the class was dismissed.

You know how when a class breaks up, in a high school or a training base, there's always a great clatter of shifting chairs, of talking, yelling, and whistling. When this one broke up there was a hush in the room. A few men talked, but their tones were subdued; they walked out carefully, not hitting the chairs, and in single file. As he reached the door one man said, "It makes you want to spit!"

Another time at the end of this class, a recruit came up to S. Sgt. John Oliver, the instructor, and said, "You know, we got a G.I. shower planned for a guy in our flight tonight. This guy is a real sourball—he never takes a bath and you can't stand to sit next to him." (In a G.I. shower a gang of men strip the victim, hold him under the shower, and scrub him vigorously with stiff brushes, usually taking off a layer of hide. Occasionally the victim ends up in the hospital.)

"That so?" said Oliver indifferently. "Well look, you're probably going to be down in this section tomorrow. I wish you'd stop around and tell us what happened."

The next day when the man came back Oliver asked him how it had gone. "The whole thing was forgotten," the recruit said. "The man who'd been the leader just never started it."

The new kind of instruction was devised by Dr. James E. Russell, of Teachers College, Columbia University, and called "Hours on Freedom." Later he explained why this session worked. The real message, he said, was in the movie. "But if you just showed that, the men would all go to sleep—they're usually so tired they'd sleep through a sex movie. It's the barracks situation that keeps them awake—by a kind of reverse psychology: they almost always end their discussion by agreeing you shouldn't beat up the crook, but down underneath nearly every man knows that he would. That hidden guilt feeling keeps him interested—and also helps give the movie its terrific impact."

But Russell did more than provoke a psychological reaction in his audience. The story of the barracks thief was chosen so that his particular audience would identify with the situation. Had he been dealing with college students, it would have been a dormitory thief; with industrial workers he would have used a locker-room thief. Of course, like a fiction writer, he could change the story to fit the audience; a journalist must go out and find a true story to do the job.

Russell was voicing a principle of good teaching. Since responsible journalism is a blend of teaching and entertainment, his method was also a good description of effective writing.

The modern interpretive piece does not preach as a sermon does. It doesn't tell people, "Do this." It identifies and explains a problem by demonstration, then demonstrates a solution, sometimes by quoting experts, more often by showing people working out their own solution. It reports the actions, emotions, thoughts of the actors. It convinces by demonstration and by reader identification, not by exhortation.

One morning I started work by rereading a piece I had written the day before. As I read the day got colder and grayer and bleaker. I dropped the last page on the desk and said, "You *stupid* jerk!"

I grabbed a piece of paper and in large black capitals printed:

DON'T TELL IT—SHOW IT HAPPENING!

I thumbtacked it on the wall above the typewriter, where I could see it every time I looked up. It stayed there for almost a year and may even have done some good.

The point is, you want your reader to become involved with your story and its characters. When you tell about them you interpose yourself, the Almighty, Invisible (hah!) Omniscience, between the people in your story and your readers. So the reader gets everything second hand. What you ought to be doing, instead, is showing the readers a movie of the characters acting and talking and struggling with their problem as they truly did. Then they get the message firsthand and, of course, it is more compelling. Gay Talese has talked of moving his "camera" from one scene to the next, to show the reader what Talese thinks is important.

In *Client-Centered Therapy,* the noted psychologist Carl Rogers wrote: "In order for behavior to change, a change in preception must be *experienced.* Intellectual knowledge cannot substitute for this." A writer wants readers to change, if only by understanding something they didn't know before. So by allowing the readers to live through a situation along with the characters involved, the writer follows Rogers' precept.

Recreating scenes of action puts quite a burden on your research ability because in order to do it, you must first see it in your own head in all its color, action, sound, and conflict. The only way to accomplish that is to take the people involved in it back over it in meticulous detail, getting the scene, the thoughts, motives, aims of the each individual. If possible you have to interview *all* the people involved so that they can check each other's memory of the incident.

Truman Capote made this point in an interview with George Plimpton at the time *In Cold Blood* was published. Plimpton asked if Capote didn't sometimes give way to the temptation to fictionalize parts of the story. Capote's answer:

No. . . . One doesn't spend almost six years on a book, the point of which is factual accuracy, and then give way to minor distortions. People are so suspicious. They ask, "How can you reconstruct the conversation of a dead girl, Nancy Clutter, without fictionalizing?" If they read the book carefully, they can see readily enough how it's done. It's a silly question. Each time Nancy appears in the narrative, there are witnesses to what she is saying and doing—phone calls, conversations being overheard. When she walks the horse up from the river in the twilight, the hired man is a witness and talked to her then. The last time we see her, in her bedroom, Perry and Dick themselves were the witnesses, and told me what she had said. What is reported of her, even in the narrative form, is as accurate as many hours of questioning, over and over again, can make it. All of it is reconstructed from the evidence of witnesses.

In the same interview Capote talked about another way in which indirection is used in first-class nonfiction. The question is, if I, the reporter, keep out of the story, how do I express my own judgments on the situation? Many journalists believe it should be done directly; their idea is, "I've done all the research and become an expert on the subject, so I should give my opinions." But they want things too simple; good nonfiction has more artistry, as Capote knew:

Of course it's by the selection of what you choose to tell. I believe Perry did what he did for the reasons he himself states—that his life was a constant accumulation of disillusionments and reverses and he suddenly found himself [in the Clutter house that night] in a psychological cul-de-sac. The Clutters were such a perfect set of symbols for every frustration of his life. As Perry himself said, "I didn't have anything against them, and they never did anything wrong to me—the way other people have all my life. Maybe they're just the ones who had to pay for it." Now in that particular section where Perry talks about the reason for the murders, I could have included other views. But Perry's happens to be the one I believe is the right one, and it's the one that Dr. Satten at the Menninger Clinic arrived at quite independently, never having done any interviews with Perry.

I could have added many other opinions. But that would have confused the issue, and indeed the book. I had to make up my mind, and move towards that one view, always. You can say that the reportage was incomplete. But then it has to be. It's a question of selection, you wouldn't get anywhere if it wasn't for that. I've often thought of the book as being like something reduced to a seed. Instead of presenting the reader with a full plant, with all the foliage, a seed is planted in the soil of his mind. . . . I make my own comment by what I choose to tell and how I choose to tell it. It is true that an author is more in control of fictional characters because he can do anything he wants with them as long as they stay credible. But in the nonfiction novel one can also manipulate: If I put something in which I don't agree about I can always set it in a context of qualifications without having to step into the story myself to set the reader straight.

Capote, of course, was a novelist before he wrote nonfiction, but good journalists who have never written novels know and use the same technique. Bob Greene, for example, used selection to make several points in a story about two fifteen-year-old boys spending a day at a shopping mall.

American Beat

By Bob Greene

"This would be excellent, to go in the ocean with this thing," says Dave Gembutis, fifteen.

He is looking at a $170 Sea Cruiser raft.

"Great," says his companion, Dan Holmes, also fifteen.

This is a Herman's World of Sporting Goods, in the middle of the Woodfield Mall in Schaumburg, Illinois.

The two of them keep staring at the raft. It is unlikely that they will purchase it. For one thing, Dan has only twenty dollars in his pocket, Dave five dollars. For another thing—ocean voyages aside—neither of them is even old enough to drive. Dave's older sister, Kim, has dropped them off at the mall. They will be taking the bus home.

Fifteen. What a weird age to be male. Most of us have forgotten about it, or have idealized it. But when you are fifteen . . . well, things tend to be less than perfect.

You can't drive. You are only a freshman in high school. The girls your age look older than you and go out with upperclassmen who have cars. You probably don't shave. You have nothing to do on the weekends.

So how do you spend your time? In 1982, most likely at a mall. Woodfield is an enclosed shopping center sprawling over 2.25 million square feet in northern Illinois. There are 230 stores at Woodfield, and on a given Saturday those stores are cruised in and out of by thousands of teenagers killing time. Today two of those teenagers are Dave Gembutis and Dan Holmes.

Dave is wearing a purple Rolling Meadows High School Mustangs windbreaker over a gray MASH T-shirt, jeans, and Nike running shoes. He has a red plastic spoon in his mouth, and will keep it there for most of the afternoon. Dan is wearing a white Ohio State Buckeyes T-shirt, jeans, and Nike running shoes.

We are in the Video Forum store. Paul Simon and Art Garfunkel are singing "Wake Up Little Susie" from their Central Park concert on four television screens. Dave and Dan have already been wandering around Woodfield for an hour.

"There's not too much to do at my house," Dan says to me.

"Here we can at least look around," Dave says. "At home I don't know what we'd do."

"Play catch or something," Dan says. "Here there's lots to see."

"See some girls or something, start talking." Dave says.

I ask them how they would start a conversation with girls they had never met.

"Ask them what school they're from," Dan says. "Then if they say Arlington Heights High School or something, you can say, "Oh, I know somebody from there."

I ask them how important meeting girls is to their lives.

"About forty-five percent," Dan says.

"About half your life," Dave says.

"Half is girls," Dan says. "Half is going out for sports."

An hour later, Dave and Dan have yet to meet any girls. They have seen a girl from their own class at Rolling Meadows High, but she is walking with an older boy, holding his hand. Now we are in the Woodfield McDonald's. Dave is eating a McRib sandwich, a small fries, and a small Coke. Dan is eating a cheeseburger, a small fries, and a medium root beer.

In here, the dilemma is obvious. The McDonald's is filled with girls who are precisely as old as Dave and Dan. The girls are wearing eye shadow, are fully developed, and generally look as if they could be dating the Green Bay Packers. Dave and Dan, on the other hand . . . well, when you're a 15-year-old boy, you look like a 15-year-old boy.

"They go with the older guys who have the cars," Dan says.

"It makes them more popular," Dave says.

"My ex-girlfriend is seeing a junior," Dan says.

I ask him what happened.

"Well, I was in Florida over spring vacation," he says. "And when I got back I heard that she was at Cinderella Rockefella one night, and she was dancing with this guy, and she liked him, and he drove her home and stuff."

"She two-timed him," Dave says.

"The guy's on the basketball team," Dan says.

I ask Dan what he did about it.

"I broke up with her," he says, as if I had asked the stupidest question in the world.

I asked him how he did it.

"Well, she was at her locker," he says. "She was working the combination. And I said, 'Hey, Linda, I want to break up.' And she was opening her locker door and she just nodded her head yes. And I said, 'I hear you had a good time while I was gone, but I had a better time in Florida.'"

I ask him if he feels bad about it.

"Well, I feel bad," he says. "But a lot of guys told me, 'I heard you broke up with her. Way to be.'"

"It's too bad the Puppy Palace isn't open," Dan says.

"They're remodeling," Dave says.

We are walking around the upper level of Woodfield. I ask them why they would want to go to the Puppy Palace.

"The dogs are real cute and you feel sorry for them," Dan says.

We are in a fast-food restaurant called the Orange Bowl. Dave is eating a frozen concoction called an O-Joy. They still have not met any girls.

"I feel like I'd be wasting my time if I sat at home," Dan says. "If it's Friday or Saturday and you sit home, it's considered . . . low."

"Coming to the mall is about all there is," Dave says. "Until we can drive."

"Then I'll cruise," Dan says. "Look for action a little farther away from my house, instead of just riding my bike around."

"When you're sixteen, you can do anything," Dave says. "You can go all the way across town."

"When you have to ride your bike . . ." Dan says. "When it rains, it ruins everything."

In the J. C. Penny store, the Penney Fashion Carnival is under way. Wally the Clown is handing out favors to children, but Dave and Dan are watching the young female models parade onto a stage in bathing suits.

"Just looking is enough for me," Dan says.

Dave suggests that they head back into the mall and pick out some girls to wave to. I ask why.

"Well, see, even if they don't wave back, you might see them later in the day," Dan says. "And then they might remember that you waved at them, and you can meet them."

We are at the Cookie Factory. These guys eat—approximately every twenty minutes.

It is clear that Dan is attracted to the girl behind the counter. He walks up, and his voice is slower and about half an octave lower than before.

The tone of voice is going to have to carry the day, because the words are not all that romantic:

"Can I have a chocolate-chip cookie?"

The girl does not even look up as she wraps the cookie in tissue paper.

Dan persists. The voice might be Clark Gable's.

"What do they cost?"

The girl is still looking down.

"Forty-seven," she says and takes his money, still looking away, and we move on.

Dave and Dan tell me that there are lots of girls at Woodfield's indoor ice-skating rink. It costs money to get inside, but they lead me to an exit door, and when a woman walks out we slip into the rink. It is chilly in here, but only three people are on the ice.

"It's not time for open skating yet," Dan says. "This is all private lessons."

"Not much in here," Dave says.

We sit on benches. I ask them if they wish they were older.

"Well," Dan says, "when you get there, you look back and you remember. Like I'm glad that I'm not in the fourth or fifth grade now. But I'm glad I'm not twenty-five, either."

"Once in a while I'm sorry I'm not twenty-one," Dave says. "I want to save up for a dirt bike."

"Right now, being fifteen is starting to bother me a little bit," Dave says. "Like when you have to get your parents to drive you to Homecoming with a girl."

I ask him how that works.

"Well, your mom is in the front seat driving," he says. "And you're in the back seat with your date."

I ask him how he feels about that.

"It's embarrassing," he says. "Your date understands that there's nothing you can do about it, but it's still embarrassing."

Dave says he wants to go to Pet World.

"I think they closed it down," Dan says, but we head in that direction anyway.

I ask them what the difference is between Pet World and the Puppy Palace.

"They've got snakes and fish and another assortment of dogs," Dan says. "But not as much as the Puppy Palace."

When we arrive, Pet World is, indeed, boarded up.

We are on the upper level of the mall. Dave and Dan have spotted two girls sitting on a bench below them, on the mall's main floor.

"Whistle," Dan says. Dave whistles, but the girls keep talking.

"Dave, wave to them and see if they look," Dan says.

"They aren't looking," Dave says.

"There's another one over there," Dan says.

"Where?" Dave says.

"Oh, that's a mother," Dan says. "She's got her kid with her."

They return their attention to the two downstairs.

Dan calls to them: "Would you girls get the dollar I just dropped?"

The girls look up.

"Just kidding," Dan says.

The girls resume their conversation.

"I think they're laughing," Dan says.

"What are you going to do when the dumb girls won't respond," Dave says.

"At least we tried," Dan says.

I ask him what response would have satisfied.

"The way we would have known that we succeeded," he says, "they'd have looked up here and started laughing."

The boys keep staring at the two girls.

"Ask her to look up," Dan says. "Ask her what school they go to."

"I did," Dave says. "I did."

The two boys lean over the railing.

"Bye, girls," Dave yells.

"See you later," Dan yells.

The girls do not look up.

"Too hard," Dan says. "Some girls are stuck on themselves, if you know what I mean by that."

We go to a store called the Foot Locker, where all the salespeople are dressed in striped referee's shirts.

"Dave!" Dan says. "Look at this! Seventy bucks!" He holds up a pair of New Balance running shoes. Both boys shake their heads.

We move on to a store called Passage to China. A huge stuffed tiger is placed by the doorway. There is a PLEASE DO NOT TOUCH sign attached to it. Dan rubs his hand over the tiger's back. "This would look so great in my room," he says.

We head over to Alan's TV and Stereo. Two salesmen ask the boys if they are interested in buying anything, so they go back outside and look at the store's window. A color television set is tuned to a baseball game between the Chicago Cubs and the Pittsburgh Pirates.

They watch for five minutes. The sound is muted, so they cannot hear the announcers.

"I wish they'd show the score," Dave says.

They watch for five minutes more.

"Hey, Dave," Dan says, "You want to go home?"

"I guess so," Dave says.

They do. We wave goodbye. I watch them walk out of the mall toward the bus stop. I wish them girls, dirt bikes, puppies, and happiness.

How better could Greene have showed us what it is like to be fifteen and male? And he did it almost entirely indirectly, by showing us what Dan and Dave look like, how they behave, how they talk, and what they talk about. With the exception of two paragraphs near the start, where Greene comments on fifteen-year-old boys, and the last paragraph, the piece depends entirely upon Greene's ability to select from among the things the boys have said and done to create a believable picture of the two, and, by extension, of all fifteen-year-old boys. He shows them dreaming of toys they cannot afford; imprisoned in their homes where there's "not too much to do": saddened by the loss of a girlfriend but too proud to play second fiddle; yearning for the day when a driver's license will set them free; caring about the animals cooped up in a pet store; and trying ineptly to meet girls.

Selection is used to accomplish other purposes, too—indirectly. Once I did a piece on the General Accounting Office, which is an arm of the U.S. Congress whose job it is to investigate the entire executive branch of the federal government. It sends its accountants and investigators out into the field to see what Uncle Sam is getting for the millions he spends on crop support programs or submarines or embassies abroad. I proposed, and *Reader's Digest* editors agreed, that it should be written as a series of little detective stories about the most important investigations the agency had run.

But it was also important to select the stories to make other points too. One was to show the vast scope and diversity of the investigations. Another was to show how the GAO ran a typical investigation, including the kinds of specialists it used. Neither of these points was stated directly; the stories themselves made them, without any comment by the writer.

The story on farms in chapter 7 is an example of a microcosm story, which is, by its nature, indirect. You tell a particular story about particular people, which gets the reader emotionally involved in them and their struggle. But in the people you pick to write about and in the things you select to say about them, you are exploring a larger, more universal issue.

The very best journalists use indirection in a similar but more sophisticated way than that. They write a story on two levels; they tell one story, but do it in such a way that they are also telling another. One of the best examples of this is a piece by Joan Didion that appears in her book *Slouching Towards Bethlehem*.

The piece, titled "Some Dreamers of the Golden Dream," is the story of a California woman, Lucille Marie Maxwell Miller, who was convicted of murdering her husband by burning him in the family Volkswagen. It reports in detail her actions, the situations that led up to it, her trial, and the trial's aftermath, so it gives full coverage to the murder. But it is much more than that; it also has an underlying message, which is that the superficial values of the mass media world—happiness is everything, buy lots of things to get status in society—lead to disillusion and death.

Didion starts by describing the San Bernardino Valley where it happened, then states her basic message:

> Here is where the hot wind blows and the old ways do not seem relevant, where the divorce rate is double the national average and where one person in every 38 lives in a trailer. Here is the last stop for all those who come from somewhere else, for all those who drifted away from the cold and the past and the old ways. Here is where they are trying to find a new life style, trying to find it in the only places they

know to look: the movies and the newspapers. The case of Lucille Marie Maxwell Miller is a tabloid monument to that new life style.

Indirection is also used to present the very idea of a story. Mass magazines must be read by millions of people or go out of business. Millions of people will not read the kind of intellectual exposition of an idea or a social or economic problem that *The New Republic* or the *New York Times* might print. So mass magazine writers must find ways to explore social problems in a way that will get read; usually that means making the point indirectly.

An editor of *Good Housekeeping* told how this worked while visiting a journalism class at Syracuse University. A graduate student asked him why the magazine didn't do more socially responsible articles on the huge problems the country faces, like race relations. The editor answered that the magazine had done thirty-five articles on race problems in the past eight years. But, he said, they were not preachments, saying white people ought to get over their prejudices, or black people ought to stop trying to make a separate society. Nobody would read those. Instead the articles made their points indirectly.

One, for example, was called, "The Pride of Five Women." It consisted of the stories of five black women who had fought their way out of poverty by their own efforts. The reader had a personal narrative to identify with, but the underlying message of the piece, aimed at white women, was that black women had as much courage, perseverance, and drive for independence as anyone else and were thus deserving of respect.

This kind of indirection is probably one of the least understood aspects of the mass media. Nobody can force magazine readers to read anything, and it is very easy for them to turn a page. Mass media writers and editors know that they must make readers *want* to read whatever it is they're trying to tell them; hence the message usually is wrapped in some kind of emotional, universal, self-interest appeal. When this is skillfully done readers gets the message, often without realizing it.

10

Leads and Endings

*M*any writers I know say they can't get to work on a piece until they've written the lead exactly as they want it to be. I've always heard these confessions with the smug warmth of superiority because I don't work that way, and obviously the way I do work is not only better, but more sophisticated, intelligent, and creative. But when I was thinking about this lead, a flash of objectivity showed me that my complacency, as often before, was phony. In fact I *do* write the lead first—not on a typewriter and not in its entirety, but I know what it's going to be and I can see it and feel its dimensions in my mind.

The reason for this grows out of the nature of a lead. It has two jobs: to start the reader reading and to state, either directly or indirectly, the underlying idea of the story. Obviously you can't accomplish the second job until you've reviewed all your research and decided what it says. In reviewing it, you've run through your mind all the possible candidates for the lead—and consciously or unconsciously evaluated the reader appeal of each. Thus, as is usual in artistry, your mind has been doing several things at once—often without your being aware of it.

Different kinds of leads do these two jobs in different ways. The anecdotal lead is probably used more frequently than any other in the mass media. The chief reason is that it is the strongest in the "hook the reader in" department. Instantly, it gives the reader people to identify with, action to watch, a problem to worry about. It's the kind Bob Greene used in the story about the fifteen-year-olds quoted in the last chapter. Both movies and television have borrowed the idea of this kind of lead in the way they start the action of a story and present at least part of its problem before they give you the title and credits.

This kind of lead can be adapted to a great variety of stories. Greene used it to introduce us to his subjects; here's an anecdotal lead that started a quite different kind of story by Claire Safran. It appeared in *Woman's*

Day and dealt with a group of parents fighting to protect their children from the effects of toxic wastes, and encountering along the way a great deal of opposition from the government officials the parents thought would protect them.

There's an empty room in the tidy red ranch house at the east end of Woburn, Massachusetts. The little boy who once slept there was just twelve years old when he died in 1981. Add his name, Jimmy Anderson, to the list of victims of the modern-day plague we call toxic waste.

Add little Robbie Robbins's name, too. Indeed, add the names of twenty-two Woburn children who have been stricken with leukemia, all but five of them now dead. Then figure in the names of their anguished parents, their grieving brothers and sisters, their terrified neighbors living with the fear that it could happen to their children as well.

It is sad to hear Jimmy's mother, Anne Anderson, tell her story. It hurts to look into her eyes, bruised with pain. "Why Jimmy?" she asked at first. "Why any child?" she asked later on. Because Anne Anderson and other parents insisted on answers, the children of Woburn are safer today than they once were. Because they are still asking questions, still demanding answers, children in other cities and towns may be safer too.

Like this one, all good anecdotal leads tell indirectly what the story is about. But a good anecdotal lead goes further and demonstrates the crux of the idea in the most dramatic terms possible. Certainly, the deaths and illnesses of the children of Woburn were the most compelling aspect of the story.

This "crux" idea is a good guide to selecting which among the many anecdotes your research has turned up is the best for the lead. If the story is about a conflict between individuals, the moment of confrontation between them is the one to use. For example, once I did a piece about a man, Dr. Earle Reynolds, who challenged the right of the U.S. government to test nuclear bombs in the atmosphere and to block off sections of the Pacific Ocean to do so. To test the law, he violated it by sailing his boat into the forbidden area while tests were going on, thus risking his own and his family's health to prove his point. The lead was a two-page report of exactly what happened when Reynolds and his family were arrested on the high seas by the U.S. Coast Guard—the moment of physical confrontation between him and the government. Why? Because the basic story was of the conflict between a man and his government and the place to start it was obviously the moment of confrontation.

Very good journalists select an anecdotal lead that expresses the mood of the story's underlying idea, though it may not report the problem or crux in overt terms. Gay Talese used this type of lead on a piece about Joe DiMaggio's life after the death of his ex-wife, Marilyn Monroe. (The piece originally appeared in *Esquire,* and was reprinted in Talese's book, *Fame and Obscurity.*

It was not quite spring, the silent season before the search for salmon, and the old fishermen of San Francisco were either painting their boats or repairing their nets along the pier or sitting in the sun talking quietly among themselves, watching the tourists come and go, and smiling, now, as a pretty girl paused to take their picture. She was about twenty-five, healthy and blue-eyed and wearing a red turtleneck sweater, and she had long, flowing blonde hair that she brushed back a few times before clicking her camera. The fishermen, looking at her, made admiring comments but she did not understand because they spoke a Sicilian dialect, nor did she notice the tall gray-haired man in a dark suit who stood watching her from behind a big bay window on the second floor of DiMaggio's restaurant that overlooks the pier.

He watched until she left, lost in the crowd of newly arrived tourists that had just come down the hill by cable car. Then he sat down again at the table in the restaurant, finishing his tea and lighting another cigarette—his fifth in the last half-hour. None of the other tables was occupied, and the only sounds came from the bar where a liquor salesman was laughing at something the headwaiter had said. But then the salesman, his briefcase under his arm, headed for the door, stopping briefly to peek into the dining room and call out, "See you later, Joe." Joe DiMaggio turned and waved at the salesman. Then the room was quiet again.

Here Talese has said a great deal about what will be the essential message of his story. The girl, of course, is a symbol for the dead Marilyn, the fishermen, for DiMaggio, who came from a family of fishermen. The gulf between them is suggested both by the fact that she is a tourist, taking their picture and that they speak a dialect she cannot understand. Joe, watching from behind a window suggests the distance of his loss of her.

The next paragraph tells about his loneliness, his tension—his fifth cigarette in a half hour—his reserve, his prominence, and the adulation he still gets as a former athlete. Quite a bit to get into two paragraphs.

The summary lead is exactly what its name says it is. It summarizes, as succinctly as possible, exactly what the article is about. Writers try to make them as dramatic and provocative as possible, but the main purpose is to tell the reader what he or she will get in the story. In this they are similar to the traditional newspaper lead which tells who, what, when, where, why, and maybe how. Here's the lead of a profile of Babe Ruth written by Roger Kahn and included in his book, *How the Weather Was*.

In his time and in his way, George Herman Ruth was a holy sinner. He was a man of measureless lust, selfishness and appetites, but he was also a man undyingly faithful, in a manner, to both his public and his game. Tradition, which always distorts, remolded Ruth as extensively in a quarter-century as it remolded Abraham Lincoln in a hundred years. Just twenty-five years after his death and thirty-eight years after his last disastrous season, only the image of holiness remains.

Kahn then goes on with a penetrating portrait of America's greatest sports legend.

Here's another summary lead, this one by Garry Wills.

For a teenaged pacifist, she did a lot of fighting. She quit her first newspaper job, on the socialist *Call*, after being reprimanded by an editor for slapping an incoherent radical at a public affair. Jailed with suffragists, she bit the notorious warden of the Occoquan workhouse and kicked two guards in the shins as they wrestled her down. It was always clear that she would leave her mark on the world; but it must have seemed, in 1917, that the mark she would leave would be a bloody one. No one could have guessed—least of all Dorothy Day herself—that she would become, with Gandhi and Dr. King, one of the principal exponents of nonviolence in our time.

Summary leads are usually short, because you figure that while you may provoke the readers' interest with your general statements, you'd better quickly get down to specific cases and people for them to become interested in. After the lead in the Ruth piece, Kahn immediately gives the reader an anecdote that occurred at Ruth's funeral, and Wills follows his lead by bringing the reader face-to-face with Dorothy Day.

Closely related to the summary lead is the one that contains a striking or shocking statement concerning something that is of immediate self-interest to millions of readers. For example, a piece I did for *Reader's Digest* on traffic courts had this lead:

> Each year more than 30 million motorists are summoned into traffic courts throughout the United States. For nine out of ten of these citizens, their day in court will be the only opportunity they ever have to observe American justice in operation. But instead of a true court of justice, the man accused of a traffic violation will too often face a mere fine-collection agency. He will probably have to wait hours in a crowded, noisy courtroom, only to appear finally before a bored, unpatient judge who is more interested in disposing of his case than in safeguarding his legal rights.
>
> "These courts," wrote a former U.S. Supreme Court justice, Charles E. Whittaker, "are so poorly housed, staffed and equipped, the proceedings so lacking in dignity and their judgments so perfunctory, that they actually create disrespect, if not contempt for all law and all courts."

This one is very close to a summary lead, but it does not suggest all the dimensions of the story, and the emphasis is on the shock value of the statements—something you can't achieve in all summary leads. Other shocking statement leads don't even try to sum up the story idea.

Here's one that William Barry Forlong put in a story he did for *Good Housekeeping:*

> It was a pleasant summer day-warm with just a hint that it would grow hot and humid later on. Doctors moved quietly among a score of patients at the Jewish Chronic Disease Hospital in Brooklyn, giving them injections under the skin of one thigh. It was just a test of their immunity, the patients had been told. There was no real danger, though they "might feel a little discomfort and perhaps see a lump for a while." But there was one thing the patients weren't told: that the injections contained live cancer cells.

This one is close to an anecdotal lead, but is so short that the anecdote is not fully realized, and constructed so that the shock comes in the last few words. (Part of the shock, incidentally, derives from Furlong's artistry in setting up a contrast: a felicitous summer day, doctors moving quietly among patients seemingly in a situation of trust and healing.)

The fourth kind of lead is one which, for want of a fancier name, we call "bam-bam-bam." In this one, you try to hook the reader in with three telescoped anecdotes, the diversity of which illustrate the scope of the story. For instance, Randy Fitzgerald started a *Reader's Digest* piece on food-stamp fraud with the following lead:

In Kentucky undercover policemen discover that federal food stamps are being traded for automobiles, drugs and automatic weapons. Among 30 suspects arrested is a 62-year-old man convicted of selling the sexual services of a 14-year-old boy for $6000 in food stamps and $1000 in cash.

In Chicago a 34-year-old woman is convicted of defrauding food-stamp and related welfare programs of $92,000 over eight years. A Justice Department official estimates food stamp fraud in the Chicago area totals $36 million annually.

In New York City five members of a family are sentenced to prison for participation in a conspiracy involving the theft of between $4 million and $5 million in food stamps, and laundering them through meat markets.

The purpose here was to catch the reader's interest with the amount of fraud, and also to demonstrate how widespread the fraud had become.

That second point—scope—is important when you're writing for national media. Most magazine writers live around New York City; the media circulate nationwide. So writers must demonstrate that the things they're writing about apply all over the country to all kinds of people. The simplistic way of doing this is with trite phrases like "from Maine to California," but professional self-respect demands a little more than that. So you select your illustrative material from different geographical—or vocational or ethnic—areas.

The trouble with the three-part lead is that it uses up, in minimal space, good anecdotal material, which is usually scarce. The three food-stamp fraud cases cited above in three paragraphs could easily have been expanded to a page or so each, and used to illustrate later points in the article. So you only use this kind of lead when you have an abundance of good anecdotes.

Writers use a descriptive lead when they think the mood of the story is of primary importance and should be established immediately. Well done, this kind of lead gets the reader emotionally involved instantly. A secondary purpose is that it locates the story geographically. The first paragraph of Joan Didion's story "Some Dreamers of the Golden Dream" in *Slouching Towards Bethlehem* accomplished this:

> This is a story about love and death in the golden land, and begins with the country. The San Bernardino Valley lies only an hour east of Los Angeles by the San Bernardino Freeway but is in certain ways an alien place: not the coastal California of the subtropical twilights and the soft westerlies off the Pacific, but a harsher California, haunted by the Mojave just beyond the mountains, devastated by the hot dry Santa Ana wind that comes down through the passes at 100 miles an hour and whines through the eucalyptus windbreaks and works on the nerves. October is the bad month for the wind, the month when breathing is difficult and the hills blaze up spontaneously. It is the season of suicide and divorce and prickly dread, whenever the wind blows.

Descriptive leads do not always present a countryside; sometimes they present people, as in a piece journalist and biographer Barbara Gelb did for the *New York Times Magazine* on director and producer Mike Nichols.

> Mike Nichols sits erect, arms folded, at a trestle table in a large-windowed, bare-floored rehearsal room, where he is directing a new play by David Rabe. Rabe sits slumped in a chair nearby, ready to leap protectively to the defense of any seeming slight to his precious words. The actors clutch their scripts—insecure, groping, desperate to please—watching Nichols for a sign of approval. Nichols, who is in a position more or less to have his pick of scripts and stars, has experienced both the joys of taking creative chances and the pitfalls of playing safe. He has been nominated for an Antoinette Perry Award for his direction of Tom Stoppard's "The Real Thing;" if he wins next Sunday, it will be his sixth Tony. And now—as he intermittently feels compelled to do, he has chosen to try a risky play.

Here, Gelb uses the description to show Nichols at work. She also shows the tension under which he is operating, and the esteem in which he is held by the actors, who watch him, seeking a nod of approval.

The "you" lead is the kind in which the writer talks directly to the readers in an attempt to convince them that their self-interest is intensely involved in this piece. It has the advantage of being as direct as a face-to-face conversation; it has the disadvantage that the reader may respond to the "you" with a "not me, Buster"—which he'd be too polite to do if you were face-to-face, but which he's quite free to do when he's alone with a magazine.

I used this kind of lead in the "What Makes Kids Popular?" piece in chapter 2. I haven't used one lately; they seem to be somehow simplistic and perhaps too manipulative.

Like all categorization, this list of kinds of leads is too clear-cut. As must already be apparent from the examples given, many leads, perhaps most, are combinations. Sometimes this is deliberate; more often it results because the writer tries to work in the most compelling material possible to get the reader started. For example, the following lead from a Ken Auletta profile that appeared in *Esquire* contains elements of the descriptive, anecdotal, and shocking-statement leads.

Snow pelted the late-model Plymouth Volare as it slid out of the city of Oswego, New York, on its way along Route 57 to Syracuse, forty miles south. Harnessed in the front seat by a three-point seat belt was the guest speaker at the State University at Oswego that night, accompanied by three undergraduates who had volunteered to drive him to his hotel, near the airport.

The four-door Plymouth barreled along at about thirty-five miles an hour, lashed by heavy winds that shoved it left and right, pounded by the thickest snowfall of the year. Suddenly, just after midnight, the car skidded out of control, spinning perpendicular to the highway, its momentum carrying it forward, slicing through knee-deep drifts, scraping and jumping a wall of ice, and coming to a halt at a forty-five-degree angle at the bottom of a ditch dividing the four lane highway.

While the car spun, the passenger in the front seat said nothing. He sat calmly holding a giant manila accordion file folder containing brochures in his lap, wrapped in the same black raincoat, gray baggy suit, and blue oxford shirt he had worn to give five college speeches in thirty hours. While the car spun, the passengers in the back seat anxiously turned to check that another automobile would not plow into the Plymouth, that the car would not skid to the right, where a steep plunge menaced. All the while, the passenger in the front seat fixed his dark, intense eyes on the feet of the driver, never wavering throughout. When the car finally jolted to a halt, the passenger cooly complimented the student who was driving, Michael Murray of New City, New York, for having kept his foot off the brake. The car might have flipped over had Murray hit the brakes. "That was a classic case of a hydroplane landing," marveled Ralph Nader.

Two types of leads used by inexperienced writers usually fail: quotations and questions. The quotation lead is generally ineffective because most quotations need explanation to be understood, and explanatory material can slow down the lead. Besides, any writer who can't write better than most people speak, is in the wrong field. Having said all that, we should point out that we have used as examples in this book two excellent stories that start with quotations: in writing all rules are made to be broken. As for questions, a good rule to follow is that a writer's job is to answer them, not to ask them.

Every cub reporter learns what a lead is the first week on the job, but nobody ever tells you anything about endings. You can spend years in the newspaper business—the great training ground for journalists—and never hear a word about endings. Probably this because the old inverted pyramid structure, used so often in news stories, written with the least important material at the end so that when the make-up editor chopped off the last couple of paragraphs to make the piece fit the hole that was left on the page, nothing much was lost. So traditional news stories went out with a whimper, but creative journalism demands that stories end with a bang—or at least a snap.

Since we seem to be hooked on categorization in this chapter, we suppose we should list the kinds of endings. Trouble is, there are only three, as far as we can see. One is the summary; another, the snapper; and the third is, well, the third kind.

The summary is a kind of retread of the lead. It's the Q.E.D. kind of thing, like your old high school geometry theorems. In the lead you make some promises to the readers—here's what I'm going to tell you about; in the summary ending you tell them you have kept the promises—here's what I have told you about.

Claire Safran used a summary ending on her piece about toxic wastes in Woburn.

The children of Woburn and Reading are safer today that little Jimmy and Robbie were. The danger has been reduced, but more needs to be done and more needs to be known about the causes. The bond of trust between people and government has been broken, and the sense of communal safety is gone. As a parent, Rev. Young is still worried. His own family lives in a different neighborhood, where he's been told that the water is "fine." Still, as he says, "When one of my children feels tired or ill, I don't think of a cold or flu. I rush the child to the doctor and hold my breath until the laboratory tests are done."

Nevertheless, he and his family stay put. So do most of the families. This is where they live, where their friends, churches and schools are. This is their home, and their major family investment. "If I knew for certain it was dangerous, I would sell my house," says Judy. "But if we knew for certain, who would ever buy it?"

For Anne Anderson, there is another question: "Where would we go?" She recalls the case of the families who were moved out of dioxin-contaminated Times Beach, Missouri, only to find themselves on another site contaminated by the same deadly chemical. "There is no place to hide from this problem," says Anne. "We will stay and fight it here."

This ending summarizes the main theme of the piece indirectly. It also returns the reader to the characters and events mentioned in the lead, giving the reader the feeling that the story has come full circle. Like all good summary endings, it wraps up the piece in a neat package.

Snapper endings are artistic, fun to write, and they fulfill an old, sound, show-business maxim, "always leave them laughing"—or crying. The snapper is usually a pointed anecdote or incident or quote that characterizes your main theme much the way anecdotal leads do. It is crisp, short, often wry, usually witty. The trouble is that when you come across an item that fills that prescription, it's usually so good you use it early in the piece. To save it for the ending requires the kind of self-restraint and foresight many writers, ourselves included, can't muster more than once every five years. Sometimes, though, you have such a wealth of colorful material that you can save a good one for a snapper. An example is the ending of a profile of Dr. Herbert R. Axelrod that Robert Boyle once wrote for *Sports Illustrated*. For thirty-five long paragraphs, Boyle had told his readers what a prodigious man Axelrod was. He was an explorer, scientist, friend of kings, writer, publisher, millionaire. Boyle then ended the piece with this paragraph:

But for all the fish, all the Mongolian gerbils, and for all the money rolling in, Dr. Herbert R. Axelrod occasionally sinks into gloom. "I'd be happy to be a pauper," he says, "if I could play the fiddle as well as Jascha Heifetz."

Simply reprinting the ending this way does not demonstrate its full impact; to get that you have to read the whole article. When you do that you don't believe Axelrod's statement, because Boyle has so thoroughly documented the man's energy and determination in making his millions that you know such a man would never be satisfied to be merely a great violinist. This is only one of the nuances that gives the ending its kick.

This kind of ending must be planned and the material held aside when the story is being outlined. This is a nice idea, but writers are not often that foresighted. What usually happens is the third kind of ending. This is the one that grows out of the story itself, naturally. It doesn't fit in any category; it evolves from the type of material you're using, the kind of story it is, and the point you're at when you finish the body of the piece and realize that now you've got to put an ending on it.

For example, take the Commando Kelly story, back in chapter 6. The whole point of the story was the two kinds of courage—the kind required to win a Medal of Honor versus that needed to survive the trials of everyday living. Partly as a suspense device, and partly because you can't expect the average reader to hold still for this kind of abstract disquisition, I merely laid the groundwork for the comparison right after the lead, then said nothing more about it until the final two paragraphs. By that time, I figured, the reader had all the facts which supported Kelly's final conclusion, so when it was given, he believed it. (I did sort of plan that one in advance.)

The third kind of ending is more a product of the writer's creativity than anything else. In a piece Norman Maclean wrote about retrievers for *Esquire,* he used such an ending. The piece actually dealt with much more than retrievers. It told of Maclean's relationship with his father. Near the end of the piece, Maclean tells of the death of his brother, and the crushing effect it had on his father, who adopted the brother's dog, and whose life was changed thereby. Maclean ended the piece this way:

> The dog and my father were inseparable, whereas before my father cared to be with dogs only during the hunting season. As for the dog, I am sure there are other cases like this, but he was the only dog I ever saw that became another dog for love of another man. For my brother he had been a duck dog, and now for my father he became a fishing dog, if one can speak of such a species. He would sit all day in the boat on the seat next to my father and peer into the impenetrable water. He not only loved but admired my father greatly—I am sure he thought the whole fishing thing was completely under my father's control, as I did when I was the dog's age and believed my father could come up with a fish whenever he was so minded. After staring a respectable length of time into the water without seeing anything but pieces of sunlight, he would bark at my father, and when my father caught a fish, the dog

would lick my father's whole face, though my father still needed part of it to see how to unhook the fish.

To the others in my family, the dog was something of a sacred object that had prolonged my father's life and helped to steady the rest of us. He was a fine dog, and after him, my father had no other dog.

Although some endings defy classification, there are a couple of rules for the latter parts of stories. In mass magazines, the ending should be up-beat if possible. Even if your story is pretty negative, you try to end with some kind of a positive thought or idea. Very seldom do you leave the reader with a "down" feeling, but if you do it should be a beaut. If your story is a tragedy and there is not even a hope at the end then, like Shakespeare in *Hamlet,* you really ought to pile the stage with corpses.

With personality pieces you often end with a summary anecdote that restates the theme of the piece. In problem stories you almost invariably end with a "what can be done" section and a short wrap-up. In "how-to" stories you often end with a summary restatement of the advantages of building a backyard swimming pool out of old newspapers for $4.69.

One final item: when you have finished the piece, stop writing. Time after time I've kept on going for two or three more paragraphs after the story was really finished. Inertia, I guess.

One time I was watching an artist paint a portrait. It was really finished, but he was fussing around with a dab here, a brush stroke there.

Finally he threw down his brush in exasperation. "Every artist," he said, "should have a man stand behind him with a big wooden mallet, to hit him smartly on the head when the painting is finished."

Same goes for writers.

11

The Body of the Story

*I*t may be an egregious kind of mechanization to presume to write a chapter about what makes up the body of a story. All you have to do is read half a dozen good articles to see that the content varies enormously. Obviously, what goes into the body depends on the kind of story it is, the quality of material available, the audience to which it is addressed and, primarily, the artistry of the writer.

You can look back at the piece about the two fifteen-year-olds in chapter 9, and see how Bob Greene uses his ability as an observer and a writer to show us the boys in their adolescent confusion and vulnerability.

Another example is the following, taken from Barbara Gelb's profile of Mike Nichols, in which she shows how Nichols works and gives a glimpse of the effect Elia Kazan's work has had on him.

Nichols nibbles on a bran muffin, sips coffee, chain smokes (without inhaling) and nods encouragingly to William Hurt and Sigourney Weaver, who are about to rehearse a love scene. She is playing Darlene, a rootless woman, bruised by love, who has a vague career as a photographer. He is playing Eddie, a marginally successful Hollywood casting director with a drug habit. "Hurlyburly," which is scheduled to open Off Broadway at the Promenade Theater on June 21, is in an early phase of rehearsal and the two young actors, though they have practiced the love scene a few times, are still feeling their way into their roles, improvising.

"Eddie and Darlene are talking about how it's lucky they didn't meet a year ago," Nichols explains. "Because, Darlene says, 'A year ago I was *crazy*.' And Eddie says, 'Oh, a year ago I was *nuts*.' Then *she* says they have to keep their hearts open, and *he* says they need time and space and no guilts. It's sort of like incantation."

[Playwright David] Rabe's dialogue for the scene gives no hint of any accompanying action, and Eddie and Darlene could be sitting across a table from each other during their exchange. But Nichols wants to find a way to "physicalize" the "underneath," as his observation of Kazan taught him to do, "so that the cliches are heard in stronger contrast." And he has found his clue in the last line of the scene, a ribald—and in a family newspaper unprintable—suggestion from Eddie to Darlene that they immediately consummate their relationship.

"I felt what would make the Event of the scene—the joke, or the irony—clearest, would be to have them—while they're in the midst of these cliches about *space* and *open hearts* and *no guilts*—be undressing each other and beginning to make love."

Sigourney Weaver slithers into William Hurt's lap, straddling him. Hurt, slouched on the sofa, begins fondling her. She pulls her sweater off. "Once I'd decided it would be a good idea for them to partly undress each other and themselves, Sigourney said she wanted Darlene to be quite aggressive," Nichols says. "It was her idea to straddle Bill. And I said, well, if she was going to do *that*—and I liked it very much, why not do it on the line, I'm *scared?* At one point, Eddie says, 'We need *time.*' And Darlene says, 'There's no rush'—whipping off her belt."

In the actor's lap, the actress unbuckles her belt and flings it away.

"We worked it out very carefully," Nichols says, watching approvingly.

Weaver kicks off a boot. Hurt tugs off her other boot. In one swift motion, Weaver zips down her dress, wriggles out of it and drops it on the floor behind her. She finally is wearing nothing but silk panties and a thin, clinging, pink knit camisole.

Hurt hastily pulls open the buttons of his shirt and shrugs out of the sleeves, as Weaver yanks her camisole over head and tosses it into the air. Naked from the waist up, the two embrace fervidly.

Nichols smiles with delight at his own handiwork and at his actors' adventurousness.

Sigourney Weaver is getting dressed. Moved by her daring, William Hurt says quietly, "You're very brave."

"You're brave too," Nichols tells the actor, smiling one of his ferociously protective smiles.

The anecdote is unusual, since Nichols, one of the characters, is commenting on the action as it occurs. But Gelb clearly recognized that by placing the quotes within the description of the actors' work, she could show readers what Nichols believes about direction, and how he helps his actors reach the goals he has set. Had she been less perceptive, the point would not have been made so well.

In addition to the artistry of the writer, this anecdote demonstrates another quality of first-class journalism: the writer must think deeply about his or her material, must have broad understanding of people, and must be perceptive enough to see the significance behind a fairly simple situation. These qualities probably cannot be taught or planned; they come from living and understanding.

So the body of a story cannot be compiled like a grocery list. But when you have read hundreds of interpretive pieces and written several score, you begin to see that there are some elements which many of the good ones share. Isolating them out helps you to ensure that the next piece you do will have at least some of the requisites of good work.

One is what, for want of a more perceptive name, we usually call the significance section. This is a paragraph or two, usually right after the lead, which tells readers why it is important to read this piece. It draws the broader significance of the story, perhaps by showing that it affects people all over the country, perhaps by showing that it touches deeply the lives of millions, perhaps by saying here is something new and important. It attempts to answer the reader's inveterate, unspoken question, "What's in this for me?" It may be a summary of all the points that will be made in the story and thus be a kind of road map of where the story is going; this helps orient the reader and, by defining precisely what is and is not going to be covered, sharpens the focus of the piece. It may be a general definition of a problem that the piece will explore specifically in terms of one person, one group, one city.

In the Gelb piece, for example, the significance section begins with a brief overview of Nichols's enormously successful career, then moves on to this:

> To watch Nichols at work is to perceive something about the making of a play that will never be discerned by its audience. To hear him talk about his work, as he did recently in full candor, is to perceive something about the making of a director and the sources of his creativity—in Nichols's case, a blend of life experiences that he applies to every project, whether a genial comedy like "The Odd Couple," or a trag-icomedy, like "Hurlyburly."

Gelb is telling her readers that the story will show them something they have never seen before—how a great director works. If they read the story, she is saying, they will learn a great deal about a man whose work most of them have seen.

A different kind of "significance section" was included in the article "What Makes Kids Popular?" which we discussed in chapter 2. The piece has a "you" lead designed to make readers identify with story. The eighth, ninth, and tenth paragraphs are the significance section, which is supposed to tell readers why this is important, and to nail down their self-interest in reading it.

In the piece on toxic waste mentioned in the preceding chapter, Claire Safran moves the reader from a focus on the children and parents of Woburn, like Jimmy and Anne Anderson, to a focus on the problem as it affects the entire country.

> When little Jimmy first became sick, no one wanted to listen to Anne's questions. City and state officials dismissed her as "an emotional mother." The tragic news had not yet broken about Love Canal, the Niagara Falls, New York, neighborhood built on a landfill that had leached out its toxic chemicals. Few people were aware of how the by-products of civilization could poison our air, our water, our land and our children.
>
> The danger is now all too familiar. Each day, a new group of parents wakes to the nightmare Anne Anderson lived with for years. From across the country come reports of children becoming ill because of asbestos in a school's ceilings, deadly dioxin in industrial-waste oil sprinkled on a dusty road or other potentially lethal chemicals seeping into drinking water. In Woburn, as in so many other places, the cleanup is not yet even begun. The answers Anne found are not final ones—but they are a beginning and they point the way for other concerned parents to follow.

Safran here is clearly telling her readers that while her story is about one city in Massachusetts, the problem exists nationwide, and reading the story will help them if ever they have to face it. It is a clear appeal to the reader's self-interest.

The food-stamp-fraud story mentioned in the preceding chapter featured a similar theme statement. The lead comprised three anecdotes about fraud. It was followed by this:

> The food-stamp program has been one of the fastest-growing of all federal programs—escalating from a $30.5-million budget and 367,000 recipients in 1964 to $11.3 billion and 22.5 million recipients today. It is also one of the most fraud-ridden and poorly run programs. Federal

investigators calculate that up to $1.6 billion a year is wasted as a result of recipient fraud, administrative error, and organized theft and counterfeiting. In many parts of the country, food stamps have literally become a second currency, used to support a thriving black market in stolen and illicit goods. Says Sen. William L. Armstrong (R. Colo.), "Theft, abuse and error in the program are not just a rip-off of taxpayers; they are a crime against the poor."

The writer, Randy Fitzgerald, is clearly telling readers that the three incidents mentioned in the lead are not exceptional, that more than one-tenth of all money in the program is wasted, and that the problem is one they should read about and understand.

Since most writers are not authorities, but reporters, they have to seek out various experts and put their knowledge at the service of the reader. The way writers do this is another of the definable elements that characterize a sound article.

In the first place, the person you are quoting about a subject has to be a genuine authority on that subject. Just having an M.D. degree, for instance, doesn't make someone an expert on everything from heart disease to cystic fibrosis; if you need a medical authority, quote a doctor on the area in which he or she has special knowledge—maybe kidney ailments, maybe new ideas in family practice. And don't be deluded by the epidemic of degree-itis that currently afflicts the country. Someone can be an expert without having a Ph.D. or even a college education.

Suppose, for instance, that you were doing a story on dishonest mechanics who gyp people on auto repairs. To prove a particular mechanic had mistreated a car, you'd have to have an honest, expert mechanic who could diagnose what was really wrong with the car, what should have been done to fix it, and how much it should have cost. He might have no higher education at all, but if he knew autos from radiator to tail pipe, he would be a legitimate expert.

When you first quote your expert in an article, you must include his or her qualifications in order to convince the reader your source *is* an expert. Usually it's easy; the person's title is often enough—the secretary of state is obviously an expert for an article on U.S. foreign policy. Sometimes you must give a title plus the person's particular expertise.

Once when I did an article on a mass murderer named Francis Bloeth, it was necessary to go back into his childhood to discover the origins of his aberration. His mother was an expert on that. But then I wanted to show that some of the things that had happened to him as a child were probably the cause of his later behavior, so I needed an authority on the causes of childhood crime. Here's the way it went:

In 1943 [Bloeth] was pronounced "a delinquent child" in Queens County Children's Court. What made him such? His mother recalls that when he was six he jumped 30 feet out of a tree, got a concussion of the brain, and after that "really started to get in trouble." But the exhaustive studies of delinquent children made by Drs. Sheldon and Eleanor Glueck of Harvard University would point to other factors in his case.

The Gluecks have found five main characteristics that separate delinquents from normal youngsters. They made up tables to predict which children would become delinquent, and the New York City Youth Board has found them to be accurate indicators. Applied retrospectively to Bloeth's life, the tables give him less than a ten per cent chance of *not* becoming delinquent.

Then the story went on to cite specific areas of parent-child relations—like discipline—that the Gluecks had found to be decisive and reported that each had been present in young Bloeth's experience.

Here the Gluecks were cited and qualified as experts and their expertise further validated in the specific areas needed by the testing program of the youth board. And this little excerpt illustrated (minimally) another technique that works well in this kind of writing. It's in the first paragraph, where I quoted Bloeth's mother on the fall from the tree as a cause of his trouble, then immediately demolished that explanation with the citation of the Glueck's study.

What we're getting into here is a problem in both credibility and ethics. Take ethics first. When you write an interpretive piece, you are really making an argument for a particular point of view. You have arrived at this point of view after going through the tough evaluative process described in chapter 6, and it represents the objective truth of the situation as nearly as you can achieve it. When you write the piece you use all the skill at your command to convince the reader that it is the truth, so your writing is *not* objective. However, while it's highly unlikely, it's just possible that your "truth" is wrong—or wrong in part. So fairness and a decent humility require that you present more than one side to a question. Thus you present the other side briefly, then counter it with stronger evidence.

A major virtue of this technique is that it makes the piece—and your argument—much more believable for the reader because what you're saying, in effect, is, "Look, I've done a thorough research job on this situation, I know all the arguments, pro and con, and I've decided the pro is the strongest."

In his book *Attitude Change and Social Influence*, Arthur R. Cohen lists other reasons for giving both sides of a story. You should do it, he says, when the audience will be exposed to the other side later on; when the audience initially disagrees with your point of view; when all the facts on both sides of the question are well known; when the opposing argument and its defenders are better known than yours.

Finally, we don't have any scientific proof of it, but we do have a strong conviction that you are more persuasive when you level with readers. Your readers may lack information, but they are not stupid. Particularly in areas where they have first-hand experience or a strong self-interest, they cannot be fooled. Try it and their most likely reaction will be, "This guy doesn't know what he's talking about!"—and they turn the page. When that happens you're out of the communications business.

There are times when leveling is not only good practice, it's the only thing you can do. Your experts disagree on some essential point and try as you will, you can't find an overwhelming weight of evidence on one side or the other. One thing you can do is tell the reader there is no agreement, quote experts, with their qualifications, on both—or all—sides of the conflict, and let the reader decide. (I've always felt, though, that this was skimping on the job, that if I just kept researching, I'd be able to make a judgment. Many times this has proved to be true. But not always.)

Sometimes when you have trouble arriving at a judgment because of conflicting expert testimony, it is because you haven't thought deeply enough about the question—or about precisely what aspect of the question is pertinent to your line of argument. This happened when I did the story on Richard Tenneson, one of the twenty-one American turncoats, mentioned in chapter 4. Tenneson gave me his version of what had happened to him in battle, but the official accounts of the battles flatly contradicted Tenneson's version. Who was right?

There didn't seem a way in the world to resolve the differences, but the more I thought about it, the more two additional elements gained importance: (1) A battlefield is impossibly confused, and what is true of the overall situation as seen from divisional headquarters may not be true at all for the individual rifleman in a foxhole; and (2) What was important in determining Tenneson's future actions was not so much the objective truth, but his truth—what he *thought* had happened. This is what would form his feelings of belonging to a larger entity and of loyalty to the army and, beyond it, the country.

So I reported the two conflicting versions of the battles, then made the above two points.

There may also come a time when, as you move merrily through the research process, you discover a fact that demolishes the argument you had planned to make. If you find such a fact, you cannot ethically ignore it. You may even have to admit that your point of view is wrong, and forget about the article. That has happened to countless writers, so if it happens to you, take comfort in knowing that you are in good company.

Probably the most important single element in the body of a story for mass audiences is anecdotes—how many you use and how well. If there's one warning editors have given me more than any other, it is, "Be sure to get plenty of anecdotes into it." There are two reasons: the specific anecdote takes a general statement and shows it to the reader in its concrete application, making it easier to grasp; secondly, in anecdotes you are writing about people doing things, so readers can see them, feel with them, see themselves in the same situation—*if* they're well done.

Writing good anecdotes demands as much logical analysis and as much creative talent as anything a writer does. They must make the general point they're supposed to make, and while this sounds obvious, it is surprising how often they do not—and the writer fails to see it. They must convince the reader that these are real people in real situations, which means they cannot be made up. Many beginning writers try this kind of fiction when they can't get real anecdotes, but every experienced editor can spot a phony at ten paces; perhaps the reason is that the writer does not have much skill at writing fiction.

Anecdotes are really miniature stories with all the appurtenances of same. They must lay the groundwork so the reader can follow the action. They must introduce characters with clear objectives, then show the characters striving toward those objectives. They usually have conflict. They move toward a climax, then usually have a denouement, just like a short story. And they have to be structured; the raw material from which they're built is seldom in final form when you get it. Warning: "Structuring" does not mean changing facts, it means perhaps rearranging their order, cutting nonessentials, emphasizing the quotes or actions that drive home the point.

For example, here are two versions of apocryphal story, the first composed by a beginning writer, the second by an experienced one:

The late Bernard Baruch was witness to a scene in New York's Central Park: A middle-aged man sat down next to a pretty young woman and propositioned her to the tune of $25. Finally his bid was accepted for four times that amount. And as the couple rose to leave the park, Baruch heard the man utter to himself, "Now that we have established the principle, it's just a matter of degree."

At a dinner party Winston Churchill was seated next to the pretty young wife of one of his top administrators. He turned to her and said, "My dear, would you spend the weekend with me for £10,000?" The woman looked shocked, hesitated, then said, "Would my husband find out?"

"Of course not," Churchill said. "I'll send him to Iceland."

"Very well," the woman said.

"Would you do it," Churchill asked, "for £10?"

"Sir! Do you take me for a harlot?"

"The principle," Churchill said, "has been established. We are now haggling over the price."

Certainly the second makes the point better. Why? Some reasons are obvious. In version one the famous character is a witness, in version two, a participant, so reader interest is heightened. In the second story you see the little drama actually being played, with direct quotes; in the first it is summarized and therefore less vivid. In version one, the punch line is not clearly related to the conflict preceding it; in version two it is. Most important, in the first story the bidder starts low and ends up high, and the story won't work that way. You've got to start high and end up low in order to set up the situation for the punch line. Finally the quote at the end is weak; "it's just a matter of degree" is much less pointed than "We are now haggling over the price."

There is also a minor element that I put into the second version for the purpose of the comparison. When I heard the original story, it did not include the business about "would my husband find out?" and the next sentence. I put these in because it seemed to me that in this situation a woman would take a little time to make her decision, and I wanted to allow her that time in the progression of the action. Of course such fictionalizing is barred in good journalism—and if you pick your anecdotes carefully it isn't needed.

Dan Greenburg is remarkably adept at handling anecdotes, as he proved in a piece called "The Ninth Precinct Blues," which appeared in the *New York Times Magazine*. The piece told of the difficulties of being a policeman in a New York city area that Greenburg calls "ugly and terrifying." Greenburg rode with the police of the Ninth Precinct, and told the story almost entirely through anecdotes and quotations. Here's an example:

One night while I am riding with Chris Reisman and Barry Noxon, two anticrime cops, in their battered sedan, a "job" comes over the radio—a "jumper." Chris floors the accelerator and we tear around the corner and over to the block, where two radio cars have pulled up with dome lights flashing. The uniformed cops are out of their vehicles, gazing upward. Six stories above us, a young man, either drunk or freaked out on drugs, dangles dangerously over the parapet, shouting incoherently about how terrible he has been to his wife.

Chris and Barry confirm that the uniformed cops have already called for Emergency Services to come with a net, and then they make a break for the front door of the building, with me following close behind. They yell for me to hug the building so I won't get hit by the man if he jumps.

The front door of the building is locked. Chris and Barry bang on the nearest window, yelling: "Police emergency! Open up!" The superintendent of the building sleepily appears and lets us into the hall. Barry, Chris and I leap up six flights of stairs in 30 seconds. At roof level, Barry gets down on his hands and knees, quietly opens the door to the roof and creeps out onto the tar paper, with Chris and me right behind him. Barry inches up to the parapet and crawls back to us.

"He's on a ledge about seven feet down," Barry whispers. He's going to see me and jump before I can grab him, unless somebody on the street distracts his attention."

Chris calls to the cops on the street on his walkie-talkie, *sotto voce*, tells them to engage the jumper in conversation and to shine a powerful light in his eyes. The cops on the street start yelling. A searchlight is turned on. Barry goes over the parapet. The jumper sees Barry a moment too late and moves to leap off the ledge. Barry reaches out and graps him. They scuffle briefly, teetering over the ledge, then Barry yanks him to safety and it is all over. The jumper curses Barry for saving his life.

Before I know it, we are back on the street. Nobody gives Barry so much as a pat on the back for rescuing the guy and nearly losing his life in the process. It is 2:30 A.M.; less than 15 minutes have elapsed since we first rolled up on the scene. On "Police Story" they'd have stretched it out to fill an hour.

Two *Daily News* photographers are firing off flashguns in the jumper's face and the just-arrived Emergency Services team is pouring out of its van. As we head for our car, an Emergency Services man passes Barry. "Thanks for doing our job, Fella," he says with mock sarcasm. Clearly, nobody is going to acknowledge Barry's bravery. I figure it's up to me. "Barry," I say, "you're a goddam hero. You know that?"

Barry shrugs. "If my timing had been a fraction of a second off," he says, "then I'd be a yo-yo."

The elements of the anecdote are the classic ones. The two cops are introduced, and, with the call about the "jumper," given their objective: to save the man. Conflict is introduced when the objective is blocked by the locked door, the slow-moving superintendent, the six flights of stairs, and the jumper's ability to spot Noxon from the ledge. But the two overcome all of the obstacles, and save the jumper; this is the climax. The denouement is the by-play that follows.

But there's much more to the story than structure: Greenburg points up the elements that show what it is like to be a Ninth Precinct cop. He never flatly states the points that he wants the anecdote to make, but he tells the story so that the reader gets them anyway.

At the beginning of the anecdote he mentions the radio call that tells Noxon and Reisman of a "job," a relatively bland term for what the two will be called upon to do. The fact that the pair use the term indicates that incidents like this are commonplace, as does the fact that the word "jumper" immediately tells them what they will face when they arrive at the scene.

He reinforces this idea with his dry description of the scene when they arrive. He shows Noxon and Reisman quickly deciding what action to take, and taking it. They seem cool, professional, and unsurprised by an event that most of us would find shocking and frightening.

Next, as they race to the door, both cops warn Greenburg to hug the building, so he will not be hit by the man if he jumps. Wouldn't that be a bizarre way to die? But one of Greenburg's points is that the bizarre and the dangerous make up a great deal of the life of a Ninth Precinct police officer.

The courage of the men becomes evident as Noxon risks his life to save a man who doesn't want to be saved. And the thanklessness of their job is driven home by the reaction to Noxon's heroism. The man Noxon has just saved curses him, the other policemen ignore him or joke about it, and when Greenburg finally tells Noxon that he is a hero, Noxon turns the compliment off with a self-deprecating smart crack.

That's quite a lot for one anecdote to do.

Good anecdotes are intensely *human* stories, stories of people doing things, overcoming obstacles, solving problems, changing, battling other people, helping them, loving them, hating them. They tell readers that the abstract idea you are presenting has very real effects on their own and other people's lives. By demonstrating those effects, in the dramas of people interacting with others, you help readers understand the situation—often their own—and help them identify with your characters and their situation. It's hardly a new technique. The Bible uses it, and the anecdotes are called parables.

What *is* relatively new—merely about twenty-five years old—is its use in journalism to add impact to the informational message. And it requires of the nonfiction writer the artistry of the fiction writer. So if you want to do it well, where do you look for your models? The fiction writers. And I've also found that the analysis of jokes helps. Jokes, after all, are short human stories with a very sharp point. Jokes evoke emotion, though only one—laughter. And jokes don't just happen, somebody writes them. So by taking them apart and seeing how they make their point, you can learn a good deal about structure and effectiveness. For example:

A man is speeding along the freeway in the pouring rain. He passes one of those ten-wheel, tractor-trailer trucks stopped on the side of the road and, out of the corner of his eye as he passes, he spots the truck driver kneeling down in front of the truck doing something with a little white kitten. Intrigued, he stops, backs up, and goes up to the truck driver in the rain. The driver has some string and is making a harness for the kitten and hitching it to the front bumper of the truck.

"Trouble?" the man says.

"Yeah. Truck broke down."

"Well, what are you doing with the kitten?"

"I'm going to get him to pull me into town."

"You think that little bitty kitten is going to pull that great big truck?"

"Sure. Why not? I got a whip."

Here the writer sets up the situation, a familiar one that any motorist can identify with, quickly in the first few sentences. Then he introduces the problem—how to get the truck to town—and builds it with the dialogue. The climax comes in the last line; there is no denouement.

But what makes it funny is the misdirection. Like a stage magician who makes sure your eyes are elsewhere when he drops in the chemical that will turn the pitcher of water into "wine," the writer sets your mind thinking along a certain direction—the stalled truck, the rain, the kitten, the harness. Then in the last line he flips your mind around to a completely new viewpoint. It startles you and makes you laugh, partly at the unexpectedness of it and partly at the truck driver's stupidity.

You can use misdirection in serious stories, too, to build up the point, heighten the impact.

Study television commercials. The good ones can set up and resolve a human situation in fifteen seconds, sometimes five. Of course they have added props of visual action and sound to help get the effect, but their basic techniques can be adapted. They have enormous compression of action; they deal only with the very nub of the situation, which is good technique in any kind of anecdote.

Getting good anecdotes is a major problem for writers. The first step toward its solution, I think, is to recognize that you must have them, and to keep researching until you have enough. The second is to use the old reporter's trick of getting a story by telling one. This does a couple of things: the story you tell outlines for your interviewees the *kind* of thing you're looking for; it starts them thinking along the lines you want; it challenges them to top your story with one of their own. I've also had good luck with the trick of taking the general subject you're talking about right down to the interviewee's own life. For instance, if I've been interviewing a social psychologist, say, on some aspect of parent-child relations, I might ask him how he handles his own children. Immediately his mind switches from dealing with broad, perhaps theoretical, considerations to the warm, personal area of his own kids. And usually, I've gotten good stories that illustrated some point that needed making; after all, he is an expert, and he's likely to have applied his expertise to his personal problems in trying to bring up decent, healthy children.

Finally, it's helpful if you keep in mind what good anecdotes are— stories about people doing things. In much of your interviewing you are dealing with abstract ideas, broad intellectual concepts; if you are constantly trying to bring these down to specific applications in the lives of people, and trying to make your interviewee do the same, you'll see the possibility of anecdotes in many of the things he or she says. Then you go after them by asking specific questions about the specific situation.

12

Dramatic Writing

*H*ere are two ways of handling the same story.

Houston, Jan. 24—An explosion sent sheets of flame roaring across waterfronts streets last night, setting fire to four houses on Avenue O and badly burning three boys.

The explosion came when high-octane gasoline, which had leaked out of a storage tank on Avenue O, suddenly burst into flame about 7 P.M. The three boys, Edward Von Kamp, 14, his brother Robert, 11, and a friend, Herman Holcombe, 12, had been in the Von Kamp home across the street from the tank when the explosion came. They rushed outside and were instantly engulfed in flames. The two Von Kamp boys were taken to the Texas Children's Hospital with third-degree burns and were on the critical list today. The Holcombe boy was taken to South Side Hospital where his condition was listed as good.

"After the second explosion, I ran out of my house and looked down Avenue O," a neighbor of the Von Kamps said. "About 50 yards away I saw a ball of fire moving toward me. Then I looked closer and saw that the ball of fire was a boy!

The neighbor grabbed the boy, Bobby Von Kamp, and rolled him on the road to smother the flames. Then he tore off the boy's charred clothing. As he worked, he could hear the clang of approaching fire engines and ambulance sirens.

Bobby Von Kamp, two weeks away from his 11th birthday, lived across the street from a gasoline storage tank on the Houston, Texas, waterfront. At 7 P.M. on January 24, 1961, he was watching television with his 14-year-old brother Edward and a 12-year-old friend, Herman Holcombe. His father, a seaman, was on a ship off the coast of Florida, his mother had just gone to the grocery store and his two older brothers were out for the evening.

As the Bugs Bunny cartoon was going off the air, the boys smelled gas. High-octane gasoline had been leaking out of the storage tank across the street. Suddenly the vapors exploded. Clouds of flame boiled through the air, licked through the open windows. The three boys dashed for the front door. Eddie held open the screen door as another explosion shook the street. He caught a burst of flames on his back. Part of the screening in the door simply melted into nothing.

The boys ran. Eddie slipped and fell. Herman said, "I'll stay," and knelt by his friend. Bobby yelled, "I'll get help!" He ran down the street with the flames streaming from his clothing.

As soon as ambulances arrived, Bobby and Eddie were sped to the Texas Children's Hospital. Herman, the least burned, was taken to another hospital.

The difference between these two stories is the difference between straight news and interpretive writing. The second, the lead of an article entitled "A Boy's Trial by Fire" by Joseph P. Blank, published in *Reader's Digest*, is also an excellent example of creative, dramatic writing.

The first story, like most news stories, focuses on the event and gives you the people only as they are affected by it. It is objective, factual, uninvolved—and leaves the reader the same way. The second focuses on the people affected by the event; it shows a little newsreel, letting you see the people acting out the event. It is also objective in that the writer takes no position, pleads no cause; it is factual—has even more facts than the first. But it is not uninvolved, and does not leave the reader that way. With its wealth of specific detail, it makes you see and identify with the boys and go with them through their surprise and shock, terror, and humanity as they help each other.

The structure of the story adds to the drama. We defy anyone to read the first paragraph and then stop: it pulls at too many basic emotions. The ball of fire rolling down the street intrigues with its mystery and evokes the primordial fear of fire out of control. The third sentence flips our minds to an entirely new understanding of the threat, then immediately triggers our sympathy for and need to protect our children.

This, of course, is the climax of Blank's little story, and he uses it as a lead to hook the reader's interest. In the next paragraph he finishes, briefly, that bit of action, then in a flashback technique, focuses on the minutes before the explosion and lets us live through it with the three boys. This is constructed, of course, as a chronological narrative and the wealth of detail—the Bugs Bunny cartoon, the screen in the door melting—allows us to experience it first hand. It builds back to the climax, skips it, and goes on to the denouement—the boys in the hospitals.

But basic to the whole story is the ancient universal drama of it. It is a story of someone fighting for life against one of humanity's great, natural enemies—fire. Because we all are unconsciously sensitive to this threat, we identify immediately with the boys' crisis. In fact, Blank has built his whole article around this universal identification. The article is about a new treatment for severe burns. "Dr. Miller found that [Bobby] was burned over 98 per cent of his body. . . . Only the soles of his feet had escaped the flames. . . . Few people have survived 50 per cent third-degree burns." To describe the new treatment, Blank takes Bobby step by step through the long process in the hospital, so that you are reading not simply about a medical advance, but about a boy's fight to live against overwhelming odds—which is the unspoken emotional agenda of the piece.

This is the essence of dramatic writing, for all drama is conflict. The deep, ancient conflicts are few and simple: man against nature; man against man; man against himself.

In the first category you get the adventure stories like those mentioned in Chapter 8. Probably included in this group are the stories of men and women struggling against the unknown, the occult, the mysteries of space—which helps explain the world's fascination with the explorations of space as well as stories of persons pushing forward the frontiers of knowledge in scientific discoveries.

The conflict of man against man lies behind many sports stories as well as political or corporation stories in which people battle one another for power and position. And, of course, it includes many men and women fighting evil, since evil is so often perpetrated or represented by other people.

But some of the latter are man against himself pieces, since "evil" may be a man's own weaknessess—fear, despair—or his primitive rages—for revenge, to conquer, to destroy. The story about the army colonel caught in a dilemma at Fort Lee, Virginia, outlined in Chapter 1, would be man against himself. Once I wrote a piece about a poor Rhode Island youth with a grade-school education who went blind as a result of an accident when he was twenty-one. In a year of rampant self-pity he went to pieces, then picked up his courage and entered a high school for the blind in Massachusetts. He graduated, went to Boston Law School, graduated second in his class, and today is a state supreme court judge. Basically it was a story of his victory over his own despair, brought on by a crippling handicap.

We are often our own enemies. A wise psychiatrist at the University of Maryland taught me this when I was doing an article on what makes people panic. "Fear of losing control of ourselves," he said, "is one of the most powerful, primitive anxieties we have." This insight not only helped me to structure the article itself, but enabled me to see the underlying drama in other human situations I wrote about later.

If you can spot the dramatic conflict in a situation that you're to write about, you can plot the article so that the dramatic story will carry your readers' interest, while its details give them the information you want them to have. We'll talk more about plotting in chapter 14.

Most writers do not make a distinction between the *story* and the *article*. Slowly, over the years of writing, they perfect their own understanding of what makes a good story, though most never consciously categorize or analyze its elements. They simply know. I never did until I started to teach and had to analyze what I'd been doing all those years. But it helps new writers, I think, if they can consciously understand the difference and the qualities that make a story. It helps in spotting those ideas which will be most likely to result in successful articles; it helps in planning the kind of material you will be seeking in your research; it helps in shaping the article after the research is finished.

Universal human conflicts are what make magazine articles timeless. Usually, within them, there is a section that is of its time, but the underlying story is ageless—like the one coming up.

Bonnie Remsberg, an excellent freelance writer, wrote it for *Family Circle*. It won the Outstanding Article Award of the American Society of Journalists and Authors in 1984. On the surface, the article is about the cancer that the nuclear weapons testing of the 1950s has brought to a small Utah town. But beneath the surface, the story deals with some of the most basic human themes and values. It is a story about fear and love, patriotism and loss. It is a story of hope betrayed, of courage and faith.

Beneath the Cloud

By Bonnie Remsberg

Utah is so beautiful, it's hard to believe that it's part of the real world. But a deadly cloud lurks over that lovely land.

Irene Houston McEwen knows that cloud well. From her white house on Main Street, in the pretty little mountain town of Panguitch, Utah, she has tracked it—and its victims—for more than 30 years. She can tell you about its beginnings and its seemingly relentless course. She can also recite the names on the casualty list—those who have sickened and died and those who have sickened and *not* died, but who live in fear for their futures and the futures of their children—born and unborn. It began at dawn on a glorious wind-swept day in January 1951, when a vast mushroom shaped orange cloud burst from the Nevada desert, 150 miles away, and floated over the valley below Panguitch and the mountains above it.

Irene McEwen watched the first explosion—and the next, and the next. She has lost track of how many detonations she actually witnessed, but she does remember that the bombs were released in series of three or four, at intervals of about three months, for twelve years.

In 1963, by our agreement with the USSR and England, all above-ground nuclear testing was abandoned. But by that time, the damage had already been done. The mushroom clouds were gone, but their legacy of cancer remained. It has meant sickness and death to an appalling number of Irene's friends and neighbors. "We didn't know," Irene says. "We couldn't have known." Indeed, in those early years of the Atomic Age, few people knew about the effects of atomic fallout. But Panguitch knows now, and so does Irene McEwen. They found out in the worst way possible.

The Panguitch Valley is a scenic pocket in the Henry Mountains, close to Bryce Canyon and the spectacular Zion National Park. In 1852, it was deemed, by a party of Mormon explorers, "a suitable place" for families to settle. Among the original settlers was a family named Houston.

Generations later, by the time Irene Houston—the oldest of five brothers and seven sisters—was born, the town was a thriving lumber, cattle and tourist center. Growing up, Irene remembers a good life, the warmth of church, family activities and weekly dances where "your father danced with you, your brothers danced with you and then, eventually, you just all paired off."

When it came her turn, Irene paired off with Clem McEwen, who, like herself, had been born in a small house near Main Street. "When we were growing up," she explains, "many people never left Panguitch. I was just lucky that Clem, who would be such a marvelous husband for me, was from one of the few families in town I wasn't related to!"

From the time she was a small, pert, pretty schoolgirl, Irene knew that she wanted to be a teacher. She studied for degrees in English, music, physical education and business, "so I would always have a job." When she was 20, she was accepted as an English and gym teacher by her home-town school system. At Panguitch High School, Irene would eventually teach all her brothers and sisters, her own children and most of the town's other young people.

Every summer, Irene took on the job of producing a community pageant. Its theme was always patriotism, and it always featured the flag. "That's the way we are here," she says. "We love our country and we schedule our lives around what's important to it." Mormon policy dictates such involvement. We're honestly more concerned with what news commentators have to say than with movie stars," Irene says.

Love of country peaked during the Second World War. "As each boy was inducted," Irene remembers, "we gave a party for him at the social hall. The next morning, everyone in town went to the bus to see him off."

Panguitch boys, including Clem, served all over the world. "One was a bombardier," she recalls, "one a tail gunner. One was in Spain and toured the castles of the Inquisition." When each one came home on furlough, Irene invited him to school to talk about what he'd seen and done. "But not all of them came back," she says. "We lost our share." (Actually, they lost more than their share. According to a town history, Panguitch's casualties, per population, were the heaviest in the state.)

Everyone in town was listening to the radio when the atomic bomb was dropped on Hiroshima. They were listening, too, three days later, when the second bomb was dropped on Nagasaki. The devastation was so great, so total, the town sensed instantly that victory had been won. "Now," Irene remembers thinking, "our boys can come home. No more will be lost."

Her first inkling of the hideous after-effects of the bomb came by way of a literary masterpiece. A year after Hiroshima, John Hersey published his classic account of events of that historic day. When his book, *Hiroshima*, appeared, Irene, a conscientious English teacher, ordered it from the library and, for three days, read it aloud to her juniors and seniors. Passages from it remain in her mind to this day.

"He wrote about how the bomb was silent," she recalls, "how you didn't hear it drop." She remembers the vivid picture of "point zero," where the bomb hit. She was particularly struck, and so were her students, with Hersey's descriptions of radiation poisoning. "I could think of nothing else," she says, "except how terrible it would be to live through."

And then the boys came home, and life resumed its normal flow.

When the United States government began testing atomic bombs on Bikini Island, in the South Pacific, Irene read about it. Later she remembers reading that those tests had become too expensive and that further tests would take place within the U.S., on the large, flat, sparsely populated Nevada desert, in what looked on a map like the middle of nowhere.

January 27, 1951, the day of the first official mainland atomic test, dawned cold. Farther down the mountains, the people went out and sat on the hillsides to watch history being made. But up high in Panguitch, where it was too chilly to sit outside at 5 A.M., Irene gathered her family and a group of students in front of her living room window for the event. "There were no leaves on the trees," she remembers, "so we had an unobstructed view. I thought how wonderful it was that we could sit in Utah and see what was going on in Nevada. I couldn't wait to get to school to tell those who didn't get up to watch what they'd missed."

It came up like an orange mushroom, then turned white on the edges as it spread. Irene and her friends saw it dissipate into the air. It floated out and out.

There was nothing else. Nothing you could see, or feel, or smell, or hear. The next morning, Clem's brother-in-law came to visit with a new "toy" he had acquired for rock hunting. It was a Geiger counter. Standing on the McEwen's porch, he flipped it on and watched the needle jump to the far edge of the gauge. "See," he said, "we've got radiation here. That's how you can tell."

Still, no one added it up. There was, simply, trust.

During those years, Irene was occupied with work, family and church. Her parents lived in the house next door. Her daughter, Melanie, and son, Clem Jr., were bright, active children. As the town grew, her husband built and managed motels. Theirs was a full life.

Once she made a routine visit to the town doctor and learned from him that lately he'd been seeing an unusual number of miscarriages. She thought it odd, but dismissed it.

Then, a year and a half after the first tests, something strange began to happen to the men of Panguitch—those strong, healthy outdoorsmen who herded sheep and cut wood, who drank the clear water and breathed mountain air. They began to get sick. And what they were getting sick with was cancer.

The first case, in August 1952, was the McEwen's neighbor across the street. He had never in his life been out of Panguitch. As he slowly sickened and then died, his sons took sick, too. "There were five cases of cancer in that family," Irene recalls. "We couldn't understand it." Later Clem's brother-in-law developed cancer. "He died a horrible death, inch by inch," Irene says.

Mormons keep detailed family histories. The dates and circumstances of births, deaths and important events are call carefully recorded. As the town's English teacher, Irene was charged with the task of proofreading those histories. It was this that made her realize that what was happening was without precedent. There was no history of cancer in Panguitch's families. "Our ancestors died of other things," she observes, "diabetes, strokes, rup- tured appendices. Women used to die in childbirth, and children of pneumonia. And some folks died of snakebite. But by and large, we were a healthy people. We just didn't have cancer."

Indeed, because Mormons have traditionally had a far lower rate of cancer than the general population, their life-style has long been studied for clues to cancer prevention. They do not smoke or drink or ingest other unhealthy chemicals. They have a low-stress environment and eat a balanced diet.

In addition to the health histories Irene had an even more dramatic look at what was happening in her town. As the community musician, she played the church organ for all funerals. At Mormon funerals, friends tell stories about the life of the deceased. The cause of death is announced. Irene heard the same story, again and again.

And then the epidemic struck home.

Irene and Clem were standing on her parents' porch one day in 1964, when Clem remarked to Irene's father that he had a sore on his tongue that had bothered him for a week. "You must go for help immediately," Mr. Houston said, and picked up the phone to make arrangements. During a long, hot trip across the Nevada desert, Clem and Irene talked about other men they knew who had developed throat cancer. Some were dead. Several others had lost their voices. Clem was lucky. Surgery took half his tongue, but he recovered and after months of arduous therapy, he learned to speak clearly again.

Irene had only begun to recover from that scare when she began hearing tragic tales about her girls, the beautiful, proud, strong girls of the Panguitch Drum and Bugle Corps.

At around the time the atomic testing had begun, a state law had made physical education mandatory for all students. Irene, who was teaching girls' gym at the time, found herself with a huge class. Since the boys' class had expanded too, there wasn't enough room inside the school to accommodate both groups. The solution was to take turns indoors and out. In order to find something for the girls to do, Irene organized a drum and bugle corps. But since the schoolyard had not yet been landscaped, maneuvers had to be held on the surrounding streets. It was there that Irene led her girls through their paces, not only during the regular gym periods, but early in the morning before school opened.

Money for bugles, drums, cymbals, batons, flags and music was contributed by the Lion's Club. "But the girls," Irene remembers, "furnished the blue and white satin for the uniforms. Three of the mothers sewed them. I'll never forget how they stood them all up in a line and pin-tucked the hems so they'd be exactly the same length."

They got so good that they entered contests and even traveled to Provo to take part in parades. "It was an exciting time," Irene remembers. Still, she felt a vague unease. She could not shake her memories of John Hersey's words. The effects of radiation, he had said, could be experienced 250 miles from the center of the bomb blast. The Nevada test site was 150 miles from Panguitch. On the mornings when the bomb went off, Irene worried about taking her girls outside. She remembers one occasion in particular: "I went into our principal's office and asked him, 'Do we have to go outside today?' He said, 'Well, it's the boys' turn inside. Where would you go? And what's wrong?' I felt almost silly when I said, 'They detonated a bomb this morning.' He was very supportive, very understanding. He said, 'I'll go with you to show you there isn't anything to worry about.' "

Looking back, Irene shudders at the memory. By the end of 1955, the principal was dead from cancer. "He was such a good guy," Irene says. "A wonderful man. I'll always remember him."

Later, the boys basketball coach also developed cancer and died.

By that time, most of the young men of the drum and bugle corps had married and started families. When the first of her girls died, Irene was deeply shocked. Then, she heard about another cancer case. Then another. One day, in 1975, a cancer screening clinic for women was announced in church. Just that morning, Irene had discovered a lump in her breast.

She remembers attending the clinic in the basement of the church. Women of the town in paper dresses. Afterwards, women crying. She remembers the cheerful, smiling face of Rama Yardley, one of the stalwarts of the Corps. By then, Rama was married, a mother. "She was blonde, very attractive," Irene says. "A capable, efficient person. She had just been told she had cancer, but that day, she was her usual optimistic self."

Within five years, Rama would be dead.

Irene herself took the advice of the clinic's doctor and went immediately to Salt Lake City, where she had a radical mastectomy. Afterward she could no longer play the piano; but she managed, once more, to play hymns on the organ. That Christmas, Clem surprised her with an organ just like the one in church.

There continued to be excessive demand for her playing. The president of a nearby college, who was the son of a highly admired local historian, died of leukemia. The doctor's wife succumbed to liver cancer. Another Drum and Bugle girl learned she had it.

In a drive around town, Irene illustrates the overwhelming cumulative effect of all this. "There isn't a block where it hasn't hit," she says, pointing. House after house, street after street. Over and over again. "It strikes—and keeps on striking," she says.

Last year, in 1982, Irene's brother had part of his intestines removed.

Clem's uncle is battling cancer now, undergoing long, debilitating treatments in Las Vegas.

There is no doubt now about what is causing it, and the courts are clogged with lawsuits. One set of suits concerns servicemen involved in the bombings and the tests. Another covers ranchers whose sheep died by the thousands from throat cancer as a result of the radiation.

Although not litigious, the McEwens have joined hundreds of other Utah residents in a lawsuit which they hope will bring the problem to public attention. They have little optimism, however, that much will change.

True, the tests have now been moved underground, but Clem and Irene are not reassured. Says she, "Now the question is, how much radiation is being released underground and seeping into the earth? How fast is it traveling?"

When maroon clouds gather over St. George, where Melanie and Clem, Jr., live with their families, and where the senior McEwens now spend their winters, Irene says, "We go out and gather the little ones in like a bunch of old settin' hens. All up and down the valley, mothers now bring in the children whenever the air looks bad."

But she bridles at the suggestion that they move away from Utah. "Our roots are here," she says. "This is our heritage, the land of our fathers. Our grandparents died for our right to be here, to live in peace and worship God the way we wanted to." Patriotism tangles her tongue as she adds, "I never dreamed that our government would do this to its own. It shreds you on the inside to realize that it not only did, but continues to do it."

Irene keeps a file, for the use of her family, of the best treatment centers for different kinds of cancer. And she tries not to worry.

When she lets herself think about the young casualties, Irene weeps first for Edna Beth Talbott.

Edna Beth was president of her seventh grade class, and one of Irene's favorites. She married another of Irene's students. When she was 27 and pregnant with her fourth child, she was told she had lung cancer. One day she came over to Irene's house and told her that 10 doctors had been called in as consultants on her case. Five had recommended an abortion; five had recommended against it. Edna Beth was left with the decision.

"My baby has the right to live," she told Irene. As the tortured young woman spoke, Irene remembers thinking, "She's telling me this because she can't face telling her own mother." Then, with a shock, the truth struck her: Edna Beth was telling her the story so that Irene could tell it at her funeral.

Edna Beth gave birth to a baby, a girl named Stormy. Then she died.

"If people could see what I saw that day at the church when they brought her casket down the aisle, with her young husband following it, those three little children hanging to his knees, that tiny baby he was carrying, that heartbroken mother and father . . . it was the saddest sight I've ever seen."

Irene *did* tell Edna Beth's story at her funeral. She astonished herself that she could remain composed. "But then," she says, "when they lowered her body into the grave, I collapsed." Since Edna Beth died in 1975, both her parents have developed cancer.

Neither Clem nor Irene likes, or wants, to come across a "cancer cripple." Indeed, they both appear healthy, vibrant and alive. Still, they live under a cloud. It casts a shadow on their lives and the lives of everyone they love. Their Melanie is pregnant now. They are all praying. Each pregnancy is a gamble; each normal birth, a triumph.

Irene knows that people in other parts of the country are beginning to be afraid of nuclear devastation. She has heard them speculate that in another war, it could reach America.

She wants them to know that it not only could. It has.

The first five paragraphs are a species of summary lead. They set the locale, introduce Irene, who will be the spokesperson and symbol of the town, establish the conflict—man against death—and set the quiet, almost elegaic, tone of the piece and the initial innocence of the people. The last two sentences state the threat and thus start the suspense that keeps you reading.

Remsberg sketches the town's characteristics, which will make the coming tragedy more poignant: "the good life, the warmth of church, family activities"; Irene even marries the boy next door. Remsberg tells us enough about Irene's actions and goals to make her real and important to us. Irene, and the whole village, represent the traditional values of the American small town, so we realize the story is not just about one isolated group of people, but about all of us.

Then Remsburg emphasizes the people's love of country—"we schedule our lives around what's important to it"—and this is verified by the sacrifices they make for it during World War II. It is important to show this, for it is this patriotism that will be the foil for the government's actions that produce the tragedy. This section ends with the irony of the promise they saw in the dropping of the first atomic bomb at Hiroshima.

The disillusionment begins with the reading of John Hersey's *Hiroshima;* Irene, perhaps alone in town, realizes its importance enough to read it to her classes. Still, the soldiers come home and life resumes its peaceful ways. And this one-sentence paragraph is another sign of Rems-berg's artistry, for it forms one side of the contrast which make the following sections so powerful.

Quietly, with no polemics, Remsberg tells us that the atomic testing was moved to the mainland because safer testing in the Pacific was "too expensive." And the people greeted the first test as a kind of celebration, an affirmation of their country's power. This ends with the two-sentence paragraph, "There was nothing else. Nothing you could see, or feel, or smell, or hear." What makes these two quiet sentences heavy with omen is the reader's knowledge of the silent death that first test exploded into the air; Remsberg knew this and was artist enough to let us see it and understand it, too.

Then comes the paragraph about the Geiger counter and the almost gleeful, "See, we've got radiation here," as though this gave the isolated town a part in an important national adventure. And this, of course, emphasizes the innocence of the people and the time.

Remsberg creates suspense with the doctor's statement that he had been seeing an unusual number of miscarriages, then builds it with the report of the healthy outdoorsmen who are getting cancer. The paragraph on the Mormon custom of keeping family histories is necessary both to prove to the reader that there is factual support for the unusual incidence of cancer and to explain why Irene would be the most aware of the creeping plague.

Now the disease strikes home and Remsberg reports it by telling the details: Clem's tongue cancer, the cases of the girls in the Drum and Bugle Corps. To help the reader understand how heavily this plague has hit, it is necessary to describe the town's involvement with the Corps; a detail like standing the girls in a line and pinning their skirts so all will be the same length makes the picture come alive. The anecdote about the principal overcoming Irene's objections to taking the girls outside particularizes the threat, then drives it home with "by the end of 1955 the principal was dead from cancer."

Now Remsberg begins to build the action by reporting the increasing number of deaths and including the lump in Irene's own breast. One dramatic device that Remsberg uses several times here is ending a para-graph, or an anecdote, with a blockbuster statement. Rama Yardley, for example: "she was her usual optimistic self" is followed immediately by "Within five years, Rama would be dead." Note, too, that in such cases Remsberg uses no adjectives; her prose is simple, factual. This unques-tionably heightens its impact; the emotional content of the statement is so strong that any attempt to heighten it with dramatic language would be too much and the statement would lose effectiveness.

Then Remsberg summarizes the devastating effects of the epidemic and builds the suspense with the paragraph describing the drive around town. Note how much more effective this description of people doing something is, than would be a simple statement of the statistics of the deaths.

Honest journalism requires that Remsberg report the growing lawsuits against the government, even though this fact undercuts the mood of patriotism and innocence that she has been building. She ascribes it to the townspeople's hope that it "will bring the problem to public attention"—which some may find questionable. And, knowing what her ending is going to be, Remsberg has a loose end to clear up: the tests have moved underground, but Clem and Irene are not reassured.

Then comes the only direct attack by Irene on the government which has allowed this tragedy to hit: "I never dreamed that our government would do this to its own." Even this is muted, and probably more effective because of it.

Remsberg presents the climax of her story with the account of Edna Beth. Because it is the climax, she must go into some detail about the relationship between Irene and Edna Beth, such as the talk they had about Edna Beth's possible abortion and the description of her funeral.

Remsberg has now all but completed her story; there remains the need to mention what the future will likely bring and to emphasize the significance of this little story by showing the broader picture. She does it with the next-to-last paragraph. Then she writes the final two sentences, which are clearly Remsberg speaking, but, consistent with the focus of the entire piece on Irene, she attributes the sentiment to her. The restraint of these two sentences unquestionably heightens their impact.

13

What Does It Look Like? How Does It Smell?

Salina, Kan.—The short, winding streets of Schilling Manor are silent in the early darkness of an autumn evening.

Homework and the chill prairie wind have imprisoned the children in the neat, one-story duplexes and small single-family homes of the development two miles west of Salina. But everywhere are reminders of their presence—an overturned tricycle silhouetted in the gathering gloom, a forgotten football nestled in a patch of brown lawn.

Dinner time is near and the lights of the tiny community are beacons of warmth and welcome. But inside the homes, the women fussing in kitchens, setting tables, urging grimy youngsters to try soap on their hands this time, have tired eyes.

Not the ordinary workaday tired eyes of too much housework, too active children and a fallen cake in the oven. The tired eyes of absence, responsibility and frequently of a fear painfully unspoken.

For in the streets of Schilling Manor there is no rush of weary husband traffic. And in the houses there is no before-dinner moment for unburdening math problems and football furstrations, no martini ritual to soothe household anxieties. The husbands of Schilling Manor are career servicemen and they are gone—most of them to Vietnam. (Douglas E. Kneeland, "Lonely G.I. Wives," *New York Times*)

*H*ere Kneeland brings his scene and his people alive by using specific details: "an overturned tricycle silhouetted in the gathering gloom," "women fussing in kitchens, setting tables," "and a fallen cake in the over." The mood is one of quiet and desperation.

Other writers have set similiar scenes many times, but this has a uniqueness that makes it stand out for the reader as something new. And that's what every writer is after when putting together a description. For there really is almost nothing that hasn't been written about before, yet creative writers are constantly presenting us with scenes and people that seem new. They do it by giving us the particular and significant details of the particular place or person. And it works because, while few situations are new, *this* situation of *this* person has some qualities that are individual and unique.

To accomplish this happy result, writers must train themselves to observe. Simple? Not so simple. The average person doesn't see a room, a landscape, a meeting, a person with much attention to detail. Unless we train ourselves to do otherwise, we get an overall impression of color, shapes, dominant emotions, an aura that serves very well for normal purposes. But as writers we must do more; we have to be able to re-create the scene for our readers, which means we must experience its overall impression, then go on to analyze it and make notes of those details that distinguish this scene or action from all others.

You do it by focusing down on details of a scene, then trying, while you're looking at them, to put together the precise words that will convey their unique flavor. For example, once I was walking around the backyard of my house in the snow while trying to think through the organization of an article. I wasn't seeing much; my mind was turned inward, wrestling with the problem. I stopped before a large azalea bush, looking at it but not seeing it. Suddenly a film seemed to drop from my eyes (I think it was really the mind's old trick of finding anything at all to interrupt hard work), and I began to see the bush. I saw that each branch ended in a little cluster of four or five twigs, and caught within their black prongs was a tiny cone of snow. The whole bush was a skeleton globe decorated with the little cones, like the whipped cream rosettes on a birthday cake. Not an earth-shaking perception, of course, but merely another of those realized pictures that a writer constantly files away to pull out and use sometime. Like now.

It seems to us that writing, which for the reader seems to flow so smoothly and fast, is the laborious putting on paper of these thousands of perceptions that have been built up one by one over the years, that a writer is working twenty-four hours a day, perceiving, analyzing, putting into words, filing away bits of reality like this. We learn to do it by doing it. And the only initial step it takes, we think, is to make an adjustment in your mind so that you not only look at things, you see them and tell yourself what they look like—or sound, or smell, or taste or feel like.

This is both the curse and the blessing of writers. A curse because once you get your mind trained to do it, it never stops and there's always a cool, detached little figure sitting up there in the back of your mind with a notebook taking down what you are experiencing. He never stops and the price you pay for him is that you never again become involved in an experience wholly, with nothing held back. The blessing is that, with the scales gone from your eyes, you perceive in vivid colors the richness and variety of the world each of us rents for a lifetime.

Writers share this ability with visual artists. His canvas before him, the painter wants to re-create the sky and water before him. The water, of course, is blue—or green or black or silver. Suppose it is blue, what color blue? What colors will he choose from his palette to reproduce the precise blue of the water? To decide he must analyze and experiment: a little cerulean blue, some white, a touch of green perhaps, some umber? When you see the finished picture you get little shock of recognition—yes, that's it, that's it—but you never know the thought and trial and failure that has gone into it.

How do you get started on the process? Well, what words would you use to describe the cry of a sea gull? Shrill? Raucous? Lonely? Strident? Happy? Angry? Resonant—with a feeling of space? Or what does a new car smell like? Exciting? Oil? Plastic? Spicy? Leather? Rubber? Paint? A combination of which of these? You can spend ten or fifteen minutes thinking about each of these, refining out the precise words that recreate the feeling you get from the experience. And this is precisely what a writer does in describing something. The description you read in five seconds probably took the writer an hour to get on paper.

Here, for example, is a description of an animal with which we are all familiar, but which we see anew through the eyes of the writer, Alexander Theroux, whose article "How Curious the Camel," appeared in *Reader's Digest.*

A camel has been described as a horse planned by committee. It has a comic munch of a face—loony, serene and disgusted all at once—with liquid eyes that shine bottle-green at night. Its eyelashes are as long as Ann Sheridan's. Its large nostrils can close against blowing sand. A ruminant, it chews its cud, and its floppy lips, seemingly insensitive to thorny plants, cover teeth long enough to eat an apple through a picket fence. You can almost chin yourself on its bad breath.

It is a large creature, reaching lengths of ten feet and standing about seven feet at the shoulder. Its smooth padfeet, each with two toes united at the sole by a web of skin, serve long, pistonlike legs able to gallop at up to 15 m.p.h. (though it much prefers to walk). It can live 40 years, spits, can travel untold miles of waterless desert. Its stomach contains a wet cud—the half-chewed slop that the animal sucks back up to its mouth with a slobbering sound as it plods along, all the while gurgling as if to remind the rider of the liquid inside its body.

There's another dimension to this business, though. The details you see and choose to write must be not only true, but significant. They must convey more in perception or emotion than they do in words. In *The Content of Writing*, Richard B. Sewall of Yale has an apt illustration—"the tailored woman down for the weekend from Smith, who forgot to clean her fingernails."

Here's another example, from "Country Boy Makes Pretty Good," a profile of Tom Brokaw written by Lynn Darling for *Esquire*.

> Yankton, South Dakota, lies on a bluff overlooking the Missouri River, a low-slung town of pickup trucks parked diagonally on broad empty streets, a place where both the Sunday morning sermon and the Saturday night saloon can count on collecting a crowd. The former territorial capital of the Dakotas, Yankton was the last stop on the riverboats' run, a jumping-off point, a town that understood the language of the last chance. It was also the place where outlaw Jack McCall was hanged for shooting Wild Bill Hickok, but that was as hot as it ever got here in Tom Brokaw's hometown.

In just over 100 words, Darling has taken her readers to Brokaw's hometown, and let them see and feel what it is like to be there. We see this "low-slung town of pickup trucks parked diagonally on broad empty streets" where "both the Sunday morning sermon and the Saturday night saloon" draw crowds—and presumably nothing else does for the rest of the week.

In his article on Ralph Nader, the lead of which is reproduced in chapter 10, Ken Auletta used different types of details to show Nader's austere style of living.

> One sees Nader's persistence in his shoes. They are low-cut black Army dress shoes with worn, slanted heels. When he served as a cook in the Army in 1959, Nader says, he purchased twelve pairs of low-cuts for six dollars apiece at the PX. He now wears the eleventh pair, and he says that to buy new heels would cost more than he paid for the shoes. Nader has not purchased a pair of dress shoes since, and he boasts of the one new pair waiting in the closet of his one-room efficiency apartment in

Washington, just off Dupont Circle. Nor has Nader purchased a pair of socks since selecting four dozen calf-length cotton-and-wool socks for thirty-five cents a pair at the PX. "I only regret that I didn't buy two dozen more," he says.

Auletta obviously obtained much of that material from an interview, but his reporter's attentiveness to detail was what made him ask Nader about the shoes in the first place. It also enabled him to write the following:

Recently, Nader accepted a tuna fish sandwich only after quizzing the activist who picked him up at the Boston airport, "Is this today's tuna?"; he grilled two different students about whether the grape punch served at Salem State College was real grape; at Oswego, he was thirsty but would not allow the red punch to touch his lips, wondered why the fish served at dinner was fried, and was shocked that anyone would touch the roast beef, saying, "Did you see how red that meat was?" Although Nader can laugh at himself, he says he eats only 14 pounds of red meat a year, can tell you how many teaspoons of sugar are in a can of Coke (nine), and has in the past referred to cigarette smokers as being "weak" in character.

While Auletta is describing behavior, rather than a town or a street, he uses the same techniques as the writers whose work we looked at above. (We'll have more to say about bringing characters to life in chapter 15.)

It's selection again. You make note of the details of the experience, then select those that evoke a common experience or present a larger reality. Perceiving the hidden glories and understanding the larger realities of a situation are what add depth to a writer's work—and, not at all incidentally, to his or her life.

One Memorial Day weekend a friend asked me to crew on his magnificent Herreshoff sloop in a race from Larchmont, around Block Island, and back. It was a slow, man-killer of a race. The breeze was so slight that you had to adjust the sails constantly, repeatedly take down one jib and put up another to catch each cupful of wind; twice we had to anchor to keep from going backward in a foul tide. In the first night and day we got virtually no sleep.

By the second night we had been becalmed off Montauk Point for nine hours. I caught a couple of hour's sleep below and came on deck to relieve the skipper at the helm at about 3 A.M. He sat in the cockpit with me for

ten or fifteen minutes, then went below for some sleep, and I was alone
with the ship.

I was cold. It was the first of June, and I was wearing woolen socks,
chinos, foul-weather pants, a Swedish fisherman's shirt, a woolen shirt, a
sweater, foul-weather jacket, wool cap and gloves; I stood behind the
wheel and shivered.

I was lonely. The sea is an alien place, not warm like the land, but cold,
impersonal, heaving with massive power, and in its depths lurks terror.
There was not another boat in sight, and the only light symbolizing other
humans was the automatic aero beacon on Block Island that swept the sky
in ominous mechanical exactness and made me think of *Wuthering
Heights*.

I was scared. I'd managed to get the boat moving on a drift of air out of
the northeast, but I wasn't sure where I was going. The light on the
binnacle was so dim and the compass card so yellow that I couldn't read it
as I stood behind the wheel. I was coming up on Block Island but didn't
know exactly where it was. I'd sailed enough to know there's a loom off the
land that makes a line in the water, but it isn't the shoreline. Many a man
has sailed his boat up onto the beach—or the rocks—deceived by that
line. I was not at all anxious to do this, because the skipper didn't think
much more of the boat than he did of his right arm, and because there
were five people below, sleeping in trust of me.

It went on like that for almost three hours. Then the light began in the
east and after a while the tip of the sun came up out of the ocean off the
starboard bow. And suddenly I could see Block Island and knew where I
was. Off to the north were three or four other boats, warm with company.
And the sun began to warm me. A little later, when I was relieved, I was
so grateful I went forward, stripped to the waist, and rolled in the sunlight
like a cat.

Weeks later, thinking about it, I suddenly knew how primitive humans
must have felt when the rising sun drove off the terrors of the night. And I
knew why sun worship played a part in so many religions. I understood
why the rising of the sun was the miracle of creation.

Much better writers than this one have used their awareness of larger
realities to add dimension to their description. Bruce Catton, for instance,
in *A Stillness at Appomattox:*

> It was the fourth day of May, and beyond the dark river there was a
> forest with the shadow of death under its low branches and the dogwood
> blossoms were floating in the air like lost flecks of sunlight, as if life were
> as important as death; and for the Army of the Potomac this was the last

bright morning, with youth and strength and hope ranked under starred flags, bugle calls riding down the wind, and invisible doors swinging open on the other shore. The regiments fell into line, and great white-topped wagons creaked along the roads, and the spring sunlight glinted off the polished muskets and the brass of the guns, and the young men came down to the valley while the bands played. A German regiment was singing "John Brown's Body."

Beside the roads the violets were in bloom, and the bush honeysuckle was out, and the day and the year had a fragile light that the endless columns would soon trample to fragments. The last campaign had begun, and a staff officer sat on a bank overlooking the Rapidan and had a curious thought: how odd it would be if every man who was to die in the days just ahead had to wear a big badge today, so that a man watching by the river could identify all those who were never coming back!

Even historians, writing nearly a hundred years after the event, by using acute observation, careful selection, and an understanding of larger realities, can write a description that lets you *be* there.

14

Mobilizing the Reader's Experience

*E*ven back in the days of "just the facts" journalism there were emotional writers. They were called sob sisters—but many were men—and they slapped it on with a shovel. Other reporters, smug in their rationalism, scorned them. But particularly in the innocence of the twenties and in the more garish tabloids, they were stars in the eyes of the circulation manager. They dealt mostly in primary emotions: sexual titillation; pity; maudlin sentimentality; bathos. There are still a few of them around in the more backward newspapers.

But even while they were still the darlings of those editors who hadn't changed their judgment of news values in half a century, the slow evolution of more sophisticated interpretive writers was showing them their age. Today the best creative journalists evoke the emotions of their readers with the deftness of a Tolstoy.

It was inevitable. Emotions play far too large a part in all our lives to be ignored, as they were by journalistic devotees of the age of reason. The mass of people perceive things far more convincingly with their emotions than with their minds, and no serious journalist could afford to ignore this weapon in the arsenal of communication. As Freya Stark said, the whole generalship of writing is in the marshalling of the reader's reserves of understanding and experience.

If you want to get philosophical about it, this development is probably the journalist's application of the ideas of existentialism. Perhaps it started with a theory that Hemingway developed in his early days in Paris. In *A Moveable Feast* he wrote: "It was a very simple story called 'Out of Season' and I had omitted the real end of it which was that the old man hanged himself. This was omitted on my new theory that you could omit anything if you knew what you omitted and the omitted part would strengthen the story and make people feel something more than they understood."

When he developed this theory he was writing a story called "Big Two-hearted River." It was about a man who takes a camping-fishing trip alone in Michigan, and he is obsessed that everything he does must be done exactly right. So you know he is trying to put some structure back into his life after some experience which has shaken him to the core. Of it, Hemingway wrote, "The story was about coming back from the war but there was no mention of the war in it." I had thought the cataclysm that had struck the man was a divorce; war never occurred to me. Thus I drew on my own feelings for an understanding of the situation, and to me the man's motivation was just as valid as the one Hemingway had in mind. This is the deepest kind of involvement by the reader, and it's what Marshall McLuhan meant when he called writing a "cool" medium.

So what has all this to do with existentialism? Webster says existentialism "regards human existence as not exhaustively describable or understandable in idealistic or scientific terms . . ." So if you can't describe human existence in scientific (read rational) terms, you convey understanding by reporting the human situation as it happened, with close attention to those aspects of it that will trigger emotional responses in your reader.

It is artistry, of course, that enables a writer to select and present the kind of material that will evoke an emotional response by the reader. But we think there are some identifiable techniques, too. One of them, surprisingly enough, is cool objectivity.

The *New York Times* uses this repeatedly when it reports, each year, its "100 Neediest Cases."

Eleanor C. is only 18, but for almost a year she has struggled single-handed to make a home for her brothers—Eric, 14, Johnny, 12, and Tommy, 9.

Two years ago the children's mother died of cancer. Last January, when their father died of a kidney ailment, Eleanor, a high school senior, immediately left school, determined to keep the family together. But she found it difficult to budget her father's veteran's benefits, and the unfamiliar household tasks were overwhelming. The boys, grieving for their parents, became unmanageable. Recently, despairing of her ability to keep going, Eleanor sought help from the agency.

An agency homemaker is now bringing order and stability into the home, and Eleanor, relieved of some of her burden, plans to complete her schooling and seek a secretarial job. A "Big Brother" has been assigned to Tommy, who seems most affected by his father's death. In the year ahead, Eleanor will need continued guidance in her valiant struggle to keep her orphaned brothers together.

There are really only two "emotional" adjectives in the piece: "valiant" and "orphaned," in the last sentence.

It seems to us that when you're dealing with material that has as much emotional dynamite as this, the impact is heightened by this kind of objective writing. If you tried to build up the effect with more adjectives and adverbs, you'd run the risk of becoming maudlin.

The strength such starkness creates was shown by a recent *Times* article by Andrew H. Malcolm. It began:

ROCHESTER—When the 69-year-old man entered the hospital here recently he thought he had only a back problem. When he left for home six days later he had chosen to die.

In between, he learned he had a fatal illness and had to make the decision confronting a growing number of aging Americans: whether to prolong his life aggressively with medical machines and modern technology or surrender to the natural dying process very soon. The patient—call him Robert Anderson, although that is not his real name— chose to give up.

'I Want to Go Home'

"I want to go home," he told Dr. Richard B. Freeman, a specialist he had met only recently.

Dr. Freeman leaned over the bed and asked, "You understand what this decision means?"

Mr. Anderson nodded, and then smiled. Dr. Freeman patted his patient's hands. And in a moment the two said farewell.

Notice the simplicity and starkness of Malcolm's prose, and the power it gives to the anecdote. A less-skilled writer might have loaded that section with adjectives and adverbs in an attempt to be sure that the reader got the point. But Malcolm knew that the story of a man's decision to die was powerful, and that the more simply it was told, the greater its effect would be.

He uses this stark writing style later in the piece, when he describes the meeting during which Dr. Freeman told Anderson that he had cancer. Malcolm is convinced that the doctor is a caring and concerned man, but again, Malcolm lets the doctor's actions prove the point.

Dr. Freeman had a cup of coffee before entering the patient's room that Wednesday morning, five days after meeting Mr. Anderson. "Hello," Dr. Freeman said, "How're you feeling?"

"I'm not off to a very good start today," said a pale Mr. Anderson. "My bones hurt a lot."

"Uh, huh," said the doctor. "Well, you've been poked and probed a good deal here."

"You'll have to speak up," said the patient. "My wife's hard of hearing—and so am I."

"That's right," said Mrs. Anderson. "Don't blame it all on me." And the trio chuckled.

Careful Choice of Words

Dr. Freeman raised the volume of his voice a notch. "I'll be as straightforward and honest as possible with you," he said. "You said you wanted that. I have a feeling you already know what's going on in your body, but let me tell you what we know and you can begin to think about what we do next."

The doctor chose his words carefully, using pauses and firm gazes to emphasize the seriousness of his words. He outlined Mr. Anderson's medical history, the back operation and the lethal calcium problem.

"Now, why did this happen?" asked the doctor. "There are many holes in your bones. Some of your ribs are broken. There are lumps on your kidneys and bladder and lungs. These are tumors. And they're spreading. You kind of thought that, didn't you?"

Mr. Anderson nodded.

"Can we do anything?" the doctor continued. "Maybe. We don't know yet what kind of tumors these are. There are hundreds of kinds. A few respond to treatment. Some go away." He paused. "Others we can't do much about."

He paused again. "We'll be very honest with you about the outlook," he went on. "But I won't have all the information for a day or so. Any questions?"

"No."

"You knew it?"

"Yup. Keep right on it, Doc."

"I will, but—are you a football fan?—well, it's fourth down, Mr. Anderson."

"Thank you very much, doctor."

"I don't know," the doctor said softly, "if 'thank you' is the right thing to say."

"What did you say, Doc?"

"Nothing," said Dr. Freeman, "I'll be back later."

Notes on a Chart

On the patient's chart Dr. Freeman noted the conversation and added: "Family and patient still have some hope. Pls do not give final negative prognosis yet. Perhaps tonite or tmw."

Again, Malcolm understands the power of his material. The writer who has a good story to tell should tell it simply. He needn't comment on it. The reader will get the point and feel the emotions if the story is told well, as this one was, from the beginning to the ending, which follows.

That evening when Dr. Freeman returned to Mr. Anderson's room to continue the grim prognosis, the patient was dozing. "Oh, good morning, doctor," said a glazed Mr. Anderson, "How are you today?"

"Nurse," said Dr. Freeman, "what have you got him on?" The answer was morphine; his pain had been too great. "So much for rational discussion this evening," said the doctor.

'The Two-Minute Warning'

The next morning Mr. Anderson was alert. "I've talked to the oncologist," the doctor said. "We can only treat some of this pain with radiation. That will raise the calcium. And then we can clean your blood every couple of days with an artificial kidney. But you might find this a miserable prolongation of things. I'm afraid things are not going to improve. The outlook is, uh, well, the two-minute warning is in."

"I understand," said the man. "We've talked about it. And I want to go home. I appreciate everything you all have done. It's been the greatest care in the world."

"I wish I could do more," said the doctor.

"Me too," said the man, smiling. "It's a very poor deal. But I'll try to put some more points on the board."

"I'm sure you will." And the doctor kissed the man's forehead.

"I'm sure I'll see you again," said the patient. But the doctor did not respond.

Outside the room he spoke to Mrs. Anderson. "I don't want to give you any false hopes," he said. "We're talking a few days to a week."

"I thought so," she said.

After arranging the immediate transfer back to the rural hospital and consulting Mr. Anderson's doctor there, a grim Dr. Freeman walked down the hall past some laughing visitors. "I don't know what's right," he said. "I just do my best."

That was Thursday noon. Sunday morning at the rural hospital, about three hours before dawn, Mr. Anderson's heart stopped. He and his wife had agreed to a Do Not Resuscitate order. When the alarm sounded, the nurses did nothing.

The death certificate said Robert Anderson died of "cardiopulmonary arrest."

The same kind of starkness was used with great effect by J. Anthony Lukas in his famous piece in the *New York Times*, "The Two Worlds of Linda Fitzpatrick." (The article is expanded and reprinted in Lukas's book, *Don't Shoot—We Are Your Children!*)

The underlying theme of Lukas's piece is that Linda Fitzpatrick's parents knew nothing at all about her "other" life, which included "crash pads, acid trips, freaking out, psychedelic art, witches and warlocks," and which ultimately led to her murder. For example, Lukas described the Fitzpatricks' decision to allow Linda to leave their luxurious Greenwich, Connecticut, home and live in Greenwich Village:

"She told us she was going to live at the Village Plaza Hotel, a very nice hotel on Washington Place, near the university, you know," her mother said.

" 'I'll be perfectly safe, mother,' she kept saying. 'It's a perfectly nice place with a doorman and a television.' She said she'd be rooming with a girl named Paula Bush, a 22-year-old receptionist from a good family. That made us feel a lot better."

The Village Plaza, 79 Washington Place, has no doorman. A flaking sign by the tiny reception desk announces "Television for rental" amidst a forest of other signs: "No Refunds," "All Rents Must Be Paid in Advance," "No Checks Cashed," "No Outgoing Calls for Transients."

"Sure I remember Linda," said the stooped desk clerk. "But Paula Bush? There wasn't no Paula Bush. It was Paul Bush."

Ruffling through a pile of stained and thumb-marked cards, he came up with one that had Linda Fitzpatrick's name inked at the top in neat Greenwich Country Day School penmanship. Below it in pencil was written: "Paul Bush. Bob Brumberger."

"Yeh," the clerk said. "She moved in here on Sept. 4, Labor Day, with these two hippie guys, Bush and Brumberger. They had Room 504. She paid the full month's rent—$120—in advance. Of course, she had lots of other men up there all the time. Anybody off the street—the dirtiest bearded hippies she could find."

In my files I have a folder labeled "Humility Department"; it contains a dozen or so clippings that I sometimes read over when I begin to feel satisfied with my own work. One of them, from a book entitled *The Last Days of Sevastopol*, by a Russian journalist named Boris J. Voyetekhov, is one of the finest examples I know of delicacy and restraint in handling emotional material.

Sevastopol is on a peninsula sticking out into the Black Sea. In World War II the German armies sealed off the mouth of the peninsula and moved down toward its tip. One detachment of Soviet soldiers was ordered to remain to cover the withdrawal of the wounded "until the last man." A captain, commanding the group, gave Mr. Voyetekhov a letter to his wife; it concluded:

I know that when I am dead, for you I will continue to live, and that nobody will edge me away from your careful heart. I know this wound will never heal. But if it happens that you meet a man fine enough for your grief whom you will love a little, and if as a result of your love you have a new life and it is a son, then let him bear my name. Let him be my continuation, though I am dead and your new friend is alive. This would not punish him, for not everybody must die, and if he cannot understand and would not like it, then leave him without sorrow or tears or longings and let it be not his but our son; and when a new Sevastopol is built, come here, and somewhere on Chersonese, somewhere near the sea, plant poppies. They grow here very well. And that will be my grave. It may be that you will make a mistake. Maybe it won't be I but another who lies there. It doesn't matter. Some one else will think of her own and plant flowers above me. Nobody will be left out, for we shall lie close, and there will be no space to spare where we lie.

15

"Get Some Narrative Into it"

One of the most frequent directions that editors gave me when I was trying to learn to write magazine articles was, "Get some narrative into it." For a long time I couldn't figure out precisely what they meant. After all, my job as a journalist, I thought, was to inform, to explain, to illuminate a set of facts, a situation; what did narrative—telling a story—have to do with this? I wasn't writing fiction, I was reporting fact.

It finally dawned on me what they meant, and when it did I had—though I didn't realize it until long afterward—one of the key differences between interpretive writing and conventional newswriting: you present your information not as disembodied facts or ideas, but in terms of people acting out those facts and ideas. And since you're showing people doing things, your job, if you have any artistry at all, is to arrange it as a story, a narrative. Suppose you want to write a piece saying that millions of Americans don't get enough to eat each day. You do it by writing about the men and women and children who live with hunger and who must struggle to survive. This allows you not only to explain the reasons for the problem, but also to work in the human story of people fighting against almost overwhelming odds. It's the human story that holds your readers' interest because they, too, probably have had to struggle to survive at some point in their lives, and they want to know how somebody else made it—or didn't. They pick up the facts and explanations you've included almost without realizing it.

This has been said before in earlier chapters, but what we haven't explored is the range of techniques that help you do the job. Narrative is one of the things a good interpretive writer borrows from fiction writers. It is telling a story, building suspense, putting your characters (and the reader) into a situation, and then taking them through it—complete with emotional involvements—to a resolution. It's not changing facts, but arranging them. It is plotting.

The skeleton of a plot goes like this: You introduce a main character, who must be admirable so the reader identifies with him and starts pulling for him. You introduce the element of conflict in your story: you give your character an objective and show him trying to reach that objective and failing. Finally, by his own efforts—usually as a result of a change in himself—he reaches his objective and collects the rewards, or pays the price. Like all skeletons, this is spare and oversimplified, but understanding it both helps you recognize a good story when you hear one, and guides your questioning when you are building a story and interviewing the people who lived the situation.

For example, when I was doing the research on the Commando Kelly piece that we discussed back in chapter 6, I began to see it as the story of a brave man, whose wife and family meant more to him than anything else, struggling to survive in a world he was not very well equipped to cope with. So, applying the formula:

* Kelly, of course, was the main character, which meant the piece had to focus on him throughout.

* I had to show he was admirable, which meant I had to get enough details so, right at the beginning, I could show him winning the Medal of Honor.

* I had to show his dominant characteristic—his love for his family—so I went after incidents and anecdotes that illustrated this.

* I had to show him struggling to preserve his family against odds, which meant I had to go after the details of his jobs, his income (showing why it was not enough to cover expenses), his unemployment and search for another job, his illness and fight against it.

* Finally, I had to show him winning his fight, which in this case meant surviving his illness, getting help to pay his bills, getting a new and better job.

You get this kind of information from interviews, but one of the key concepts of narrative writing is that you don't always present it in exactly the way you got it. For example, I got the details for the lead of the piece—Kelly and his first wife finding out she had terminal cancer—from the only survivor, Kelly himself. But I didn't present it as a long quote from Kelly. Instead, using the details he gave me, I recreated the scene itself so the reader could watch it unfold, instead of getting someone's account of it, secondhand.

In the *New York Times* interview mentioned earlier, Truman Capote told how he did the same sort of thing when he was writing *In Cold Blood:*

On the other hand, in that same first part [of the book], there's a scene between the postmistress and her mother when the mother reports that the ambulances have gone to the Clutter [the murder victims'] house. That's a straight dramatic scene—with quotes, dialogue, action, every-thing. But it evolved out of interviews. . . . Except in this case I took what they had told me and transposed it into straight narrative terms. Of course, elsewhere in the book, very often it's direct observation, events I saw myself—the trial, the executions.

As Capote said, it is possible to achieve great accuracy for purposes of reconstruction by careful and assiduous interviewing. For example, I once did a story for *Redbook* about a man, Earle Reynolds, who thought the testing of atomic bombs in the atmosphere was a threat to the world's children. (The story about the children of Utah in chapter 12 would seem to indicate that he was right. And the continuing protests about nuclear weapons testing would seem to prove a point made earlier, that many magazine stories are, in essence, timeless.) The United States had sched-uled a series of such tests in the western Pacific Ocean and had barred all shipping from the area. Reynolds decided to protest the testing by sailing his boat into the prohibited zone, getting arrested, and thus forcing the whole issue into courts for a ruling.

I wanted to start the piece with the scene of the actual confrontation between Reynolds and his government—the moment of his arrest by the Coast Guard. I had to be able to visualize the scene in order to recon-struct it.

First I went aboard Reynold's boat, the *Phoenix*, and looked it over in detail—size of the cockpit, location of main hatchway to cabin, which bunk each member of the family slept in, location of the radiotelephone, and so forth. Then I borrowed the group interview technique, mentioned in chapter 5, that S. L. A. Marshall had told me about. I got all those who had been aboard the boat that night into Reynold's apartment and spent hours going over with them exactly what had happened, minute by minute. They checked each other; where one's memory of what had happened proved faulty, another would point it out:

"Then I got up and went on deck. . . ."

"No, you didn't; not then. It was later. Because I was at the helm and the first one up was Earle; you came up a minute or two later."

"Oh yes, that's right. I remember now, I was awake, but I didn't get up right away. . . ."

After I had taken the group through the entire scene (as well as what happened in the next few days) I had one side of the story. I needed the other, so I went down to Pearl Harbor and went aboard the Coast Guard buoy tender *Planetree*, which had made the arrest, looked over the ship, and interviewed her captain. Again, I took him through the confrontation minute by minute. Then, having both versions of the same set of actions, I reconstructed the scene:

The first move came at about eleven P.M. when they were 19 days out of Honolulu. Ted Reynolds, a thin, very mature 19-year-old, was on watch. "It was perfect trade wind sailing," he said. "The seas were moderate—about four or five feet high—and *Phoenix* was slipping along beautifully. It was very dark and suddenly off to the southeast I saw a light, the first since Honolulu. I immediately called the skipper."

The skipper, Dr. Earle L. Reynolds, a noted scientist, swung out of his bunk just below the cockpit and came on deck. He flipped on *Phoenix*'s masthead light and he and Ted watched the other light on the horizon. In a few minutes they could make out a green running light, too, so they knew it was a ship and was heading for them. Earle Reynolds went below and called to the ship on the radio, but got no answer. His calling aroused everybody else aboard the 50-foot *Phoenix*—Earle's wife, Barbara, Jessica, their daughter, 14, and Niichi Mikami, a Japanese friend. All crowded into the small cockpit aft and watched the other ship approach. She was the Coast Guard buoy tender *Planetree* returning from a four-month trip into the far Pacific, and her captain, Commander Armand J. Bush, had been ordered to intercept the *Phoenix*.

She came on, looking bigger and more ominous as she approached the little *Phoenix*. She kept coming until she was so close her tall sides cut off the wind from *Phoenix*'s sails, and the little boat became unmanageable, unable to get out of the way. The Reynolds stopped breathing; they knew the heavy steel *Planetree* could crack their boat like a walnut.

Earle Reynolds went back to the radio and called again, "Please talk on the radio." No answer. (Commander Bush told me later he hadn't heard Reynolds. This seems unlikely, and Bush added, "Even if I had heard him I wanted to talk face to face. That way I knew who I was talking to.")

But *Planetree* didn't quite hit the *Phoenix*. Slowly she came to a stop beside and astern the wallowing ketch. Over the noise of the slapping sails, the wash of the seas and the rumble of *Planetree*'s idling engines Bush called, "Are you all right?"

"We're fine, thanks," Reynolds replied.

Bush gave him their position, then gave him the position of the prohibited zone where the U.S. Atomic Energy Commission was testing nuclear bombs. He quoted the AEC regulation forbidding American citizens to enter the zone and said the area ahead was dangerous. Then he asked, "Are you going to enter the zone or go around?"

"Enter," Reynolds called back.

"Where?"

"Fourteen degrees north."

No more was said. The *Planetree* dropped astern for the rest of the night and followed at a distance of three or four miles.

Like many narratives, this story was written on two levels—the intellectual argument against nuclear testing and the human drama of a family risking their lives and freedom to protest a governmental act they believed to be wrong.

In putting the story together it was necessary to work on both levels. For example, in both I had to handle motivation: *why* did they do this? On the intellectual level I did it by reporting that Earle Reynolds, a noted physical anthropologist, had been sent by the National Academy of Sciences to Hiroshima to study the effects of atomic radiation on the growth and development of children; the deleterious effects he found helped explain why he made the protest. On the human level I tried to handle it by concentrating on Reynolds's wife, Barbara. She not only had an active social conscience, she was determined to hold her family together, and if Reynolds was to sail into the forbidden zone, she would go along.

It was also necessary to carry the narrative along on two levels—both climaxing in the decision to make the trip. I tried to handle the "intellectual" by showing Reynolds doing a research study of the effects of testing in the atomsphere, then bringing his findings home each night and talking them over with Barbara and the kids. In the process the case against testing was made by reporting the specific things Reynolds learned. On the "human" level I showed Barbara and Earle arguing out the decision on whether to take the children along on the protest voyage. In the course of the argument the danger becomes clear and suspense grows.

I think I didn't succeed very well. It's difficult to report the drama of a decision that somebody makes because it is an internal process; you have to get inside a person's mind and first understand, then try to show the battle of the pros and cons. Writing about thoughts doesn't make very sensational reading; about the best you can do is try to find actions that reflect the thoughts and write about them. In this case I tried to do it by showing Earle and Barbara talking out the pros and cons. Rereading it later, I saw that it slowed the narrative down and wasn't very convincing.

Another technique you use in narrative is to play it like an accordion. You can't possibly report everything that happened during the time span your story covers. You need to lay certain foundations for the story—like "qualifying" Earle as an expert on radiation effects or explaining Barbara's role. You must tell enough about your characters' backgrounds so readers feel they know them. Much of this material is purely factual and when it is, I think the thing to do is compress it into the shortest possible space. You pack your sentences full; this alone helps give a feeling of pace and movement. For example, in the section on Earle's background, I reported that both his parents were killed when he was in high school so he had to get a job and support himself; but he also took correspondence courses at the University of Chicago in an effort to get a college degree. Then this paragraph:

> One June when he got back his examination paper in a course in anthropology from the University of Chicago, the professor had scribbled on it, "You better come up and see me." That autumn Earle and Barbara arrived in Chicago with no money and a determination to get Earle a degree. The professor helped get him a job on a research project and Barbara, who had graduated from Teacher's College, Columbia University, got a teaching job. This pattern of work and study marked their lives—except for time out for Barbara to have two of their three children (Tim and Ted)—for the next six years while Earle earned his bachelor's degree in anthropology from Chicago, then his master's and doctorate from the University of Wisconsin.

But your readers, I think, won't hold still for too much of this, so you have to get through it quickly, then give them a break by telling a story. And the stories must be given enough space so they can involve the reader's emotions. For example, after the "compression" section on their background, I got into the explanation of the relations—and conflicts—within the family. Because the piece was for *Redbook*, a women's magazine, I concentrated on Barbara. The situation was this: in Hiroshima, Earle had built a boat and decided to fulfill a lifelong dream of sailing around the world. Then this:

> Barbara didn't want to go. She was afraid of the water—her father had drowned in a sailing accident while she was a child. But she also knew how determined Earle was. Sitting in the cockpit of the *Phoenix* at Honolulu a few weeks ago, she explained:
> "I knew he was going to do it and if he did it would be an important experience in his life. Well, if a marriage is to be good, there ought to be as few important experiences as possible that haven't been shared by

both partners. So I said I'd go along." She looked off toward the rugged black mountains of Oahu for a moment, then with a rueful smile, added: "I also thought if I sailed with him to Honolulu, I could get him to sell the boat and go back to normal living."

She couldn't. From Honolulu the family sailed around the world in the *Phoenix* and during the four years it took, they all had experiences that made their ultimate protest voyage both possible and likely.

If a family is to break with accepted behavior it must have great internal strength—and freedom. Thus the most important thing Barbara learned—and the hardest—was to cut her roots, to break with the idea that a family ought to have a home in one place, that children ought to be brought up in a particular place and have normal playmates and schooling, that there should be a steady income and insurance policies and money put aside for retirement. To break, too, with the many things that make up security for most women: her own furniture and dishes and silver, curtains at windows, the solidity of her home and her place in the community.

"Now," Barbara said, "our roots are in the family itself, not in any *place*. We are self-contained and self-nourishing. We have our fights and disagreements, but we have learned to know each other as individuals and to like each other. Ted and Jessica, for instance, are five years apart and had their own groups of friends ashore and had little contact with each other. But on the trip they found things in common and ways they could have good times together."

"We talked over everything—we were always short of money and we didn't hide it from the children. We all discussed things and decided together how much we'd spend and for what. And then of course we learned to work together for the safety of the ship, and learned what each could do so that we became an interdependent unit."

Five paragraphs on the "human" explanation; in the middle of it one "compression" paragraph on a voyage that covered four years. (That hurt; I had pages and pages of good material about that voyage, but of course it didn't belong in the story, so I had to forget it.)

How do you select the scenes to be expanded? They must be significant parts of the story. The lead of the piece was one such, and it was worth expanding because it showed the actual confrontation, which is what the story was all about. This last was another because it showed Barbara's motivation, her intelligence, and the strength of her self-discipline, all of which made her more real to the reader and more admirable, which a protagonist in a story ought to be.

This trick of personalizing an idea is used over and over again in all the mass media—newspapers, magazines, television documentaries, films.

It's what Remsberg did in the story about Utah, what Malcolm did in the story about the man's decision to die, what Lukas did in the Linda Fitzpatrick story. There is a definite procedure for writing these stories, which, for want of a better name, we call microcosm stories.

The idea comes in one of two ways: (1) You spot a trend or a problem or an issue that affects hundreds of thousands of people; (2) You spot an event that has deeper implications reflecting the same kind of widespread problem or issue. In either case your procedure is basically the same, though it varies in details. Take the first:

You've made an observation that *seems* true; the first thing you have to do is find out whether it really is true. For example, once I was talking with the director of a mental hospital in Connecticut, and at one point he wandered off the subject. The thing that drove him up the wall, he said, was what happened to his patients after they were released. Here we have people who have broken down under the pressure of too much stress, he said, we put them back together again, and then they go out and run into much more stress than they had before they came in. Why? Because they've been in a mental hospital, they're "crazy." Employers won't hire them, friends, family, and acquaintances treat them differently—either shun them completely, or go to the other extreme and treat them so gently that the patients know they're under suspicion. The trouble, he said, is that the public generally is afraid of mental illness and doesn't understand that a person can be cured after a mental breakdown just as surely as they can be cured of pneumonia.

This sounded logical, and I thought there might be an article in it. But first I had to find out whether the director knew what he was talking about. I checked around with other hospital directors, with psychiatrists, and other mental health experts, and they agreed the problem did exist pretty much as the Connecticut man had outlined. As we talked about it, there began to emerge a pattern of the specific kinds of things the released patients faced; getting a job was a major difficulty, because of employers' suspicions. Working out normal relations with other people was another, including for single persons the whole question of whether to marry, whether to tell the intended about the illness, and whether to have children (would they be mentally unstable?). Probably the biggest problem was the enormous blow to—perhaps the complete destruction of— the patient's self-confidence: "I've lost control of myself; it has been *proved* that I can't run my own life. How can I ever again believe that I can make it from here on out?"

This pattern of specific problems had to be the outline of the article; these were the major points that had to be dealt with. It seemed that the best way to do the piece would be through a personal narrative—find someone who had lived through the experience, who had dealt with the separate parts of the pattern, then write the story in terms of his or her experience. Since I was working on *Redbook*, the patient should be one with whom our readers could easily identify. It should be a young woman, preferably married with young children; in addition, of course, it would have to be a woman who was not afraid of being identified in print, who was willing to talk about her experience, and who was articulate.

How to find such a woman? You usually start the search by locating some person or organization or institution that has broad knowledge of the kind of people or situations you're interested in. In this case I went to the National Association of Mental Health, which had local chapters all over the country. I told the public relations director what I was trying to do and asked her if she would circularize their local chapters to find such a woman. She did. About a month later she came up with half a dozen candidates, plus a good deal of information about the experiences of each.

The one who seemed most promising was a young woman in San Francisco. She didn't fit our formula exactly—she was married, but had not been when she had her breakdown, and she had no children—but she was willing to talk, and her experiences illustrated the major points of the pattern. So I went to San Francisco and spent hours and hours interviewing her.

She was a brave woman. Going back over her initial breakdown, her experiences in the hospital, and her later fight to win back a place in the "normal" world was excruciatingly painful for her. She was often in tears and once was so shaky I was afraid she might have a relapse. But she was convinced that the story might help others in the same situation, and she found the courage to go through the ordeal. I didn't dare subject her to the additional stress of taking notes; after each interview—one lasted from 7 to 11 P.M.—I rushed back to the hotel and spent hours reconstructing the interview as nearly verbatim as possible.

I'll never forget one thing she said: "The thing that hit me the hardest was when they took away my keys in the hospital."

"Your *keys!* Why?

"Because your keys are your life. There's the key to the office, that's your job. Your key to the apartment, that's your home, your security. The key to your car, that's your freedom."

Once I finished the interviewing, it was simply a job of writing the narrative of her experience, using the skeleton plot mentioned earlier, and making sure that the major points covered in the story fitted the pattern of the overall problem.

The preliminary work on this kind of story often takes longer than the interviewing after you've found your person. In this case it took six or seven weeks; once it took a year and a half to find the right man. (Of course, I was doing other articles in the meantime.) But sometimes this kind of story works the other way: you turn up the personal story before you've identified the problem. As you explore the story, you begin to see the dimensions of the problem looming in the background. (If nothing looms, you have only a personal adventure story, which is much less significant and is not really an interpretive piece. It's a straight news story or feature.)

That's what happened with the story of Francis Bloeth, a mass killer. He killed three people, capriciously and at random, in a week. Long Island was terrorized; people were afraid to go out at night, all-night restaurants and gas stations closed down, people who had never had guns bought them. Then a few days after the last murder, police arrested Bloeth and a couple of days later he confessed. The papers gave complete coverage to all aspects of the affair and when it was over and Bloeth was in jail awaiting trial, the story seemed to be over.

I suppose it was the terror that made me think more about the incident, and the more I thought the more it seemed that there was a deeper story that needed to be told. Every institution our society has erected to protect itself from a man like this had had its hands on Bloeth and had let him go to kill three people. That became the underlying theme of the piece, and of course I had to verify the hypothesis by interviewing a flock of experts before I could be sure that it was sound. Once that was done, and I understood the deeper issues involved, I could write the story, using Bloeth's life as the narrative that carried the pattern of the problem.

There's a danger in this technique—a danger that you get so carried away by the human narrative that you rely too heavily on your own observation of the underlying problem. You don't check it out thoroughly enough with the experts who have a much broader and deeper view than you do, and you end up with a strained, or even false, article. Once I thought I spotted a good story idea—that the people who bought new homes at inflated suburban prices were paying more than their fair share of property taxes. The reasoning was that since they paid higher prices than had owners of older homes of equal size and value, their assessed valuations, based on the higher prices, would be greater and thus their taxes would, too.

It sounded reasonable and comparisons on the tax rolls seemed to bear it out. So did other information I gathered from a few, rather restricted, studies I was able to locate. I was about to start the search for two specific cases I could use in a comparison article when I interviewed a man at the

Census Bureau in Washington. I was working on another story, and when we finished that subject I mentioned the tax idea to him, to keep the conversation going. He said, "Yeah, I know it sounds logical, but it's not true." How did he know? "Well," he said, "we thought it was true, too, so we did a nationwide study. Found out it wasn't, that old houses get sold often enough so that they, too, reflect the inflated prices and so do their assessments." I took a look at the study, verified that it was a sound one, and watched my story go down the drain.

It was chastening, as it always is, to find that you're not as brilliant as you thought, but it's much better to find out at this stage than after you've gone roaring into print fat, dumb, happy—and dead wrong.

16

How To Handle Dull Stuff

*O*ne day when he was editor of *McCall's*, the late Dan Mich called and asked me if I'd like to do an article on varicose veins. This was not a subject that I'd been aching to cover for my whole life and Dan sensed it. Well, he said, I know it's not the most attractive idea in the world, but it is important; millions of women are afflicted by the ailment, hate it, and there have been some new medical developments in treatment. So how about it?

I didn't like the idea, but I respected Dan's judgment, and I'd learned that once you started research on a subject, however unlikely, your interest usually grew. So I said I'd do it.

I blew it. The research was sound and structurally the piece was OK, but it was about as interesting to read as a Pentagon memo. If I'd had any sense, I'd have called Dan when the research was finished and told him I couldn't handle it. But false pride plus the free lance's inveterate need for money kept me from doing it.

This was one of those times when you don't live up to your expectations for yourself so you don't talk about it, but the failure keeps nagging at you. Because of this, I think I finally figured out what I'd done wrong, and the more I thought about it, the more it seemed the mistake applied to more than this one incident.

Certain stories that journalists have to handle are about as interesting as a discarded beer can. They have to be written because they contain a good deal of information that is important to large numbers of people. Like the annual income tax story in April, the analyses of city or federal budgets, a new discovery in genetics, obituaries, or a revision of the city charter. Normally when you're assigned one of these, you approach it with resignation and, if you're a competent journalist, you do a competent job. You get all the information in, accurately, in some kind of logical order and as concisely as you can manage. So it's clear and complete and sound, but exciting it ain't.

We think you can do better. What it takes is a change in approach and, of course, imagination and the other attributes of creativity.

Your first triumph over the material comes in your attitude toward it. If you approach it as necessary drudgery, your story will be dull. If you look at it as a challenge, are determined to make it something special, and use your imagination to identify the special something, you'll probably start getting the ideas that will result in a fresh handling. And it will be rewarding because this kind of creativity always gives a glow of satisfaction.

Judith Crist clued me in on this. When she was first working on the old *New York Herald Tribune*, she, like most beginning reporters, was given obituaries to write. She hated it. She used the considerable force of her personality to try to convince the editor to give her something else to do and failed. So, she said, she took a new look at what she was doing. Suddenly, she said, she saw the job in a whole new light: here was a person's life spread out before her; it was finished and now could be looked at whole and evaluated for its direction, its accomplishments, its failures, and its drama. With this approach the material became not a dull recountal of facts, but a living document, the story of a human life. "Besides," she said, with a glint in her eye, "I realized that I had the last word."

Immediately her work began to take on color and movement.

What Crist had done for obituaries was to complete the first step in winning a victory over all dull material—to *think* about it, analyze it, try to relate it to other things in history or humanity, to figure out where it's going, its effect on the country, on people—if it's important it *must* affect many people—and on what kinds of people. Then go see some of those people and write the story of how and why it affects them.

But before you can convince your readers that the subject is important you must enable them to understand it. In his bestseller, *The Soul of a New Machine*, Tracy Kidder uses a familar analogy to describe one part of the workings of a computer:

". . . the main issue was the computer's storage system. Here, in packages of symbolic bits, are kept both information for the computer to manipulate and also many of the instructions that tell the computer what to do with that data. The system resembles that of a region's telephone system; phones are of no use unless they are distinct from one another, and an item in a computer's storage system is of no use unless it has its own "phone number," its own unique symbol, known as an address. A 16-bit machine can directly generate symbolic addresses

only 16 bits long, which means that it can hand out to storage compartments only about 65,000 unique addresses. A true 32-bit machine,
however, can directly address some 4.3 *billion* storage compartments."

Another example of making potentially dull material as interesting as
possible comes from the *Manhattan, Inc.* piece by Peter Wilkinson, the
outline of which we looked at in chapter 3.

Early in the piece, Wilkinson had to describe the kind of white-collar
crime that pervaded the garment district of New York. The section could
have been a plodding description, the kind often seen in newspaper
stories, but Wilkinson used his talent as a writer to make it interesting.

Dirty, rambunctious, and overflowing with trucks, people, and push-
carts, New York's garment center is a huge production machine fueled
by the energies of hundreds of tiny, family-owned companies making
everything from silk shirts to the hangers to display them on.

Accordingly, "making a living" in the garment center means playing
by a unique set of rules. Competition, a desperate need for ready cash,
and greed have left the area a playground for operators with muscle or a
scam. Payoffs, funny loans, and sundry other shakedowns take place
daily—all in the interest of keeping the machine humming at its own
manic pace.

In this haven of the minor malfeasance, a more lucrative scam has
been spawned on Fashion Avenue. Government agents call it "phony
invoicing." It is a complicated game in which a businessman solicits bills
for goods he doesn't want and never receives, pays them, and takes back
up to 90 percent of what he paid, in cash, from a cooperative conspir-
ator.

Folks on the street call it "buying green," and it is a fine way to raise
business expenses, pay less tax, and fill pockets with wads of money—
legitimately earned or, in some cases, creatively embezzled and beg-
ging to be laundered. The beauty of the plan is the paperwork—
reassuring piles of official-looking documents to hoodwink nosy IRS
agents. Dozens of apparel firms (some existing only on paper or as a
name chiseled on a battered office door) are known to provide this
"phony paper," taking commissions of 6 to 20 percent for their trouble.

The areas of science and technology are among the most important in
today's society. Every day, major breakthroughs occur in the physical
sciences, and seemingly every hour, they occur in the computer sciences.
These advances often quickly have an effect on readers, so the job of a

science writer is important. It is also difficult, because as important as scientific advances may be, they usually must be described in technical terms, and technical terms have a nasty habit of sending readers on to the next article.

To avoid that, the best science writers use all of the writer's weapons. They make their articles as interesting as they are important. Doing so requires hard work, but the result makes the work worthwhile. The following is an excerpt from a *Time* article about two pilots, Dick Rutan and Jeana Yeager, who had flown an experimental aircraft called *Voyager* for four and one-half days, and more than 11,600 miles without stopping for refueling, and who planned to fly the plane around the world nonstop. Writer Michael D. Lemonick began the article with an anecdote about the flight, but soon had to describe some of the unique technical qualities of the aircraft. The story could have become dull or confusing at this point, but Lemonick's writing glistens and carries the reader through the section.

But the mission's undisputed star was *Voyager,* a distinctive, almost ethereal craft, whose shell weighs only 938 lbs.; add engines and other equipment, and it is still shy of a ton—lighter than most small cars. The rest of its takeoff weight of nearly 6,200 lbs. (which will be closer to 12,000 lbs. for the around-the-world flight) is mostly fuel, distributed evenly in 17 tanks, located in the wings, fuselage and "outriggers" that flank the cabin.

Voyager began life in 1981 as a sketch on a napkin at the weather-beaten Mojave Inn, near the airport. The sketcher was Burt Rutan, 43, an engineer with an established reputation for building quirky-looking but aerodynamically ingenious planes. With his brother Dick and Jeana Yeager (no relation, believes Jeana, to famous Test Pilot Chuck), Rutan had decided to attempt the around-the-world flight.

The key to such a marathon would clearly be a lightweight, efficient, flying fuel tank. Eighteen months and many sketches later, when *Voyager* assumed its basic shape, it was a textbook example of feather-weight design and construction. The shell is made from quarter-inch-thick panels of Hexcel honeycomb, a resin-coated, paper-like polymer, covered with graphite fibers embedded in epoxy. The panels weigh just 4 oz. per sq. ft. but have remarkable tensile strength; the ends of the craft's thin, 110-ft. single wing can flex up and down as much as 35 ft. without breaking.

That section is a study in clarity and in making potentially dull material interesting. The reader never becomes bored or confused. Lemonick used words like "ethereal" and "quirky-looking," and mentions the napkin incident to give the piece a human tone.

One of the keys to making unfamiliar concepts understandable to the reader is simplicity. A reader will find it much easier to grasp "4.3 billion" than "4,300,000,000." In statistical stories it's always easier on the reader if you do the arithmetic—not, "this year's budget for the Department of Social Services was $68,474,387, up from last year's $44,674,256," but "this year's budget was $68 million, up a third from last year."

And it helps to reduce big numbers—there don't seem to be small ones anymore—to the smallest possible. Instead of writing "750,000 of the one million school children in the city are black," write, "three out of every four school children in the city are black"; it's even clearer than saying "75 percent are black."

When you have a number of concepts to get across in a complex story, you can provide a roadmap for the reader by numbering the paragraphs containing each. "There were four major reactions to the governor's proposal. 1——. 2——. 3——. 4——." Then later in the story when you want to refer back to one or the other, you use the numbers. This device helps clarify things for your readers: they see the four different viewpoints all at once, then can go on for fuller explanation in successive paragraphs if they want to. The trouble with this device is that it's too mechanical; as you switch from concept to concept without transitions, the flow of the story is wiped out. But there are stories so complex that clarity is a greater virtue than flow.

The same objection applies to the question-and-answer format, although it is used a great deal by people who want to get across much factual information quickly and concisely. It gives you great control over your material and saves the space taken by transitions. But it cannot be done successfully without deep and careful thought.

When we're reading "Q and A" pieces, our most frequent reaction is that they're not asking the questions we want answered. Many of the questions are set-ups—put there only to give the writer a chance to say something in the answer that he or she wants to say. We usually quit reading at that point. The key to successful use of the Q and A format is to think long and deeply about your readers' interests and to frame the questions they would want answers for.

We think "Q and A" is too clumsy a device to use in an interview—as *Playboy* uses it, for example. In an interview story your purpose is to give the reader an understanding of a person, his or her thinking, personality, experiences, and role in society. The "Q and A," while revealing, imposes a mechanical structure on what should be a human story. You can see how much the writers chafe under the *Playboy* formula when you notice that the answers get longer and longer, the questions fewer, so that the interviews become less like "Q and A"s and more like those in which the subjects reveal themselves by talking. This—allowing the subject to talk—was one of the devices introduced years ago by the *New Yorker* in their profiles, and it works beautifully when it's artistically done. (We'll talk more about that in the next chapter.)

17

How Do You Bring Them Alive?

*O*f all the kinds of interpretive writing, profiles may be the most interesting to do and the most difficult, both for the same reason—you're attempting to re-create a human being.

They're interesting because you are getting under the skin of another person (let's say a woman), learning to understand her with all her ambitions and hangups, the satisfactions of her successes, and joys at the unexpected beauties that have entered her life, her self-contempt at her failures, the contradictions of her personality, the drama of her conflicts, her courage and cowardices, the main direction of her life, the ultimate tragedy of her entrapment in her own inadequacies, or perhaps the inspiration of her ultimate victory over forces that should have been too strong for her.

And these are the same things that make writing a profile so difficult. For you must try to understand all these dimensions of your subject's personality and then encompass them in the pale, two-dimensional medium of words. There are never enough words within the length limits you cannot exceed. And to find the precise words to convey the color and contradictions of a person is a damnably difficult chore you never fully master. To do the job superlatively, which is what all writers want, all that is required of you is that you be a great artist.

Of course you never make it. But then, if you're any good as a writer, you're never satisfied with anything you do; that comes with the territory. (That also is what makes writing such a good way to spend your life; as your skills increase, the ceiling of your aspirations keeps getting higher. Probably the worst thing that can happen to you is to bump your head against the ceiling when you're halfway through life.)

So how do you arrange to come close? The job breaks down into two stages that, like many aspects of writing, go on simultaneously but must be explored one at a time. The first is the research—getting under the person's skin; the second is pulling it all together, figuring out what the main thrust of her personality is and what, from among all the material you have, will best illustrate it.

The research job is shaped like a spiral; you start outside the person, go round and round her, getting closer all the time and finally finish at the center, with her. You start by reading. Has she written anything? Read it. Nobody can write anything without revealing herself. Has anybody written about her? Read that—with your notebook beside you, so you can note the questions that pop into your mind to ask her. Some writers also note the perceptions that they get about the person—not as final conclusions, but as impressions to be verified or denied as your understanding grows.

Then you start interviewing. You talk to the person's colleagues, her coworkers, her boss, her secretary, her employees. You talk to her family—her parents, her brothers, her children—recognizing always that they are biased by their emotional attachments to her. You talk to her friends—current friends and, if you can find them, friends during earlier stages of her life, when she was in school or starting her career. Then you talk to her enemies, to offset the bias of others and recognizing that they, too, are biased. You talk to people who can be objective about her—if there are any—either because enough time has passed to dim their emotional attachment, or because their relations with her were of the kind that required them to be objective—like a college professor who had her as a student.

During each interview you recognize that you are getting only one aspect of the woman's life, though, of course, you probe for as many aspects as each interviewee has been exposed to. You go after anecdotes, things the woman did in certain circumstances, because anecdotes are mostly what your story is going to be made up of. And after each interview you sit down and think about what has been said and note down questions that you will later ask another interviewee or the subject herself.

You may talk to twenty or two hundred people in this process, depending on how exhaustive your story is going to be and on whether you're doing one side of the person or a full, rounded portrait. That "one side" needs explanation: it does not mean you set out to do a biased picture, like a hatchet job. It does mean your original story idea may encompass only one aspect of the person's life. For example, let's say you're doing a piece on the particular style of acting of Robert Redford and you want to show how he developed it. Then, of course, you concentrate on that side, see the people who would have first-hand knowledge about it, and forget the rest. But even that kind of limited approach requires you to interview many more people than you expect.

Finally, you see Redford himself. You are armed with all the questions you have noted down after all the other interviews, plus those you thought of when you were reading books or articles about him. You spend as much time with him as he will allow—a day, a week. If possible you live with him, you meet him in the morning—paying due attention to what he's like before breakfast—go to work with him, eat with him, watch how he acts toward his co-workers, the director, his wife, his kids. You pay close attention to the way he dresses, the furniture in his office, and the pictures on the walls; you listen to the way he talks, catch the rhythms of his speech, his inflections, his individual phrasing and favorite expressions; you note the way he walks and skis; you describe to yourself the precise way he smiles and the expression his face wears in repose, the shape of his mouth and eyebrows and the way he moves his hands when he talks—or keeps them clenched in his lap or stiffly along his thighs; you watch his eyes and the way they change as emotions or thoughts filter through them; you open the shutter of your perceptions to catch the nuances of his relations with other people, the way he reacts to them and they to him; you try different gambits on him and watch how he reacts—flattery, argument, opposition, the put-down, agreement.

This is what Tom Wolfe calls "saturation reporting" when he talks about the "new journalism"; it is an essential in doing profiles, but new it isn't. Interpretive writers have been using it for more than a quarter of a century. Nevertheless, Wolfe and Breslin and Talese and several others use it beautifully, and some of the things they have written after using it have reached heights of sophistication and artistry that many earlier practitioners did not approach.

This is an almighty difficult process, and it is absolutely essential to work through it if your piece is to have any focus. Once in my early days of free-lancing, I was doing a profile of the late Chester I. Barnard, then head of the Rockefeller Foundation. I had read everything he'd written, most of it privately published and covering an enormous range of subjects. I had interviewed all the people, I had spent hours and hours with him, I had gathered all the facts of his career. It had been remarkable.

He'd been a poor boy in New England who had worked his way through Harvard by leading a jazz orchestra and had quit a couple of months shy of graduation because he thought he'd gotten all he could, and the degree didn't mean anything to him. He had joined the telephone company and shortly had become such a master of the complex mathematics of rate-making that he'd been on the government's wartime telephone board while still in his twenties.

He'd been the youngest president of a phone company in history. He had a large library of music and was an accomplished pianist, so determined on perfection that he'd take out a piece of music and play it over and over again until he felt he'd done it as well as he possibly could, then go on to the next. He taught himself French by writing a dozen French words and their English translations on three-by-five cards; he carried them around in his pocket and pulled them out to study them while waiting for a bus, riding home from the office, waiting for an appointment. When he knew them all, he'd throw the card away and make another.

He'd written a book called *The Functions of the Executive,* which revolutionized the theory of how to manage an organization so that it accomplished its goals. He was an expert on Napoleon, the Catholic Church, and on the foundation, development, and organization of Islam. He was such a lousy golfer he'd quit in disgust at himself. During the Great Depression, when food riots wracked city after city, he'd organized one of the first government welfare operations in the country. He was an accepted member of half a dozen conservative clubs of top executives, and he'd gone to Russia and written a pamphlet on what he learned that shook the clubs to their foundations and got him called communist. He'd been a member of an ultra-select group of five men who had drawn up a plan for the control and use of atomic energy, both national and international. It's still being followed. He had been called "one of the six finest minds in the world."

He was iconoclastic, witty, irreverent; talking to him about the problems of the day was like watching a brilliant beam of light played on a dark roomful of writhing monsters. He was fascinating and so diverse that I couldn't encompass him. After struggling for days to pin down the main thrust of his life, I finally called for help. I went up to see Charley Ferguson, the editor at *Reader's Digest* I was working with then, and talked out the problem.

Fergie said, "Before you can start to write a profile you've got to complete this sentence: John Smith is the man who ———."

So I went home and spent more tortured days trying to complete the sentence. I finally did it, but not very well and the resulting piece was not as sharply focused as it should have been. Fergie's sentence had clarified the problem and given me a direction in which to work. I believe he was right; you've got to complete it before you can start to write.

Once you've completed the sentence, how do you proceed? Very much as you do in any other piece. The organizational structure can, but need not, be the same conceptual pattern outlined in chapter 7. Because you're writing about a person, your lead is usually an anecdote which illustrates the point made when you completed the sentence, like the leads about Joe DiMaggio and Mike Nichols in chapter 10.

Or you can use a summary lead, like the one Garry Wills used in his profile of Dorothy Day.

Then you go ahead and reveal the subject, let's say a man, mostly by showing him in action, point by point—with the points being those aspects of his life and personality that seem to you the most significant. It's a tough and delicate job of selection. You may or may not take him through his life chronologically—probably not, because the most illuminating anecdotes didn't happen chronologically. You usually end with an anecdote that sums up the man.

But one thing is absolutely essential; you've got to show his bad side as well as his good, his weaknesses as well as his strengths (or if the main thrust of your piece is negative, his strengths as well as his weaknesses). Without this, you're doing either a puff piece or a hatchet job, and in either case the reader doesn't believe you. Readers *know* nobody is perfect or all bad, and they figure if you make a man that way you're being dishonest.

Creating a balanced piece is not easy to do for two reasons: One is that by the time you've learned enough about your subject to understand him, you like him—because we think you almost always like those persons you really understand. The other is that it's difficult to find anyone who will be critical of your man—especially if he is a person of power, or a person who has accomplished things in his life—because people who have accomplished enough to be worthy of a profile usually have more positive than negative traits.

I had a terrible time with this when I did the piece on the late President Kennedy. For one thing he was a genuine golden boy. For another, I liked the guy. For a third, his public relations people had built one of the fanciest, gold-plated, stainless steel fences around him I'd ever tried to get through. This was while he was in the Senate, and about the only deleterious thing I could get about him was a crack a colleague had made to him one day: "What we'd like from you, Senator, is a little less profile and a little more courage." (Clever, but not quite fair, because I was convinced Kennedy had great courage.)

I went to Boston and talked to Republicans and to members of those wings of the Democratic party that were anti-Kennedy. I didn't get much, probably because the Democrats were afraid of his power and the Republicans were respectful of it, and most people who knew him liked him. Finally I went to Harvard and looked up some of his old professors. Most of them liked and admired him too, but they were more objective, and one or two of them had revealing insights into the sources of his ambition and the kinds of obstacles he'd had to struggle against in his early years. And that was a key.

If a man is truly admirable, if his life has been mostly positive, if he has had many more successes than failures, you can humanize him, make him believable to the reader, by identifying the things he had to fight to overcome and then by showing him doing it.

One of Kennedy's traits, for example, was his great need to win, implanted by his father ("My father was never interested," he said once, "if you came in second") and by his competition with his brothers. Honed since childhood, this need became a spartan self-discipline which drove him several times in his life to go beyond what should have been the limits of his physical endurance. Once at Harvard he was in the infirmary with grippe and fever when the trial heats for a coming swimming meet with Yale were announced; he sneaked out of the infirmary and took part in the trials. His health suffered for the rest of the term. When he campaigned for the Senate in 1952, he had an open wound in his back, the legacy of the PT-boat smash in World War II, and had to get about on crutches. Yet many times he'd address a late-night rally in one town, then get in the car and try to sleep as he was driven to the next town. There, at seven in the morning, he'd be at a factory gate to shake hands with the workers as they came in. Not once during the campaign, his aides told me, did he mention the pain. This kind of need to win may be a virtue or a vice in your personal lexicon, but showing a man coping with it can do nothing but humanize him.

Another technique for adding balance to a profile is to allow the person to reveal himself through quotes. In her profile of Mike Nichols, Barbara Gelb let Nichols tell of his attempts to get over his own vanity.

"Having fame is wonderful," Nichols says, if you can control its tendency "to make you feel like a baby."

The struggle with his baby feelings was at its most pronounced during Nichols's years as a performer, when, he says, his vanity all too often would take over and cause him to behave petulantly. "It's—you know—'I don't like the way the ads look,' or, 'One of the lights is out, I'm not being lit properly.' As a director, those things concern me for the *project,* not for *me.* When you're worried about it for *you,* that's something I'm very uncomfortable with."

In a *Rolling Stone* cover story, one of Glavin's former students, Rob Hoerburger, used good description ending in a quote to prove one of his major points about rock star Phil Collins. Hoerburger had earlier described Collins as rock's Cabbage Patch kid, an unlikely star, a plain, homely singer surrounded by MTV glitz. He also showed that Collins's style of living differed markedly from those of his fellow rock stars. He began that section by desribing Collins at home during a week in which his wife was away.

He looked a bit haggard, admitting that he didn't sleep well alone. The cats didn't get fed for three days, because Collins, who wasn't used to feeding them, kept forgetting to buy cat food. And with only a week to go before they moved into a new home, there wasn't a single gold record packed, not even a box in sight.

Collins did, however, air out the hot-tub room and start up one of two mountainous jukeboxes he had stocked with his favorite 45s, mostly vintage Beatles and Motown—although looking through the dusty glass that shielded the titles, he had some trouble remembering them. The house itself is small by rock-star proportions, really just an oversize cottage with a second floor. It would be hard to imagine Eddie and Valerie living there, for instance, but Collins, like the house, fits right in with the gentrified populace. Driving around Guildford on an unusually warm day in December, his fuzz face might have been the only thing to give away his identity—Guildford seemed a place where men shaved twice a day. Otherwise, in his cotton-checked trousers and argyle sweater, he was a natural, waving to an elderly bicycling couple who let him pass on the lane. This wasn't the typical MTV look, and Collins often feels less comfortable around his more chic pop peers. At the Band Aid taping, he found himself surrounded by photogenia—Sting, Duran Duran, Culture Club—as he sat behind the drums in his argyles. "I looked around and everyone had leather trousers on, jumpers with three-quarter sleeves that would have been girls' ten years ago. I'm so unfashionable, it's embarrassing."

The quote at the end of the section finishes it nicely, but the strength of the section lies in Hoerburger's description of Collins's life.

So while quotes gathered in interviews may reveal a great deal about people, their actions usually reveal more. In the Barbara Gelb article on Mike Nichols, Gelb starts one section with a quote from an interview, then uses an anecdote to show Nichols practicing what he preaches.

Nichols often makes things clear for his actors by illustrating bits of motivation with incidents from his own life. "Partly, I do this because it's all I *know*, and partly because I very much want to encourage them to pour *their* lives into what they're doing. I believe that the process can illuminate a scene and it also lets us learn a little more about each other, so that we can work together a little better."

In a scene, for example, where Eddie manifests blind jealousy over a fancied betrayal by Darlene, and Sigourney Weaver is at a loss how to react, Nichols asks her, "Have you ever been with an insanely jealous person?" He is thinking of a year in his own life, and just such a relationship.

"I know a great deal about that kind of jealousy," he says. "If, for instance, we were watching a movie together and there was a woman on the screen, I had to sit very, very still, or I would be excoriated for a long time afterward. It was a *scalding* experience, and I learned from it that jealousy is entirely the problem of the person *undergoing* it, and it's not really attached to *you* at all."

And he gives the actress a startling image to think about: "Being with an insanely jealous person is like being in the room with a *dead mammoth*."

Here Gelb, like Hoerburger, does what the best writers always do. She makes the point by showing her subject in action.

Epilogue

*T*he life of the nonfiction writer is filled with defeats and victories, frustration and fascination, risks and rewards.

The writer works with his own ideas and his own opinions. He can use his power, which is literally the power of the press, to influence the attitudes of millions of persons. For centuries writers have helped alter the course of the country's history. In fact, the writings of Samuel Adams, Tom Paine, and others helped spark the fight for the country's independence. In the early part of this century, the muckrakers, including Lincoln Steffens, Ida M. Tarbell, Samuel Hopkins Adams, and Ray Stannard Baker wrote of corruption in government and abuses by business, and created a demand for the passage of laws that governed such things as child labor, the quality of food and drugs, and truth in advertising. During the seventies, Bob Woodward and Carl Bernstein of the *Washington Post* unearthed the facts behind the Watergate scandal, facts that eventually led to the resignation of President Nixon. Today, writers like Claire Safran and Bonnie Remsberg, whose work we have seen in earlier chapters, continue the tradition of informing Americans of abuses by business and government.

The muckrakers were investigative journalists, but many more writers perform a different job. They help people by giving them information they need. It may be information on ways to solve a particular problem, like how to deal with a dyslexic child. It may be the information that helps explain a complex issue that is important to their lives, like a new tax bill or the effects of air pollution. It may be information that enlarges their readers' lives, like the Barbara Gelb piece mentioned earlier, which broadens readers' appreciation of a play by demonstrating the thought, trial and error, hard work, and inspiration that go into its production.

But presenting this kind of information in ways that will penetrate the readers' normal defenses is extraordinarily hard work, most of which comes under the headings of self-discipline and self-knowledge. Self-discipline means not being satisfied with the first way you write a sentence, but working it over until it says *precisely* what you want it to say. It means forcing yourself to think, to analyse a body of recalcitrant material: what does all this information add up to? how do these facts fit together—and where don't they? what does this story *say?*

Self-discipline means learning to handle the fears that every writer has. The most frequent of these is: what if it doesn't work this time; what if I can't handle it well enough so it will be published? Such fears either swamp you or you surmount them; if they swamp you, you say you have writer's block. You surmount them by bringing them up and facing them—which requires some self-knowledge. Facing them, you analyze them: what am I really afraid of? suppose this comes true, what's the worst that can happen? if that happens, will I die? will I starve? Anything less usually seems manageable.

Such fear usually stifles your creativity, and preventing it is where self-knowledge comes in. Creativity is a product of your unconscious mind; knowing this often allows you to trigger that mind force. And this not only usually solves the problem you face, but also produces one of the great rewards of writing. Creativity is seeing familiar things in a new or different way, and this, in turn broadens both your own and your readers' understanding of life's predicaments.

There are other rewards. An early one is the ego-satisfaction at seeing your name in print. This is joyful—and transitory. Next you want to see it in print over something you consider good, and will consider good a year from now.

A big and lasting reward is knowing that you have helped people to understand and appreciate their own lives; that you have had influence enough to get a bill passed or to stop a bad one; that knowledge you have passed along will help someone suffering with a dread disease, perhaps even to save a life.

These are some of the reasons why, despite all the hard work, all the struggles and frustrations, most writers would have no other job.

INDEX